EVIL

EVIL

*The Science Behind
Humanity's Dark Side*

Julia Shaw

ABRAMS PRESS, NEW YORK

Library of Congress Control Number: 2017949741

ISBN: 978-1-4197-2949-2
eISBN: 978-1-68335-208-2

Printed and bound in the United States
10 9 8 7 6 5 4 3 2 1

Abrams books are available at special discounts when purchased in
quantity for premiums and promotions as well as fundraising
or educational use. Special editions can also be created to
specification. For details, contact specialsales@abramsbooks.com
or the address below.

Abrams Press® is a registered trademark of Harry N. Abrams, Inc.

ABRAMS The Art of Books
195 Broadway, New York, NY 10007
abramsbooks.com

To the insatiably curious

CONTENTS

'He who fights with monsters should look to it that he himself does not become a monster.'

Friedrich Nietzsche,
Beyond Good and Evil

INTRODUCTION:
THE HUNGER

THE FAMOUS NINETEENTH-CENTURY German philosopher Friedrich Nietzsche wrote in 1881: '*Böse denken heißt böse machen*' – thinking evil means making evil.[1] Only when we assign something the label 'evil', only when we think that something is evil, does it become so. Nietzsche argued that evil is a subjective experience, not something that is inherent to a person, or object, or action.[2]

This book explores some of the science behind this sentiment, ranging across a spectrum of concepts and notions that are often associated with the word evil. It is a study of human hypocrisy, the absurdity of evil, ordinary madness and empathy. I hope to challenge you to rethink and reshape what it means to be bad.

Over the past thirteen years, as a student, lecturer and researcher, I have enjoyed discussing the science of evil with anyone who is willing to listen. What I like most is destroying the fundamental conceptualisations of good and evil as black and white, replacing them with nuance and scientific insight. I want us all to have a more informed way of discussing behaviour that at first we feel we cannot, and should not, begin to understand. Without understanding, we risk dehumanising others, writing off human beings simply because we don't comprehend them. We can, we must, try to understand that which we have labelled evil.

Let's start by doing an evil empathy exercise. Think about the worst thing you have ever done. Something that you are probably ashamed of, and that you know would make other people think less of you. Infidelity. Theft. Lying. Now imagine that everyone knew about it. Judged you for it. Constantly called you names arising from it. How would that feel?

We would hate for the world to forever judge us based on the acts we most regret. Yet this is what we do to others every day. For our own decisions we see the nuances, the circumstances, the difficulties. For others we often just see the outcome of their decisions. This leads us to define human beings, in all their complexity, by a single heinous term. Murderer. Rapist. Thief. Liar. Psychopath. Paedophile.

These are labels bestowed on others, based on our perception of who they must be, given their behaviour. A single word intended to summarise someone's true character and to disparage it, to communicate to others that this person cannot be trusted. This person is harmful. This person is not really a person at all – rather some sort of horrible aberration. An aberration with whom we should not try to empathise because they are so hopelessly bad that we will never be able to understand them. Such people are beyond understanding, beyond saving, evil.

But who are 'they'? Perhaps understanding that every single one of us frequently thinks and does things that others view as despicable will help us to understand the very essence of what we call evil. I can guarantee that someone in the world thinks you are evil. Do you eat meat? Do you work in banking? Do you have a child out of wedlock? You will find that things that seem normal to you don't seem normal to others, and might even be utterly reprehensible. Perhaps we are all evil. Or, perhaps none of us are.

As a society, we talk about evil a lot, and yet we don't really talk about it at all. Every day we hear of the latest human atrocities, and superficially engage with constant news chatter that makes us feel like humanity is surely doomed. As journalists often say, if it bleeds it leads. Concepts that elicit strong emotions are distilled into attention-grabbing headlines for newspapers and shoved into our social-media feeds. Seen before we get to breakfast and forgotten by lunchtime, our consumption of reports of evil is phenomenal.

Our hunger for violence in particular seems greater now than it ever has. In a study published in 2013 by psychological scientist Brad Bushman and his colleagues which examined violence in movies, they found that 'violence in films has more than doubled since 1950, and that gun violence in PG-13 films [12A] has increased to the point where it recently exceeded the rate in R-rated films [15]'.[3] Movies are becoming more violent, even those which are specifically for children to watch. More than ever, stories of violence and severe human suffering permeate our daily routine.

What does this do to us? It distorts our understanding of the prevalence of crime, making us think crime is more common than it actually is. It impacts who we label evil. It changes our notions of justice.

At this point I want to manage your expectations regarding what this book is about. This is not a book that dives deep into individual cases. Whole books have been dedicated to specific people who are often referred to as evil – like Jon Venables, the youngest person ever to be convicted of murder in the UK and labeled by the tabloids as 'Born Evil', or serial killer Ted Bundy in the US, or the 'Ken and Barbie killers', Paul Bernardo and Karla Homolka, in Canada. These are fascinating cases, no doubt, but this book is not really about them. It is about you. I want you to understand your own thoughts and proclivities more than I want to pick apart specific examples of other people's transgressions.

This is also not a philosophical book, a religious book, or a book about morality. It is a book that tries to help us understand why we do terrible things to one another, not whether these things should happen or what the appropriate punishments for them are. It is a book filled with experiments and theories, a book that tries to turn our attention to science for answers. It tries to break down the concept of evil into many pieces, and to pick up each one to examine it individually.

This is also not a comprehensive book about evil. A lifetime would be insufficient for such a task. You may be disappointed to learn that I will spend almost no time discussing crucial issues like genocide, abuse of children in care, children who commit crime, election fraud, treachery, incest, drugs, gangs or war. If you want to learn about such issues, there are many books out there for you, but this isn't one of them. This is a book that seeks to expand on the currently available literature and bring in the unexpected. This book provides an overview of important and diverse topics related to the concept of evil that I think are fascinating, important, and often overlooked.

MONSTER HUNTING

Before we slip into the science of evil, let me explain who I am and why you can trust me to walk with you through your nightmares.

I come from a world where people hunt monsters. Where police officers, prosecutors and the public collectively take their pitchforks and search for murderers and rapists. They hunt because they want to maintain the fabric of society, to punish those who are perceived to have done wrong. The problem is that these monsters sometimes don't actually exist.

As a criminal psychologist who specialises in false memories, I see cases all the time where people search for an evil perpetrator even though no transgression has actually taken place. False memories are recollections that feel real but are not a representation of something that actually happened. They sound a bit like science fiction, but false memories are all too common. As false-memory researcher Elizabeth Loftus has said, instead of being an accurate record of the past, memories are much like Wikipedia pages – they are constructive and reconstructive. You can go in there and change them, and so can other people.

In extreme situations our memories can end up so far from reality that we can come to believe that we have been the victim or witness of a crime that never took place, or that we perpetrated a crime that never happened. This is something I have studied directly in my lab. I have hacked people's memories to, temporarily, make them believe they did something criminal.

But I don't just study this in the lab. I also study it in the wild. I sometimes get mail from prisoners. These letters are quite possibly one of the most interesting things I receive by post. One letter came in early 2017. The letter was written eloquently with beautifully legible handwriting, both of which are rather unusual characteristics for a prison letter.*

It explained that the sender was in prison because he had stabbed his elderly father to death. He hadn't just stabbed him once though; he had stabbed him fifty times. The perpetrator was a university lecturer at the time of the murder, with no criminal record. He's not the kind of guy we would expect to go around stabbing people.

So, why did he do it? I was startled when I learned the answer to this. The reason for the letter was to ask me to send him my book on false memories, as it 'was not yet available at the prison library'. He had seen it mentioned in *The Times*, and said that he wanted, he needed, to know more about this area of research. The reason he wanted to know more was that he had come to realise, while in prison, that he had killed his father because of a false memory.

Here's what he claims happened. While undergoing treatment for alcoholism, it had been suggested to him that one thing that explains alcohol dependence is a history of childhood sexual abuse. He had it repeatedly suggested to him by therapists and social workers that he must have been abused. While he was undergoing therapy, he was also the primary carer for his elderly father. He was exhausted. One evening, while taking care of his father, he claims that the memories all rushed back. In anger, and as an act of revenge, he committed the murder. Once in prison he realised that

---

* Details of this case have been altered to protect his identity.

these events never actually happened, and that, instead, he had been led to falsely believe and remember a terrible childhood that never was. He's now sitting in prison, not denying the act, but having difficulty understanding his own brain, his own behaviour. He had thought, for a period of time, that his father was evil. He then committed a terrible crime. If we believe his version, can we really say that he is evil?

I sent him my book, and in return he sent me a letter and a painting of a pink flower. I keep it on my desk. It's a reminder to me that through research and science communication we can give understanding and humanity back to a group that is too often deprived of both.

It is easy to forget that the complexity of the human experience does not stop just because an individual has committed a crime. A single act should not define a person. Calling someone a murderer because they once made a decision to murder someone seems inappropriate, oversimplified.

Convicts are people too. For 364 days of the year a person can be completely law-abiding, and then on the 365th they can decide to commit a crime. Even the most heinous convicted criminals spend almost all of their time *not* committing crimes. What do they do the rest of the time? Normal human stuff. They eat, they sleep, they love, they cry.

Yet it is so easy for us to write off such people and to call them evil. And this is why I love doing research in this area. And it's not just memory that fascinates me in understanding how we create evil. I have also done academic work on the topics of psychopathy and moral decision-making, and I taught a course on evil where I explored topics as diverse

as criminology, psychology, philosophy, law and neuroscience. It is at the intersection of these disciplines that I believe
the true understanding of this thing we call 'evil' lies.

The problem is that instead of facilitating such understanding, heinous crimes are generally seen as more of a
circus show than something we should try to understand.
And when we do try to lift the curtain to see the humanity
behind the exterior, others often stop us from taking a good
look. Discussing the concept of evil is still largely a taboo.

EVIL EMPATHISERS

When attempts at empathy and understanding are made,
there is often a particularly vicious utterance that is used to
shut them down; the implication that some people should
not be empathised with, lest we imply that we too are evil.

Want to discuss paedophilia? That must mean you are a
paedophile. Mention zoophilia? So, you are saying you want
to have sex with animals. Want to talk about murder fantasies? You are clearly a murderer at heart. Such
curiosity-shaming tries to keep a distance between us and
the people who are perceived to be evil. It's 'us', the good
citizens, versus 'them', the baddies. In psychology this is
called 'othering'. We other someone when we view or treat
them as inherently different to ourselves.

But such a distinction is not only adverse for discourse
and understanding, it is also fundamentally incorrect. We
may think that our labelling of others as evil or bad is rational,
and our behaviour towards such individuals justified, but the
distinction may be more trivial than we expect. I want to
help you explore the similarities between the groups of people

you consider evil and yourself, and to engage with a critical mind to try and understand them.

Our reactions to deviance may ultimately tell us less about others and more about ourselves. In this book I want to encourage a curiosity, an exploration of what evil is and the lessons we can learn from science to better understand humanity's dark side. I want you to ask questions, I want you to be hungry for knowledge, and I want to feed your hunger. Come with me on a journey to uncover the science of your living nightmares.

Let me help you find your evil empathy.

'There is no such thing as moral phenomena,
but only a moral interpretation of phenomena.'

Friedrich Nietzsche,
Beyond Good and Evil

1

YOUR INNER SADIST: THE NEUROSCIENCE OF EVIL

On Hitler's brain, aggression and psychopathy

WHEN WE TALK about evil we tend to turn our attention to Hitler. This is perhaps unsurprising, as Hitler perpetrated many of the acts that we associate with evil, including mass murder, destruction, war, torture, hate speech, propaganda and unethical science. History, and the world, will forever be stained with his memory.

A nod to the pervasiveness of our automatic connection between general badness and Hitler is even reflected in everyday human interactions. In disparaging discussions, people who say or write things that others disagree with are often described as 'Nazis' or 'like Hitler'. Godwin's Law suggests that every online comment thread will eventually lead to a Hitler comparison. These in-passing comparisons trivialise the atrocities committed, escalate discussion to a point of no return, and often effectively shut down conversation. But, I digress.

Because of the variety and depth of the devastation Hitler was both directly and indirectly responsible for, entire books have been written about his motivations, his personality and his actions. People have long wanted to know why, and how, he became the man we know from the dark pages of our history books. In this chapter, instead of dissecting the particulars of his actions, I want us to focus our attention on just one question: if you could go back in time, would you kill baby Hitler?

The answer to this one question tells me a lot about you. If you answer 'yes', then you probably believe that we are born with the predispositions to do terrible things. That evil can be in our DNA. If you answer 'no', then you probably have a less deterministic view of human behaviour, perhaps believing that environment and upbringing play a critical role in how we end up as adults. Or, perhaps, you said 'no' because killing babies is generally frowned upon.

Either way, I think that the answer is fascinating. I also think that it is almost certainly based on incomplete evidence. Because do you really know whether terrible little babies become terrible adults? And is your brain actually that different from Hitler's?

Let's do a thought experiment. If Hitler was alive today, and we put him into a neuroimaging scanner, what would we find? Would there be damaged structures, overactive sections, swastika-shaped ventricles?

Before we can reconstruct his brain, we need to first consider whether Hitler was mad, bad or both. One of the first psychological profiles of Hitler was written during World War II. It is considered to be one of the first offender profiles ever, and was written by psychoanalyst Walter Langer in 1944 for the Office of Strategic Services,[1] a US intelligence agency and early version of what would later become the Central Intelligence Agency.

The report described Hitler as 'neurotic', that he was 'bordering on schizophrenia', and made the correct predictions that he was striving for ideological immortality and would commit suicide in the face of defeat. However, the report also makes a number of pseudo-scientific assertions that are unverifiable, including that he enjoyed masochistic sex (being hurt or humiliated) and had 'coprophagic tendencies' (the desire to eat faeces).

Another attempt at a psychological profile was published in 1998, this time by psychiatrist Fritz Redlich.[2] Redlich conducts what he refers to as a pathography – a study of the life and personality of a person as influenced by disease. In studying Hitler's medical history and the medical history of his family, along with speeches and other documents, he argues that Hitler showed many psychiatric symptoms, including paranoia, narcissism, anxiety, depression and hypochondria. However, although he finds evidence for so many psychiatric symptoms that he 'could fill a psychiatry textbook', he argues that 'most of the personality functioned more than adequately' and that Hitler 'knew what he was doing and he chose to do it with pride and enthusiasm'.

Would he have wanted to kill baby Hitler? Or would he have placed more importance on Hitler's upbringing? Redlich argues that there was little to suggest during childhood that

Hitler would become a notorious, genocidal politician. He argues that, medically speaking, Hitler was a fairly normal child, who was sexually shy and did not like torturing animals or humans.

Redlich also argues against the idea that little Hitler had a particularly troublesome upbringing, and criticises psycho-historians for assuming that he did. It seems that we cannot assume this to be the cause of his later behaviour, and the unsatisfying answer to whether Hitler was mad seems to be 'no'. It turns out that this is often the case. Just because someone has committed heinous crimes does not mean that they are mentally ill. To assume that everyone who commits such crimes is mentally ill removes personal responsibility from the perpetrators of such acts, and stigmatises mental illness. So, how are people like Hitler capable of such horrors?

Working towards a 'neuroscience of human evil', psychological scientists Martin Reimann and Philip Zimbardo came up with a different idea as to why we are capable of horrible acts. In their 2011 paper, 'The Dark Side of Social Encounters',[3] the authors try to establish what parts of the brain are responsible for evil. They state that two processes are most important – deindividuation and dehumanisation. Deindividuation happens when we perceive ourselves as anonymous. Dehumanisation is when we stop seeing others as human beings, and see them as less than human. The authors also explain dehumanisation as a 'cortical cataract', a blurring of our perception. We stop being able to really see people.

This is apparent when we talk about 'the bad guys'. The statement dehumanises. It assumes that there is some homogenous group of individuals who are 'bad', and who are different from us. In this dichotomy, we, of course, are 'the good guys' – a diverse group of human beings who make ethically sound decisions. This dividing of the world into good guys and bad guys was one of Hitler's preferred approaches. Even more distressing was the development of the argument that those targeted were not even made up of 'bad people', that they were not even human. A dramatic example of dehumanising was seen in Hitler's genocidal propaganda, where he described Jewish people as *untermenschen* – subhumans. The Nazis also compared other groups they targeted to animals, insects and diseases.

More recently, the United Kingdom and United States have seen a string of vitriolic public statements about immigrants. In 2015, British media personality Katie Hopkins described migrants arriving in boats as 'cockroaches', a term that was publicly criticised by the UN's human-rights chief, Zeid Ra'ad Al Hussein. He retorted, saying, 'The Nazi media described people their masters wanted to eliminate as rats and cockroaches.'[4] He added that such language was typical of 'decades of sustained and unrestrained anti-foreigner abuse, misinformation and distortion'. Similarly, on 1 May 2017, the 100th day of his presidency, Donald Trump read aloud as part of a speech the lyrics of a song about a snake originally written in 1963 by Oscar Brown Jr.[5]

> On her way to work one morning
> Down the path alongside the lake
> A tender-hearted woman saw a poor half-frozen
>   snake.

His pretty colored skin had been all frosted with the
   dew.
'Oh well,' she cried, 'I'll take you in and I'll take care
   of you.'
. . .
Now she clutched him to her bosom, 'You're so
   beautiful,' she cried,
'But if I hadn't brought you in by now you might
   have died.'
Now she stroked his pretty skin and then she kissed
   and held him tight
But instead of saying thanks, that snake gave her a
   vicious bite.

Trump uses the story as an allegory about the dangers of
refugees. He is comparing refugees to snakes.

   This kind of oversimplified grouping of an imagined
enemy is echoed over and over in politics, partly because it
is so catchy. With a bit of help from a leader and some
inspiring rhetoric, harmful ideologies readily flourish. And,
while we all sometimes fall into this trap, some of us are
particularly prone to being influenced by such poisonous
imagery.

   This is where we really begin our imagined reconstruction
of Hitler's brain. Given his particular propensity for dehumanising, the parts of the brain responsible for this may
have been particularly affected. According to Reimann and
Zimbardo, deindividuating and dehumanising 'could potentially involve a network of brain areas, including the
ventromedial prefrontal cortex, the amygdala, and brainstem
structures (i.e., hypothalamus and periaqueductal gray)'.

Helpfully, they provide an image of their model, which I have reconstructed for you.

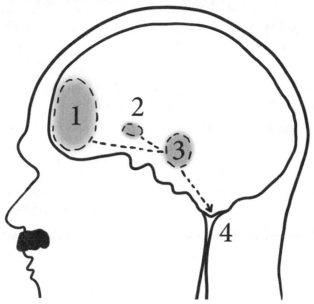

Hitler's brain: the proposed pathway to evil, which involves the ventromedial prefrontal cortex (1), the amygdala (2), the brainstem (3) and central nervous system (4).

Their model suggests that what starts as a feeling of anonymity, of not being to blame for what we do because we feel like we are simply part of a larger group, ends with an increased ability to do harm to others. Here's how they propose evil works in the brain.

Deindividuation. The person stops thinking of themselves as an individual, and identifies as an anonymous part of a group. This leads them to feeling like they are not personally accountable for their behaviour. This is related to a decrease in the activity of the ventromedial prefrontal cortex – vmPFC (1). Reducing the activity in the vmPFC is known to be linked with aggression and poor decision-making, and can lead to disinhibited and antisocial behaviour.

Dehumanisation. This decreased activity is accompanied by an increase in activity in the amygdala (2), the emotion part of the brain. This is linked to feelings such as anger and fear.

Antisocial behaviour. Then, these experienced emotions go via the brainstem (3) to trigger other sensations (4), like increased heart rate, blood pressure and gut feelings. These changes are essentially the body getting into fight-or-flight mode – anticipating bodily harm and getting ready to survive.

It is argued that this pathway is enhanced in those who have an underactive vmPFC, and has been seen repeatedly in studies of offenders. Research has shown that murderers and psychopaths in particular have decreased activity in the vmPFC. Just as an underactive thyroid means that your metabolism is defective and you are more likely to become overweight, it is thought by researchers, including Reimann and Zimbardo, that an underactive vmPFC means that your moral judgement is defective and you are more likely to commit crime and do other antisocial acts. As Reimann and Zimbardo summarise, 'Research on aggression suggests that decreased activation of frontal lobe structures, particularly the prefrontal cortex, or lesioning of this brain area can be a central cause for aggression.'

If we were to peek into Hitler's brain, it would probably look normal at first, but when asking him to make moral decisions we might see an underactive vmPFC, combined with indicators of his general paranoia and anxiety. However, given that he did not have any major abnormalities or brain damage that we know of, it seems very unlikely that I could tell the difference between a scan of an average healthy brain and a scan of Hitler's. Knowing nothing about you, I probably would not be able to tell apart a scan of your brain and of Hitler's brain.

Instead of thinking of some people as particularly bad, and others as good, let's rethink this and flip the question: rather than asking if a few specific people are predisposed to being sadistic, we should ask: do we all have a sadistic predisposition?

EVERYDAY SADISM

According to a 1999 paper by psychological scientists Roy Baumeister and Keith Campbell, 'Sadism, defined as the direct achievement of pleasure from harming others, is the most obviously intrinsic appeal of evil acts.'[6] They argue that the existence of sadism makes other theories or explanations of evil obsolete – 'People do it because it feels good; enough said.'

Inspired partly by Baumeister's work, and further arguing that sadism is actually pretty normal, are Erin Buckels and colleagues.[7] In a paper published in 2013, they argue that 'current conceptions of sadism rarely

extend beyond those of sexual fetishes or criminal behavior
. . . Yet enjoyment of cruelty occurs in apparently normal,
everyday people . . . These commonplace manifestations
of cruelty implicate a subclinical form of sadism, or, simply,
everyday sadism.'

As part of her research Buckels and her team conducted
two ingenious experiments. As they describe in their paper,
'Needless to say, it is not possible to study human murder
in the laboratory. We therefore turned to a proxy behavior
more amenable to ethical research, namely, killing bugs.'
Needless to say, indeed. So, instead of asking participants
to murder people, they asked them to murder bugs. Of course
we all know that bugs aren't really a proxy for people – we
have probably all killed bugs – but this task might still be
able to tell us something about who is willing to be sadistic
and who isn't.

How did it work? The researchers recruited participants
for a study on 'personality and tolerance for challenging
jobs'. Once they arrived at the lab, the participants got to
choose to do one of four tasks that mirrored real jobs. They
could either be an exterminator (kill bugs), an exterminator's
assistant (help the experimenter kill bugs), a sanitation worker
(clean toilets), or a worker in a cold environment (endure
pain from icy water). The group they were most interested
in were the participants who chose to be exterminators. This
group was given a bug-crunching coffee grinder and three
cups, each with a live bug.

What was particularly creative about this study was its
design. According to the team, 'To maximise gruesomeness,
we designed a killing machine that produced a distinct
crunching sound. To anthropomorphise the victims, we gave

them endearing names.' The names were written on the side of the cups – Muffin, Ike and Tootsie.

Do you think you would choose to kill the bugs? To hear them get crushed alive, just because you had been asked to do so? In this particular study, just over a quarter (26.8 per cent) of participants chose to kill the bugs. The next question is whether you would enjoy killing them. According to the study results, the higher participants ranked on sadistic impulses, the more they enjoyed killing the bugs and the more likely they were to kill all three bugs rather than stop before their task was complete. These were normal people, many of whom took pleasure in killing the living critters.

A quick test: as I described the methodology, did you worry about the wellbeing of the bugs at any point? Maybe you were even chuckling away to yourself, thinking how much fun killing bugs is. Hmmm . . . you would probably score in the researchers' higher range of subclinical sadism. Luckily for Muffin, Ike and Tootsie, 'unbeknownst to participants, a barrier prevented the bugs from reaching the grinding blades'. The researchers assure us that no bugs were harmed in the making of this science.

The team also conducted a second, completely different, experiment. This one was all about hurting innocent victims. Here, participants played a computer game against an opponent who they believed to be another participant in a different room. They had to press a button faster than their opponent, and the winner got to 'blast' their opponents with a noise, the loudness of which the winner got to control. Half of the participants got to blast right away after winning, while others had to do a short but boring task before they were allowed

to administer the noise. The boring task involved counting
the number of times a particular letter appeared in nonsense
text. It was easy but tedious. Their imaginary opponent
always chose the lowest blast level, so that there would be
no need for retaliation.

Would you blast your opponent? How loud would you
go? Finally, would you be willing to work for the opportunity
to hurt them? The study results show that while many of us
would be willing to hurt an innocent victim, only those who
scored higher on sadism increased the sound once they
realised that the other person did not fight back. Those were
also the only people willing to do the boring task in order
to hurt their opponents.

It appears that many 'normal' people are willing to be
sadistic. The results led the researchers to argue that we need
to get to know ourselves better if we want to really get an
understanding of sadism. 'For the phenomenon of sadism
to be fully addressed, its everyday nature and surprising
commonness need to be acknowledged.'

What are the common characteristics of these kinds of
sadistic behaviours? One common theme that appears is
aggression. When you hurt something else, for example
when you kill a bug, you are acting aggressively. Similarly,
in order to get sadistic pleasure, it seems that most of the
time one must first do something aggressive. So let's back
it up a bit. What other kinds of aggression are there? Let's
start with a type of aggression that you have probably felt
but never understood: a weird feeling that you want to hurt
tiny, fluffy animals.

CUTE AGGRESSION

One unexpected situation in which our sadistic tendencies seem to show themselves is in the presence of cute animals. Have you ever seen a puppy that was so adorable that you just couldn't handle it? Where you felt like you wanted to take your hands and squeeze its floppy little face *really* hard? Some animals are just so cute that we feel a bit like we want to hurt them. Kittens, puppies, baby quail, we want to squeeze them hard, pinch their cheeks, bite them, growl at them.

But why does this happen? Aren't psychopaths and serial killers known for hurting animals? Researchers assure us that most of us don't actually want to harm animals, so although it sounds sadistic, these emotions are not indicative of some deep, dark secret lurking inside you. You probably love Fluffy, and don't actually want to hurt him. However, this does not resolve the issue of why our brains tempt and torture us with a quasi-aggressive reaction. This feeling of wanting to hurt things that we find cute is so common that there is a term for it – 'cute aggression'.

Oriana Aragón and colleagues from Yale University were the first to study this bizarre phenomenon, publishing a paper about it in 2015.[8] They conducted a number of studies on the idea. Participants in one of their studies were shown pictures of cute animals and handed a large sheet of bubble wrap. 'We hypothesised that if people have the impulse to squeeze while viewing cute stimuli, and we provide them with both cute stimuli and something to squeeze, that indeed they will squeeze.' Participants who viewed pictures of baby animals popped significantly more bubbles than those who saw pictures of adult animals.

The authors then wondered whether perhaps the aggression people felt would go away if the participants had something akin to an animal on their laps – something which would be an outlet for their feelings. For this, the researchers created a pillow 'made of extremely soft, silky fur material', and had half of their participants hold it while looking at cute pictures of animals. They reasoned that if provided with something to squeeze and caress, people might not have the aggressive emotions.

They found the opposite of what they were expecting. Participants showed more cute aggression because the researchers had 'added a tactile stimulus of cuteness'. They concluded that this may be indicative of what could happen if their participants had actually handled baby animals: 'When considering people handling actual small, soft, fluffy animals, [the added stimulus] may lead to an increase in these aggressive expressions.' In other words, seeing pictures of kitties online is squeeze-worthy, but handling them in person feels like it is *just too much*.

According to the research team, this also extends to babies. See how you respond to the following statements, which are from a longer list that Aragón and colleagues gave to their participants.

1. If I am holding an extremely cute baby, I have the urge to squeeze his or her little fat legs.
2. If I look at an extremely cute baby, I want to pinch those cheeks.

3. When I see something I think is so cute, I clench my hands into fists.
4. I am the type of person that will tell a cute child, 'I could just eat you up!' through gritted teeth.

If you agree with any of these statements, then you suffer from cute aggression not just towards kitties and puppies, but also to baby humans. This too can make for weird emotions, where parents might worry about their own feelings towards their children. (Why do I feel like I want to hurt my baby when I would never actually do her any harm?) It's one of many dark thoughts parents can have and don't want to share with anyone else, for fear of being labelled a bad parent, a bad person. But when this happens, don't be alarmed. This feeling seems to be quite normal, and isn't entirely surprising. Cute aggression is likely a by-product of an adaptive human characteristic. If we think something is cute, we generally want to keep it alive, we want to take care of it. This is probably also what has encouraged us to keep cute animals as pets in the first place.

This is particularly likely to happen when we see something that fits the 'baby schema' – large, wide-set eyes, round cheeks and small chins.[9] It doesn't matter if it's not actually a human baby, or even a real animal. We think cartoons are cute if they fit this schema, we can feel this about stuffed animals, and Google designed its first self-driving car to fit this format so that we would be less scared of the new technology.

In the cute-aggression research, the authors propose that because this cuteness creates in us such strong, positive feelings, our brains are overwhelmed by an expression of care, which the brain tries to counteract with an expression of aggression. This happens because humans sometimes have 'dimorphous displays': we don't always respond to things with a single emotion, but with two emotions simultaneously. And these can consist of both positive and negative emotions that are all muddled up.

Dimorphous emotions happen when we feel so over-whelmed by emotion. Probably to avoid emotional overload that could cause harm to it, the brain throws in a counter-acting emotion – like crying when we are really happy, or smiling at a funeral, or wanting to squeeze something we really care about. That means next time you want to squeeze a cute animal, it probably doesn't mean you are sadistic towards cute things, it is more likely to mean that your brain is overloaded and trying not to short-circuit.

Let's tie this back in with evil. Having a tendency to actually hurt fluffy animals or little babies is probably well within many people's conceptualisation of evil. But, loving them *so much* that your brain has to protect itself from exploding with joy? That probably isn't.

Speaking of aggression towards things we love, a target of mine is my significant other. I like to playfully slap him, squeeze him and annoy him. But at what point does this stop being cute and start being aggressive? Should I be worried? Should he?

It turns out that the term cute aggression might be a misnomer, not fitting with commonly accepted definitions of aggression at all. Cute aggression probably really isn't aggression at all, it just *looks* like aggression. This is even something the researchers who coined the term accepted. So if that isn't real aggression, what actually *is* aggression?

US-based psychological scientist Deborah Richardson has been studying aggression for decades. Together with Robert Baron, in 1994 she defined aggression as 'any behaviour directed toward the goal of harming another living being'. Aggression, they argue, has four necessary characteristics.[10] First, aggression is a behaviour. It's not a thought, idea or attitude. Second, aggression is intentional. Accidents don't count. Third, aggression involves wanting to harm. You need to want to hurt someone. Fourth, aggression is directed towards a living being. Not robots or inanimate objects.

As Richardson explains, 'Breaking a plate or throwing a chair to express general annoyance would not be aggression. Trying to hurt your mother by breaking her prized antique plate or throwing a chair *at* your friend in hopes of hurting him *would* be considered aggression.'

When we look past the playful, pseudo-aggressive behaviours we sometimes have in relationships to more serious aggression, the question becomes: why do we hurt the ones we love? Well, anger appears to be a key motivation. In a 2006 study on aggression towards loved ones by psychologists Deborah Richardson and Laura Green,[11] participants were asked to discuss their aggression towards a person with whom they had been angry in the last month. Thirty-five per cent stated they had been angry with a friend, 35 per cent with a romantic partner, 16 per cent with siblings and 14 per cent with a parent. The report also found that most of these people acted aggressively towards the people they were angry with. Our loved ones are easily accessible, often stir up strong emotions in us, and we are often dependent on them in some way.

This seems to be a potent mix for becoming the targets of our aggression.

For romantic partners specifically, motives for aggression and violence also include retaliation for emotional hurt, to get a partner's attention, jealousy and stress.[12] We hurt those we love for so many reasons. Some of those reasons are difficult, deeply rooted and hard to control. But there are a few things that we can control to reduce our likelihood of acting aggressively.

One may involve simply grabbing a snack.

According to a 2014 study by Roy Bushman and colleagues,[13] self-control requires brain food in the form of glucose (sugar). Because aggression can result from poor emotional and physical self-control, they wanted to explore the link between glucose and aggression. They asked 107 married couples to measure their sugar levels every morning before breakfast and every evening before bed for three weeks. The researchers also measured their aggression levels towards their partner by giving each participant a voodoo doll along with 51 pins, and telling them, 'This doll represents your spouse. At the end of each day, for 21 consecutive days, insert between 0 and 51 pins in the doll, depending how angry you are with your spouse. You will do this alone, without your spouse being present.'

The researchers also measured aggression at the end of the study by giving participants the ability to blast their spouse with a noise through headphones. The noise was specifically selected to be a mixture of sounds that most of us hate, including fingernails scratching on a chalkboard, dentist drills and ambulance sirens. According to the researchers, 'Basically, within the ethical limits of the laboratory, participants controlled a weapon that could be used to blast their spouse with unpleasant noise.' Luckily for the spouses, and unbeknownst to the participants, the noise did not actually reach the spouses' ears, but was recorded by a computer instead.

Participants who had lower glucose levels stuck more pins into the voodoo doll and blasted their spouse with louder and longer noises. The researchers concluded that eating regularly and keeping up your glucose levels should help to reduce aggression and conflict in relationships. So, next time you feel like fighting with a partner, eat something first. Have a chocolate bar. Make sure you are actually angry and not just *hangry*.

Putting food aside, our style of aggression seems to also depend on our victim. In their study on aggression towards loved ones, Richardson and Green also found that 'when people are angry with a romantic partner or sibling, they are likely to confront them face-to-face. However, when people are angry with a friend, they are likely to avoid direct confrontation by delivering harm circuitously – for instance, by spreading rumors or talking behind his or her back.'[14] Clearly, aggression can take many forms.

Let's now pick apart the definition of aggression a bit further. What are the different kinds of aggression? In 2014 Richardson summarised over two decades of her own research on aggression.[15] She argued that there are three main types of aggression. The first, direct aggression, involves striking out with hurtful words or actions, for example by yelling at someone or hitting them. This can be picking a verbal fight with an intimate partner, mocking a friend to hurt them, or being hurtfully sarcastic. In more extreme forms, this can lead to intimate partner violence and assault.

The second, indirect aggression, is less obvious. Indirectly aggressive behaviours involve attempting to hurt someone by going through an object or another person. This can include actions like damaging someone's possessions or spreading rumours. Indirect aggression also includes the concept of social aggression, which is harming someone by damaging or disrupting their relationships.[16]

Finally, there is a third form of aggression. The third type is by far the most common, and it involves hurting someone by being non-responsive – passive aggression. For your own enjoyment I have the entire set of passive-aggression items from the revised Richardson Conflict Response Questionnaire.[17] I encourage you to use this as a moment of introspection. Think about someone you love. A parent, a sibling, a lover, a friend. Now think about your history with that person, and whether you have done any of the following in an attempt to hurt them, punish them or make them otherwise unhappy:

- Did not do what the person wanted me to do
- Made mistakes that appeared to be accidental
- Seemed uninterested in things that were important to the person
- Gave the person the 'silent treatment'
- Ignored the person's contributions
- Excluded the person from important activities
- Avoided interacting with the person
- Failed to deny false rumours about the person
- Failed to return calls or respond to messages
- Showed up late for planned activities
- Slowed down on tasks

If you said yes to any of these, then you have been passive aggressive to someone you love. With friends we may intentionally ignore an apologetic text message, with parents we may show up late to frustrate them, and with lovers we may withhold sex to punish them for perceived wrongdoing. Why do we do these things? One reason might be that this kind of behaviour is easy to deny. If you are found out and accused of being passive aggressive in an argument, it's the kind of behaviour where you might say 'What? I didn't *do* anything.' We can tell ourselves that, because this is aggression through inaction rather than action, we are blameless. In reality though, passive aggression can be just as harmful to relationships and the psychological wellbeing of others as the other types of aggression.

It seems that both sadism and aggression can be everyday emotions. But surely there must be a difference between someone who passively aggressively doesn't put the dishes away, and a person who spreads vicious lies, or someone who assaults people on street corners?

According to psychologist Delroy Paulhus and colleagues, 'In common parlance, aggression is a trait, that is, a stable and enduring style of thinking, acting, and feeling.'[18] A trait is when you say that someone *is* something: 'Sam is aggressive.' This means that in everyday conversations we often speak of aggression as something that is a fundamental part of a person.

But Paulhus and colleagues claim that aggression is not itself the underlying personality flaw. We may focus on aggression as a trait that makes us evil. But perhaps aggression isn't even a trait. It's simply a manifestation of various other traits, a collection of emotions and actions that result from being human, and that everyone is capable of. Although we may not like to think of it this way, aggression is normal, not evil.

But some of us do have a cluster of personality traits that make us more likely to be aggressive. These traits are collectively known as the 'dark tetrad'.

THE DARK TETRAD

In a paper published in 2014,[19] Paulhus uses the phrase 'dark personalities' to refer to a set of socially aversive traits in the subclinical range. The traits are subclinical because the person does not meet enough of the criteria to be diagnosed with any of the disorders in a clinical setting (by a psychologist or psychiatrist). People with dark personalities are able to 'get along (even flourish) in everyday work settings, scholastic settings, and the broader community'. The 'dark tetrad' is a collection of such 'dark personality' traits, including psychopathy, sadism, narcissism and Machiavellianism.

When it comes to diagnosing people with personality disorders, researchers and clinical psychologists often talk about thresholds. For example, to be classified as being a psychopath you need to score at least 30 (or 25, depending on who you talk to) out of a possible score of 40 on the psychopathy checklist.[20] With this cut-off, anyone who scores 29 or lower is considered not to be a psychopath. However, as you can imagine, the difference between a score of 29 and one of 30 is mostly arbitrary, and the matter of much dispute among scientists. To deal with this, scientists have increasingly treated psychopathy as a continuum. Today, scientists mostly want to know what happens as people score higher on psychopathy, not just whether they meet a cut-off. The same is true for sadism, narcissism and Machiavellianism. Within this research, one of the key questions has become: as people score higher on these measures, do they become more likely to hurt people?

Before I continue, I want to issue a warning. Research on each of these traits is compelling, but also fraught with problems. By using terms like 'dark' or even 'psychopathic' to describe human beings, we run the risk of dehumanising them. We also run the risk of accepting the idea that a certain person *is* bad. That wrongdoers cannot change because evil is in their DNA. It feels like medical monsterisation. So, approach the next section with caution, and resist the urge to think that those who have dark-tetrad traits are 'bad'.

First up, we have psychopathy. In 1833 Dr James Prichard formulated an early version of what we now call psychopathy. He called it 'moral insanity'.[21] People diagnosed with moral insanity were thought to make bad moral judgements, but had no defects in their intelligence or mental health. Psychopaths, too, are often clever and sane, and are more likely to do things that are widely considered to be immoral. Today, the most commonly used definition of psychopathy comes in the form of the Psychopathy Checklist Revised (PCL-R).[22] The first psychopathy checklist was created in the 1970s by Canadian psychologist Robert Hare, as a more structured way for psychologists and researchers to diagnose someone as a psychopath. Based on the checklist, some of the defining features of psychopathy are: superficial charm, lying, lack of remorse, antisocial behavior, egocentricity and – most importantly – a lack of empathy.

Most would argue that the defining feature of psychopathy is the lack of empathy. A lack of empathy is strongly linked with crime. Such a diagnosis means that when the person commits crimes or breaks rules they aren't weighed down by things like remorse or sadness. Empathy really gets in the way of hurting people. Psychopaths can be particularly ruthless, and I have more than once heard them referred to by academics matter-of-factly as monsters. There seems to be the consensus that there are offenders and then there are psychopathic offenders. They seem to live in a separate, scary, category.

Is this empathy deficit rooted in the brain? According to a 2017 synthesis (a meta-analysis) of neuroimaging research on psychopaths, 'Recent brain-imaging studies suggest abnormal brain activity underlying psychopathic behaviour.'[23] It seems the brains of psychopaths are different from the brains of non-psychopaths. The article concludes that 'psychopathy is characterised by abnormal brain activity of bilateral prefrontal cortices [the front part of the brain] and the right amygdala [near the middle of the brain], which mediate psychological functions known to be impaired in psychopaths'. In other words, neither the decision-making part of the brain nor the emotional part of the brain are working quite right. Because of findings like these, some have argued that you could, at least partially, blame the brain when a psychopath makes the decision to commit a crime.

But, just like we could probably not look into Hitler's brain and spot a monster, we also could not look at the brain of a psychopath and say they are going to be aggressive. This is illustrated by the case of James Fallon. Fallon studies the brains of psychopathic killers. After scanning the brains of many of his participants, he held in his hands the image of a clearly pathological brain. As it turned out, this brain was his own. 'I've never killed anybody, or raped anyone,' said Fallon in an interview in 2013. 'The first thing I thought was that maybe my hypothesis was wrong, and that these brain areas are not reflective of psychopathy or murderous behaviour.'[24]

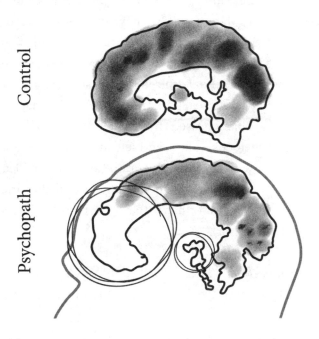

The brain of a psychopath. Fallon's brain (bottom), viewed from the side, shows a lack of activity in the parts of the brain involved with empathy and making good decisions. It is a classic example of a psychopathic brain.

He then asked his mum about it, and found that hidden in his family tree were at least eight people who had probably killed someone. Based on this, and after further research on himself, he accepted that he might actually be a psychopath. He labelled himself a 'pro-social psychopath', someone who has difficulty feeling empathy but behaves in socially accept- able ways. In 2015 he even published a book about it called *The Psychopath Inside*.[25] Not all psychopaths are created equal, it turns out, and certainly not all psychopaths are criminals. Even someone born with the brain of a killer might never kill anyone, although they are more likely to do so.

Second on our dark tetrad, we have narcissism. According to American psychological scientist Sara Konrath and her colleagues, 'Some individuals think they are great and special people who should be admired and respected by others. Such people are often called narcissists . . . The narcissistic personality is characterised by inflated views of the self, grandiosity, self-focus, vanity, and self-importance.'[26] So, how can we spot a narcissist? Konrath and her colleagues conducted eleven separate studies, and found that there is one very useful questionnaire that can help us identify a narcissist. Here it is:

The Single-Item Narcissism Scale (SINS)
To what extent do you agree with this statement: 'I am a narcissist'?

(Note: The word 'narcissist' means egotistical, self- focused, and vain.)

1	2	3	4	5	6	7
not very true of me						very true of me

That's the whole thing. If there were an award for shortest personality measure, this would win it. Why does it work? According to Brad Bushman, one of the co-creators of the scale, 'People who are narcissists are almost proud of the fact . . . You can ask them directly because they don't see narcissism as a negative quality – they believe they are superior to other people and are fine with saying that publicly.'[27]

While narcissists may believe themselves to be great, others do not always agree. Those of us who are high on narcissism are often seen to be arrogant, argumentative and opportunistic.

But it seems that not all narcissists arc as fundamentally convinced about their own superiority as Bushman implies. Narcissism has been classified into two types, grandiose and vulnerable. While grandiose narcissists are seen as being show-offs, egotistical and assertive, vulnerable narcissists are seen as complaining, bitter and defensive. The vulnerability and particularly dislikable characteristics of the second group seem to come from not fully buying in to their own superiority.

Grandiose narcissists can be frustrating, but vulnerable narcissists can be dangerous. In 2014, Zlatan Krizan and Omesh Johar wrote about narcissistic rage – an explosive mix of anger and hostility.[28] Only vulnerable narcissism appears to be linked with this particular type of anger. The authors explain that over the course of their research they have found that 'narcissistic vulnerability (but not grandiosity) [is] a powerful driver of rage, hostility, and aggressive behaviour', and that this is 'fuelled by suspiciousness, dejection, and angry rumination'. This shows that those of us who mask our insecurities with a façade of superiority are particularly at risk of doing harm to others.

Next on the dark tetrad we have Machiavellianism, which is the least well known of the tetrad traits. The name is based on the Italian Renaissance diplomat and writer Machiavelli, who, in his book *The Prince*, advocated that, to obtain their goals, some people are willing to use all means necessary. The ends justify the means, and it's fine if it involves manipulation, flattery and lying.[29] In their 2017 paper, Peter Muris and colleagues defined Machiavellianism as 'a duplicitous interpersonal style, a cynical disregard for morality, and a focus on self-interest and personal gain'.[30] Rather than lacking empathy like the psychopath, or feeling superior like the narcissist, this is a more functional social strategy. It's about power and personal gain.

Machiavellianism is typically diagnosed with a tool called the MACH-IV.[31] Muris and colleagues go on to explain that there are three parts of Machiavellianism: 'manipulative tactics (e.g., "It is wise to flatter important people"), a cynical view of human nature (e.g., "Anyone who completely trusts anyone is asking for trouble"), and disregard for conventional morality (e.g., "Sometimes one should take action even when one knows that it is not morally right")'. Ultimately, the idea is that someone who scores high on this trait is willing to do whatever it takes to achieve their goals.

Finally on the dark tetrad, we arrive back at the topic we've already discussed at length – sadism. This was a recent addition in 2013, and was actually a by-product of the bug-crushing study we discussed earlier (surely you remember Muffin, Ike and Tootsie?). It was after this series of everyday sadism experiments that Erin Buckels and her colleagues proposed to change what was known as the 'dark triad' to the 'dark tetrad' (psychopathy, sadism, narcissism and Machiavellianism).[32] Darkness gained another dimension.

Those of us who score high on any one of these dark traits, but particularly those who are high on all of them, are far more likely to break society's rules. Dark tetrad does as dark tetrad wants. But is this always a bad thing?

THE GOOD SIDE OF YOUR BAD SIDE

Many of the traits that look exceptionally negative on the surface might have some value once we lift them up and actually inspect them. Research on the dark tetrad shows that these characteristics actually help some of us succeed. Our researcher with the brain of a psychopath, Fallon, claims that his psychopathy makes him more ambitious. Similarly, aspects of Machiavellianism, particularly the willingness to do whatever it takes to get to the top, may help someone to thrive in a corporate setting.

Along the same vein, in 2001 a paper was written entitled 'Is narcissism really so bad?' (which sounds *exactly* like a title a narcissist would choose).[33] In it, researcher Keith Campbell concludes that 'narcissism may be a functional and healthy strategy for dealing with the modern world. The notion that narcissists are fragile, depleted or depressed simply does not square with current research on normal samples.'

What about sadism? That's a bit more tricky. It seems to me that in the constant battle between our senses of morality, empathy and desire to survive, a bit of sadism may well have also been good for us. Getting some pleasure from cruelty may have made it easier for us to kill animals, kill humans, or do other unpalatable things on which our survival depended. When empathy gets in the way of hurting others, sadism might help us do what we need to do.

Perhaps there is a good side to your bad side. Intuitively, however, it still feels as though there must be people, and acts, that are *unequivocally* evil. So far, we have not found them. From this chapter it seems that there is no such thing as an evil brain, an evil personality or an evil trait. We can hunt for them all we want, applying psychological tests and societal labels, but ultimately we find ourselves knee-deep in complicated and nuanced aspects of humanity. Even one of history's archetypes of evil, Hitler, was a human being with a neurological profile probably not as different from ours as we may wish to believe.

Throughout this book we will explore many aspects of human behaviour that have negative consequences, are at odds with our values, or are labelled evil. We will not shy away from that which makes us uncomfortable, and we will repeatedly ask ourselves one main question: 'Is it evil?'

As a kid I used to love the *Scooby-Doo* cartoons. Arriving in their 'Mystery Machine' van, the team of four kids and their talking dog would be summoned to find a monster who was terrorising a local neighbourhood. They would then run around looking for clues as to who the monster was, and at the end they would capture and unmask him. It was always some normal person in a costume. There were no monsters.

Like the Scooby crew, we may find ourselves inadvertently hunting for an easy fix, an easy excuse, an easy word – evil. But instead we will find that there are no simple explanations for why humans do bad things, that there are many, and they are marvellously nuanced.

Although there may be differences between the brains of those who do 'bad' things and those who don't, acknowledging the similarities between us can be far more striking than aggressively highlighting the differences. It seems that for all of us, our brains make us capable of great harm. So, if it cannot be easily identified in the brain, what is it that stops many of us from acting out sadistic impulses? For example, what's the difference between you and a murderer? Well, to this issue we turn next.

2

MURDER BY DESIGN: THE PSYCHOLOGY OF BLOODLUST

*On serial killers, toxic masculinity
and ethical dilemmas*

WE LOVE KILLING. Which is great, because we need to kill to survive. Hungry? Kill something to eat. Sick? Kill the bacteria before they kill you. Threatened by something? Kill in self-defence. Not sure what it is? Kill it, just in case.

We love killing so much that our species is referred to as a 'super predator'. This is because humans kill more in terms of quantity and diversity than any other predator. According to a 2015 review of behaviours by different kinds of predators, the conservation scientist Chris Darimont and colleagues concluded that humans kill so much that we 'alter ecological and evolutionary processes globally'.[1] The team also concluded that we kill so much that it is unsustainable.

While all this killing is going on, there is one kind of killing that we care about most – that is, killing members of our own species. But we care about it in a weird way. While on the one hand we condemn murder, many of us also fantasise about it.

Some of us fantasise about throwing our boss out the window, about forever silencing that screaming baby, or dream about a scenario where we stab an ex-lover right in the heart. I regularly feel like I want to kill people – you know, *just a little bit*. Especially when they are dawdling at airports.

The normality of murder fantasies – or 'homicidal ideation' as it is sometimes referred to by researchers – was first established by Douglas Kenrick and Virgil Sheets at Arizona State University. Back in 1993 these two psychological scientists asked participants whether they had ever had a murder fantasy.[2] Perhaps surprisingly, the majority said yes. In their first study, in fact, 73 per cent of men and 66 per cent of women said yes. To confirm that this wasn't just a particularly murderous sample, and to gather some more details about what the fantasies focused on, a second study was conducted. Similar rates were found. This time, 79 per cent of men and 58 per cent of women claimed they had murder fantasies. Who did the participants want to kill? Men were more likely to imagine killing strangers and co-workers, while women preferred family members. Another popular target group were step-parents . . . like a horror-movie version of *Cinderella*.

Why does this happen? According to scientists Joshua Duntley and David Buss, fantasizing about killing is an evolutionary strategy, albeit one with questionable usefulness in much of the modern world.[3] It is part of our evolved psychological design. Murder fantasies are a product of the human capacity for abstract thought and hypothetical planning – if I did this, what would happen? They allow us to play out entire scenarios. They help us to always be prepared for the worst, and to entertain ways of improving our quality of life by getting rid of people who stand between us and our goals.

And it is when we mentally rehearse these situations that most of us quickly realise murdering someone probably isn't what we actually want to do, that we don't want the devastating consequences. Those who don't have this capacity to mentally test potential future behaviours and their likely consequences might act more impulsively, and live to regret it. As we will learn, dealing impulsively with frustration is a major contributor to murder.

But some of us don't just fantasise about murder, we actually go through with it. So, who are these people? Why do people murder each other? If we ask our evolutionary psychologists Duntley and Buss, they would argue that this is because sometimes it makes sense to kill people, at least from an evolutionary standpoint. Humans murder because they have been designed to do so.

According to their Homicide Adaptation Theory, when we weigh the costs and benefits of killing another member of our species, there is quite a bit that can be gained from killing, particularly for men. In a paper they published in 2011, they write: 'Killing historically conferred large fitness benefits:

preventing premature death, removing cost-inflicting rivals, gaining resources, aborting rivals' prenatal offspring, eliminating stepchildren, and winnowing future competitors of one's children.' Although risky, as murder is often detected and can endanger the person who murders, they conclude that murder was at times still a winning strategy.

Before we continue, let's talk about definitions. The term 'murder' is typically used to describe the *unlawful* killing of another person. In other words, it does not include killing in self-defence or in state-sanctioned situations like the death penalty or in war. The death can be the result of wanting to kill the person, or wanting to hurt them really badly and it resulting in their death. This is the necessary *'mens rea'* ('guilty mind') for a killing to be regarded as murder.

A broader term is 'homicide'. This typically includes both murder and manslaughter, the latter of which is a lesser crime that still involves killing another person but in which either (a) there was intention to kill, but there are mitigating factors such as loss of control or diminished responsibility ('voluntary manslaughter'), or (b) there was no intention to kill, but there was gross negligence or the killing happened as part of another inherently criminal and dangerous act ('involuntary manslaughter'). This we will only touch on in passing.

Exact differences between manslaughter, murder and homicide can be complicated and differ between countries. So, when I use the term homicide I am going to use the same definition as the 2013 United Nations global review on homicide, arguably the most comprehensive such review to date.[4] They define it as 'unlawful death purposefully inflicted on a person by another person', i.e., intentional and unlawful murder.

The UN report makes it clear that it is important to study homicide not just because it is 'the ultimate crime' but because it creates a ripple effect which goes far beyond the loss of life, and 'can create a climate of fear and uncertainty'. Homicide rates can affect entire communities, making people scared to go out at night, or to visit certain neighbourhoods. The report highlights that homicide 'also victimises the family and community of the victim, who can be considered secondary victims'. It's not just the person who is killed that matters, but their families and friends who have to suffer the consequences.

Compared to other kinds of crime, studying murder is relatively easy. If a person is killed, found dead or goes missing, the chance of this being reported is very high, and the 'dark figure', the number of unreported crimes, is quite low. This stands in contrast to crimes such as rape and sexual abuse, for which we often have very few reports, resulting in a very large dark figure. Because of this, according to the UN report, it is 'the most readily measurable, clearly defined and most comparable indicator for measuring violent deaths around the world'. The report further states that this transparency makes homicide 'both a reasonable proxy for violent crime as well as a robust indicator of levels of security within States'.

According to the UN review, in 2012 almost half a million (437,000) people were murdered around the world. This rate has fluctuated over time. While the media might have us believe otherwise, we can see from the study that, after a peak between 1991 and 1993, recorded homicide rates have since generally dropped around the world.

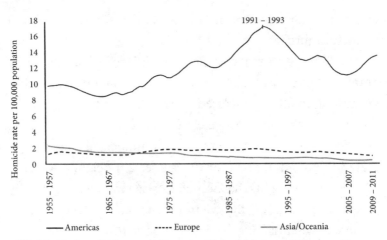

Worldwide homicide rates, from the United Nations Office on Drugs and Crime, *Global Study on Homicide, 2013*

From a graphical representation of their findings, we can also see that there are enormous differences in homicide rates in different parts of the world, with the Americas having a rate that is about ten times higher than Europe and Asia/Oceania. This does not mean that people in different countries are inherently more violent, but is instead due to the complex interplay of social factors. Murder rates can differ in relation to the affluence of the countries (their GDP), culture and oppression, political or social conflict, and access to weapons. Particularly in places like the USA, easy access to guns is often seen as a major contributor to murder rates.

The report also looked into the types of people who commit homicides. Most murder is committed by men against men, with an astonishing 95 per cent of perpetrators and 79 per cent of victims being male. We also know that most people who commit murder (in terms of raw numbers) live in the Americas. Favourite murder weapons differ based on country. In the Americas, 66 per cent of murders are committed with a firearm. Those convicted of murder elsewhere in the world are more likely to use sharp objects like knives, or other ways of killing – including using blunt objects, physical force or poison. Finally, when men kill women, the women they kill are likely to be their intimate partners or family members. While 47 per cent of females were killed by intimate partners or family members in 2012, only 6 per cent of men were.

This gives us a very basic picture of what homicide looks like around the world, but it does not answer the far more interesting question of why people kill each other. To this, we turn next.

THE BANALITY OF MURDER

I really dislike typologies that try to label people who have committed murder based on the crime scenes they leave behind, or their perceived subconscious motivations – 'By golly, I think this murderer is motivated by power. He probably still lives with his mum. Clearly, he is a deranged psychopath.' I partially blame TV shows for making it seem that this kind of offender-profiling is interesting or useful – I think it is neither.

However, I do rather like a functional typology. In this regard, what researchers Albert Roberts and colleagues put together in a paper published in 2007 bears examination.[5] Here they argue that 'homicide is not a homogeneous behavior. Homicide perpetrators are not the same in terms of motivation, environmental factors, demographics, and interpersonal dynamics. Different factors of complex

combinations precipitate homicides.' Note that their taxonomy leaves out murders committed for political reasons.

Despite this complexity, they found that most homicides
fit quite well into a four-fold typology that is based on only
the most essential elements of the crime. The first type is
'altercation or argument precipitated homicides' – in other
words, fights that escalate, sometimes for ridiculous reasons.
They are impulsive responses to minor frustrations. Some
examples taken from the paper include:

- Argument and fight over $4.00. Victim died from beating.
- Defendant hit victim in the head with a 2x4 because they
  were fighting over a bike. Shot victim over argument over
  dog.
- Shot victim after argument over glasses.
- Beat victim with a bat and dumped his body in the woods.
  Argued over drugs.
- Defendant shot victim after some altercation they had
  earlier in the day.
- Beat victim with baseball bat over money.

These seem like some pretty standard fights that got
completely out of hand, and in the heat of the moment
someone was killed. It's safe to say the response of murder
in these situations is not proportionate to the magnitude of
the argument. It goes to show that murder motives are based
on the perception that the violence is justified in the moment,
rather than what most people would see as reasonable justification later on.

The second type of homicide is a 'felony homicide'. This
is where someone intentionally kills another during the

commission of a serious crime. These murders are typically committed during a robbery, burglary or kidnapping. Here, the ultimate goal is not to kill the person, but to get access to money or other gains. The person who is killed is either in the way, like when a perpetrator is trying to burgle a house and the owners happen to be home, or is part of the crime, like holding someone ransom and then killing them.

Third are 'domestic violence or intimate partner violence induced homicides'. Here, the people who have committed murder kill a family member or partner. Some examples of motives are:

- Shot victim. He believed she was unfaithful.
- Shot wife after she left him.
- Stabbed his wife to death because he thought she was cheating on him.
- Defendant used car to run over and kill husband who had beaten her badly.
- Shot and killed victim after years of emotional abuse.
- Defendant stabbed boyfriend in chest with kitchen knife after argument.

These murders are not committed in order to gain money, but are due to the complexities of human emotion and power in relationships. Here, it seems that our murder fantasies are closest to what ends up happening. Killing an ex-boyfriend, stabbing someone who cheated on you, running over an abusive partner – these are the situations where our emotional pain translates into the desire to inflict physical pain on the other person. We may want cathartic release, to make the other person hurt as much as or more than we do.

The final type that Roberts and colleagues include are 'accident homicides'. This exclusively involves killing people while driving under the influence of alcohol or other drugs. This last one is a bit of an odd one out, because it is the only type where the person does not actually intend to kill anyone. It also would not fall within the definition given by the UN report, but does fall within the general idea of unlawful killing. However, as those who have lost someone as the result of the recklessness of drunk-driving will attest, losing someone this way is often not much different from having the victim stabbed or shot. Anger and desire for vengeance can be comparable, even if reasons for killing are not.

When we think of a 'murderer', we think of a mugshot of a guy with a teardrop tattoo on his face, snarling at us. Instead, what this typology shows us is that the situations in which homicides often occur are really quite mundane. Many of us have had a heated argument with a partner or felt slighted by someone who wouldn't pay back a small debt. The only difference seems to be that these murders happened when the perpetrator acted on what many of us just fantasise about. In the case of 'accident homicides' it is even more banal. Plenty of us might do exactly the same thing, getting into a car drunk or high, but – due to nothing other than luck – the consequences end up being completely different.

Making matters even more complicated, most people who murder someone never murder anyone ever again. Reconviction rates for homicide, also known as recidivism rates, are very low. According to a review of the literature published in 2013 by forensic psychologist Marieke Liem,

'Studies that assess specific recidivism (i.e., committing another homicide) alone find recidivism rates ranging from 1 to 3 per cent.'[6] Can we really call someone who killed a person once in the heat of an argument a *murderer* for the rest of their life? Or were they just a murderer at the time they committed their crime?

But, before we address this, let's examine one of the curious facts of murder first. As both men and women are clearly capable of homicide, why are most murders committed by men?

TOXIC MASCULINITY

Up until this point I quite like the evolutionary argument: homicide can be adaptive. But our evolutionary research friends, Duntley and Buss, go on to argue something far more controversial.

They argue that 'men, not women, have evolved bodies and minds designed to kill'. They argue that this is because, 'over evolutionary time, the greater reproductive variance among men selected for more extreme and risky male strategies to acquire and retain mates . . . sex differences in the use of risky strategies, such as violence and homicide, are an outcome of this unique selection pressure on men . . . men who failed to take risks would have been at a disadvantage in competition for mates and, therefore, less likely to leave descendants'. Men, they argued, have more to gain genetically from murder than women. This doesn't excuse murder, of course, but it might help to explain why murder happens so often.

In line with the idea that men are predisposed to aggres-

sion and thereby murder, a meta-analysis of research by John
Archer in 2004 showed that 'direct, especially physical,
aggression was more common in males than females at all
ages sampled, was consistent across cultures, and occurred
from early childhood on, showing a peak between 20 and
30 years'.[7] The review found that this wasn't because men
were angrier than women, but that 'the overall pattern indicated males' greater use of costly methods of aggression
rather than a threshold difference in anger'. This fits with
what our evolutionary theorists propose: men are more likely
to take risks than women, including acting on aggressive and
homicidal impulses.

However, Archer also argues that the same data can
support a more social view. He writes that while it could be
that these differences are found around the world because
men are born like this – 'the sex difference is characteristic
of the human species' – it could also be because of social
roles: 'Gender roles are consistent across cultures.' This is
decidedly a more nuanced view.

This brings me to my point of contention with evolutionary
theories of aggression and murder. They can quite readily
be used to argue 'Well, that's just how men are.' To counter
this, first of all, humans have the capacity for inhibition. This
means men can *choose* to not act aggressively. Predispositions
don't make some people commit murder; their own decisions
do that. It's a bit like the idea that guns don't kill people,
people do. Second, maybe men murder more because society
raises boys to be more disinhibited, aggressive and physically
active than girls.

There is ample research on this, and I also have a relevant
story that I want to share. I had a friend when I was growing

up in Canada. Our status as best friends was consolidated on the first day of Grade 3, when she gave me a colourful bangle and declared that we would be friends for ever. Even though she lived almost an hour away, my parents regularly drove me to see her for playdates. On one such playdate it was her tenth birthday. We had been told to wait in her bedroom until we were called. We were excited about what her parents had planned. They called us after what seemed like an eternity, and we came running into the living room, delighted to find a pile of beautifully wrapped presents waiting for my friend.

Despite her excitement, she sat down obediently on the couch adjacent to the pile, waiting for her parents to allow her to proceed. Before she could even open the first one, her five-year-old brother stormed into the pile and started tearing the presents apart. There was gift wrap everywhere. My friend couldn't contain her disappointment and started crying, while her parents sat by idly, clearly amused by the spectacle. They never interfered. My friend was devastated for weeks. Even at the time I recognised the double standard. It was my introduction to misogyny.

Whenever people say that boys will be boys, that sexist comments are just locker-room talk, or that men are just naturally more violent than women, I think of stories like this one. Society often gives too much leeway to destructive, aggressive and violent actions carried out by men. This is bad for women, like my friend whose birthday was ruined, but it might be even worse for men.

When we rationalise male aggression as natural and normal, we accept that men are more likely to be convicted of crimes, end up in prison, and be victimised by other men.

But why should our prisons be filled with men? Is this not a disastrous situation for males? Gender inequality in how we educate boys and girls on violence and aggression is hugely problematic. If we want violence and murder rates to go down, this is something we can, and *must*, change.

Social arguments aside, there is often one more factor that people bring up when they discuss gender differences in the commission of murder and other violent crime. It is the argument that testosterone hijacks men's brains and makes them act out. Let's look at the evidence for this.

In 2001, James Dabbs and colleagues published a paper showing a correlation between the amount of testosterone in the saliva of people convicted of murder and the severity of their crimes; the more testosterone, the more ruthless the homicide.[8] According to their study, this ruthlessness was shown because 'among inmates who committed homicide, those high in testosterone more often knew their victims and planned their crimes ahead of time'. The acts were considered more ruthless when they were not just reactive, but were more calculated and planned.

Why? Neuroscientist Sarah Cooper and colleagues published a study in 2013 in which they examined this.[9] They treated half of their sample of male rats with testosterone for four weeks, and then had them complete a task. They gave the rats the choice between two levers. The 'safe' choice involved a small amount of food, while the 'risky' lever paired a large amount of food with an increasing shock to the rat's feet. The testosterone-treated rats preferred the risky option. According to the researchers, 'Increased preference for the large reward, despite risk of footshock, is consistent with increased risk tolerance.'

The researchers did this study in part to help us better understand 'roid rage', when men who take certain steroids (anabolic–androgenic steroids, which are synthetic derivatives of testosterone) act more impulsively and aggressively. They found that, in line with our evolutionary argument, higher levels of testosterone make some of us more likely to take risks. Risks like acting aggressively or murdering someone.

Before I go on to explain that the link between testosterone and violence is actually a bit more complicated than these studies make it seem, I want to share with you the curious origin of the notion that testosterone and aggression are linked. It all started in 1849, with a German doctor, six cockerels, and a four-and-a-half-page research paper.[10]

Here's what happened. On 2 August 1848, Arnold Berthold thought it was a good idea to cut off the testes of six male chickens to see what happened. For two cockerels, he detached one of the testes and left it loosely bobbing about next to the still-attached one. He then removed both testes from the four other cocks. For two of these cocks, who we shall call Christian and Frederick, Berthold did something absolutely crazy. He surgically inserted Christian's testis *into Frederick's intestines*. Similarly, Christian got Frederick's testis inserted into him. Ah, medicine in the 1800s!

According to his original paper,[11] Berthold found that the two cockerels who had had their testes removed entirely were 'not aggressive' and 'fought with other cockerels rarely and then in a half-hearted manner'. The four other cockerels exhibited normal behaviour – 'they crowed lustily' and 'often engaged in battle with each other and with other cockerels'. He also found that the testes placed within the intestines of

Christian and Frederick had attached themselves to the intestinal tissue.

The doctor speculated that this must mean that something in the testes was absorbed by the blood and transferred to other parts of the body, causing aggression. Later this substance became known as testosterone. This innocuous paper would go on to become the foundation of modern endocrinology (the study of the system that controls hormones). It would also go on to revolutionise how we think about aggression in males, and the role of hormones in human violence.

Seems pretty simple. Add testosterone, get more aggression. Remove testosterone, get less aggression. However, this notion has been repeatedly challenged, most recently by a review of the research in 2017 by Justin Carré and colleagues.[12] They found that 'the relationship between testosterone and aggressive behavior is much more complex than previously thought'. After reviewing studies in humans and animals, in and out of the lab, they concluded that 'despite evidence linking testosterone to human aggression and/or dominance behaviors, these relationships are either weak or inconsistent'. So, the apparent truism that males are more violent and aggressive because of their testosterone levels may actually be overblown.

The authors even suggest that we might have the testosterone–aggression link somewhat backwards. What is potentially more interesting is how behaviour affects the production of testosterone, and *then* how testosterone affects behaviour. As the authors summarised, 'More robust is the finding that testosterone concentrations change rapidly in the context of human competition – and that such changes in testosterone concentrations positively predict ongoing and/ or future human aggression.' This means that as we compete with one another, our testosterone levels increase, and this increase can lead to more aggression.

This is supported by a number of studies, most notably a series conducted on sport competitions. One of the first to show that competition increased testosterone levels was published by Allen Mazur and Theodore Lamb in 1980, and involved a small sample of male tennis players who showed an increase in testosterone after a victory, and a drop after being defeated.[13] Carré and his colleagues explain that this is because 'testosterone is highly responsive to competitive interactions . . . Winners typically have elevated testosterone concentrations relative to losers.' They further explain that 'acute changes in testosterone may serve to promote competitive and aggressive behaviors'. Perhaps testosterone may be better linked with the useful side of aggression, the side that helps us win competitions, rather than more criminal forms of aggression. Testosterone helps us to earn Olympic medals and job promotions.

So, next time you hear someone say that testosterone makes people violent, please correct them.

I am now going to switch gears a bit. It's time for some empathy exercises, and a new question.

When is homicide the 'right' thing to do?

TROLLEYOLOGY

Not all killing is created equal. For example, it may be justified to intentionally kill someone if you are a soldier, are acting in self-defence, are saving someone else, or are killing for the greater good. We kill for the greater good when we fight in the name of justice, freedom or rights. So, when is killing bad? Some might argue when the harm caused by killing someone outweighs the benefits of doing so. Of course, the 'benefits' that can come out of killing someone can be entirely subjective.

To showcase this, let us use a classic thought experiment, the trolley problem. It has been modified in many ways over the years, but the modern version is typically credited to Philippa Foot in 1967.[14] There is a whole body of research just on different types of the trolley problem, an area of study called 'trolleyology'.

Here is the general scenario: a trolley is running out of control down a railway track. In its path are five people who have been tied to the track by a madman. Fortunately, you can flip a switch that will lead the trolley down a different track. Unfortunately, there is a single person tied to that track. Would you flip the switch?

In moral dilemmas like this, both in written scenarios and in virtual-reality situations, researchers find that the vast majority of us try to save as many people as possible. According to a paper published in 2014 by Alexander Skulmowski and colleagues, in such situations 'cognitive responses predominate due to the impersonal nature of the situation'.[15] They argue that 'impersonal dilemmas lead most people to exert a *utilitarian* (or, more broadly, *consequentialist*) judgment: they tend to bring about the best overall consequences at the cost of the well-being of single individuals'. This was even true when the scenario happened in virtual reality. In their own study, they had participants repeatedly complete a VR computer game where they had to decide whether to let a train they were controlling kill ten people, or to make it change track and kill one person. Ninety-six per cent of participants sacrificed one to save ten. Participants completed this scenario ten times, and most made the same decision every time. Greatest good for the greatest number was the general decision when they were being rational and impersonal.

But the researchers then changed the scenario slightly and made the following appear: the trolley is running out of control down the track. There is a fork in the track. On the left side there is a man standing on the tracks. On the right is a woman. Whichever path you choose, that person will be killed. Do you steer the train left or right?

Skulmowski and colleagues alternated where the man and the woman stood, but they found a general tendency towards sacrificing men. This was particularly true for male participants, 62 per cent of whom killed (or let die) another man. The authors believed that this was because of social desirability – protecting and saving a woman is seen as more favourable in the eyes of society than saving a man. It seems that we don't just want ourselves to feel like we are doing the right thing, we also want others to agree that we made the most ethical decision. We want to look good. Be praised. Be seen as heroes.

But this changes as soon as we make the situation personal.

Let's try another variation. A trolley is running out of control down a track. In its path are five people who have been tied to the track by a madman. You are standing on a bridge over the track and there is a very large man standing next to you. If you push the large man off the bridge you will stop the train. He will die but you will save the five people on the track. Do you push the large man off the bridge?

If here you hesitated, and thought that you couldn't live with yourself if you murdered someone with your bare hands, you are not alone. 'In comparable personal dilemma situations that require direct physical force to sacrifice the single person, people tend to be more passive and let the five people die.' Studies show that far fewer of us are willing to push someone than to pull a lever, even if the ultimate outcome for the person sacrificed – death – is the same.

Let's change the situation one final time, in line with what researcher April Bleske-Rechek and her colleagues did in 2010.[16] Here are four variations that Bleske-Rechek and her team would have given you had you participated in her version of this thought experiment.

A trolley is running out of control down a track. In its path are five people who have been tied to the track by a madman. Fortunately, you can flip a switch that will lead the trolley down a different track.

Version 1: Unfortunately, a seventy-year-old female stranger is tied to that track.

Version 2: Unfortunately, your twenty-year-old male cousin is tied to that track.

Version 3: Unfortunately, your two-year-old daughter is tied to that track.

Version 4: Unfortunately, your romantic partner is tied to that track.

Do you save a stranger, your own daughter, the love of your life? The researchers found that, 'As expected, men and women were less likely to sacrifice one life for five lives if the one hypothetical life was young, a genetic relative, or a current mate.' When faced with personal sacrifices, emotional sacrifices, we quickly change how we think we should behave. We may feel that *no* lives are as important as the lives of our loved ones. Even if we had to sacrifice 1,000 people to save our own child, we might morally, or at least instinctively, feel that it is the right thing to do.

According to neuroscientist Joshua Greene and colleagues, who have studied what moral decision-making looks like in the brain, the way we deal with this kind of dilemma changes because emotion plays such a big role in these decisions.[17] When we are making moral decisions purely based on logic, on what they call 'controlled cognitive processes', we are more likely to make utilitarian decisions that maximise the greater good.

However, 'automatic emotional responses' like the emotions that go along with the thought of having to kill someone, or losing a daughter, can hijack this process. When we have this kind of emotional interference, we are far more likely to make judgements that are selfish. Rather than weighing up killing five people against killing one, we weigh up the emotional impact on *ourselves* of killing our own daughter, or letting five strangers die.

But, there is more that neuroscience can teach us about how these dilemmas look in the brain. In 2017, a team of scientists published a study reviewing all existing neuroscientific studies on moral decision-making and moral evaluations.[18] They identified that some brain areas are commonly active when we make moral decisions. They found that all types of moral decision-making involve increased activation of the left middle temporal gyrus, medial frontal gyrus and cingulate gyrus.

They also found that 'making one's own moral decisions involves different brain areas compared to judging the moral actions of others'. Our brains react differently if we are asked whether we should save the drowning man, or whether someone else should save him. In making our own moral decisions, we use three additional parts of the brain – 'moral response decisions additionally activated the left and right middle temporal gyrus and the right precuneus'. The last of these, the precuneus, is a brain region that is involved in higher-level thinking, including thinking about who we are (the self) and consciousness.

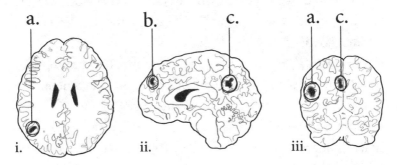

Moral decision-making. The left middle temporal gyrus (a), the medial frontal gyrus (b) and cingulate gyrus (c) were active for all types of moral decisions. Seen here as a slice from the top (i. axial), a slice from the side (ii. sagittal) and from the back (iii. coronal).

Neuroscience has given us but a tiny glimpse into how humans make moral decisions. It has highlighted the role of emotion, and how our brain needs to work harder to make decisions involving our own actions. There is, however, no specific part of the brain than makes us moral creatures. According to Garrigan and her colleagues, 'There appears to be no evidence for a uniquely "moral brain" as brain areas that show increased activation during moral tasks are also involved in other functions.' Even the exact role of emotion is still disputed, as is the applicability of hypothetical dilemmas to decisions that people need to make in reality. In reality, you probably wouldn't stop and think whether you should save your daughter. You would just jump in and do it. The five strangers would be unlikely to get much thought at all.

So, if we look at killing from a hypothetical perspective, it seems that it is fine as long as it is in the name of the greater good, or to save someone. This leads me to killing that is in a league of its own, committed by people who don't think they are doing the right thing, and are not working based on the socially desirable set of utilitarian rules set out by society. They plan their attacks, sometimes revel in them, and execute them with precision. These people aren't just caught in banal situations, murdering because a dispute got too heated, or because they felt they had to kill people for the greater good. I'm talking, of course, about serial killers.

THE MILWAUKEE MONSTER

In 1994, Jeffrey Jentzen and colleagues from the Medical College of Wisconsin published a report based on their involvement as forensic experts in the case of the serial killer Jeffrey Dahmer.[19]

Their involvement began on 23 July 1991, when police

came across a naked and handcuffed young black man running down the middle of the street. The man took them to the house of Jeffrey Dahmer, where they found several human body parts. They called the Milwaukee medical examiner's office, who started an investigation of the scene. Dahmer immediately cooperated, and even helped the team to understand how he committed the murders.

According to the report, 'Dahmer lived in a small, cramped, sparsely furnished single-bedroom apartment . . . The apartment itself was clean, well maintained, and relatively odorless.' As the forensics team worked their way through the small apartment, they found a shocking amount of body parts. Human heads were found in his freezer and fridge, along with dissected human hearts, a torso and, according to the report, 'a plastic bag containing 31 sections of skin . . . Skin pieces were irregular, but somewhat square.' They found a cooking pot with the hands and genitals of one victim, and cleaned skulls in the kitchen cabinets. In the bedroom they found more body parts – five skulls, a cleaned skeleton, an intact scalp and hair, and 'desiccated genitalia that had been painted a Caucasian flesh tone'. Helpfully for the forensics team, Dahmer had even put together a photo album entitled 'Photographic Diary', with neatly displayed and catalogued Polaroids of the victims before they were killed, and in various stages of dismemberment.

During the autopsies, the forensics team noticed something even weirder – neatly drilled holes in some of the victims' skulls, and evidence that acid had been injected into their brains before death. Upon speaking to Dahmer, they found that this was 'an attempt to render the victims helpless and use them as involuntary zombies'. The thirty-one-year-old Dahmer, it seems, was trying to make himself a sex zombie.

Dahmer was found to be sane by two juries, and was convicted of murdering sixteen young men. He had lured them back to his apartment, drugged them, raped them, cut them into pieces, preserved the body parts by boiling or freezing them, and kept photos of the process as 'mementos to keep him company'. If there was an evil checklist, he'd tick all the boxes.

But, was he evil? Relatives of his victims called him 'Satan', the judge sentenced him to fifteen life sentences (you know, just to be sure, in case he survives the first one), and Dahmer himself said that he wished he could be given the death penalty for the suffering he caused.[20] In some ways his wish was granted when, only two years after being imprisoned, one of his prison-mates bludgeoned him to death with a broomstick. Dahmer was found in a pool of his own blood in the prison toilets – the murderer was murdered by another convicted murderer.

It is difficult to come up with any explanation of his behaviours. He seemed entirely motivated by his own gratification and sexual desires. But the softer side of him seemed to just want a companion. He said himself that part of the reason he killed his victims and kept the bodies was because he was lonely and 'didn't want them to leave'.[21]

Did he have a broken brain? Was he missing empathy? We don't know, but we do know that he was found sane in psychological assessments, seemed to understand that what he was doing was wrong, and empathised with his victims. Yet he was able to overcome all of these inhibitions because, according to him, he was so lonely.

Loneliness is a relatable human characteristic, even if serial murder is not. Going a step further, we could look at the big-picture social and cultural factors that might lead to someone feeling so lonely, and why, for example, the United States has by far the most serial killers per capita of anywhere in the world. According to sociologist Julie Wiest, who has written extensively about serial killers, the culture of America fosters serial killing, particularly because of the incredible notoriety given by the press to people who commit murder.[22] Serial killers are sensationalised, they have fans, they become celebrities overnight.

According to criminologists Sarah Hodgkinson and colleagues, in a review of serial-killing research published in 2017, 'Serial killing has an enduring fascination with the public, but the discourse is dominated by reductionist and individualised accounts. These accounts perpetuate a number of misleading stereotypes about the serial killer and hides the diversity this form of homicidal behaviour takes.'[23] Serial killing is such a low-frequency event that it is difficult to get useful data that can help us see patterns. On top of that, the academic literature on serial killing is limited. Hodgkinson and colleagues argue that we need to talk about why people commit acts of serial killing 'within wider socio-cultural contexts' – in order to understand serial killers we must first try to understand the societies they live in.

Serial killing is a crime that is hard to understand, and it is made harder by the lack of available data. Although it is difficult to know, serial killers are thought to largely kill for the same reasons as those who have only one murder victim – some kill because they enjoy it, others because they are lonely, and others over perceived slights.

When we start to scratch below their scary surface, even the worst killers turn out to be human beings. And, looking at the data, it seems that humans largely kill for the same reasons that they do many other things – to find human connections, to protect their families, to achieve their goals, to acquire things they think they need. They do it to deal with basic human emotions like anger and jealousy, lust and greed, betrayal and pride.

Those who study the brains of convicted murderers might argue that these individuals exhibit fundamental human flaws in a stronger or more disinhibited way, but if we believe our evolutionary researchers from the beginning of this chapter, we find that probably all of us are capable of murder. If your murder fantasies were deeper, and you had less to lose, you too might act on them. Maybe the only difference between you and a serial killer is a fully functioning prefrontal cortex, enabling you to inhibit behaviours when another cannot.

We fear death, so it comes as no surprise that we fear those who murder. But, as Socrates once said, 'Nobody knows death; nobody can tell, but it may be the greatest benefit of mankind; and yet men are afraid of it, as if they knew certainly that it were the greatest of evils.'[24] Let us not confuse our fear of death with justification for dehumanising people who have inflicted it.

'He has conceived the evil enemy, the Evil One, and this in fact is his basic concept, from which he then evolves, as an afterthought and pendant, a "good one" – himself!'

Friedrich Nietzsche,
On the Genealogy of Morality

3

THE FREAK SHOW: DECONSTRUCTING CREEPINESS

On clowns, evil laughs and mental illness

WE SOMETIMES USE terms that ascribe negative traits to people we don't really know. That guy is creepy. What a weirdo. She's freaking me out. We say these things as though creepiness, or weirdness, or freakiness is something that a person *is*, rather than the result of a situation. But if we stop and think for a minute, what actually is creepiness? Do people know when they are creepy? Are *you* creepy?

Until recently there was no actual science to help us understand creepiness. It was only in 2016 that Francis McAndrew and Sara Koehnke published the first empirical study on the topic.[1] They wanted to put their fingers on this seemingly elusive concept. As they wrote, 'Given its pervasiveness in everyday human social life, it is very surprising that no one has studied it in a scientific way.'

So, what is going on when we feel that someone is creepy? McAndrew and Koehnke argue that being 'creeped out' is the result of an in-built threat detector. A detector that lets us know something is off by giving us feelings of confusion and unpleasantness, or feeling 'the chills'. But describing what creepiness feels like isn't good enough. The researchers asked, if it is a threat detector, what is it warning us about? They argued that creepiness 'cannot just be a clear warning of physical or social harm. A mugger who points a gun in your face and demands money is certainly threatening and terrifying. Yet, most people would probably not use the word "creepy" to describe this situation.'

So, they set out to discover what we interpret as 'creepy'. The first thing their 1,341 participants were asked to do was to consider the following scenario: Think of a close friend whose judgement you trust. Now imagine that this friend tells you that she or he just met someone for the first time and tells you that the person was 'creepy'.

Participants then rated the likelihood that the person had one of 44 different behaviour patterns or physical charac- teristics. They found that almost all (95.3 per cent) of the participants stated that men were more likely to be creepy than women. They also found a number of 'creepy' features or behaviours that were strongly linked to one another, and may be at the core of creepiness. Participants rated the following as the most likely characteristics of a creepy person:

1. The person stood too close to your friend.
2. The person had greasy hair.

3. The person had a peculiar smile.
4. The person had bulging eyes.
5. The person had long fingers.
6. The person had unkempt hair
7. The person had very pale skin.
8. The person had bags under his or her eyes.
9. The person was dressed oddly.
10. The person licked his or her lips frequently.
11. The person was wearing dirty clothes
12. The person laughed at unpredictable times.
13. The person made it nearly impossible for your friend to leave the conversation without appearing rude.
14. The person relentlessly steered the conversation towards one topic.

A number of other characteristics were also associated with creepiness, including being extremely thin, not looking your friend in the eye, asking to take a picture of your friend, watching your friend before interacting with them, asking about details of your friend's personal life, being mentally ill, talking about their own personal life, displaying inappropriate emotion, being older, and steering the conversation towards sex. That's *a lot* of different things that can make someone, particularly men, appear creepy.

What do creepy people do for a living? Apparently the creepiest professions are (in this order) clown, taxidermist, sex-shop owner and funeral director. The least creepy profession? Meteorologist.

On top of these many factors, it is generally believed that creepy people don't have insight into their own creepiness. In fact, 59.4 per cent of participants thought that creepy people don't know they are creepy. On top of this, most thought that creepy people cannot change.

What does all this mean? The authors asked the participants about the general nature of creepy people, and most of the characteristics tapped into three core factors: they make us fearful or anxious; creepiness is seen as part of the personality of the individual rather than just their behaviour; and we think that they may have a sexual interest in us.

The authors further explain that 'while they may not be overtly threatening, individuals who display unusual patterns of nonverbal behavior, odd emotional responses, or highly distinctive physical characteristics are outside of the norm, and by definition unpredictable. This may activate our "creepiness detector" and increase our vigilance as we try to discern if there is in fact something to fear or not from the person in question.' The characteristics captured in the list suggest that the creepy person your friend is interacting with is hard to predict. Creepiness, it turns out, is probably our reaction to not knowing whether or not we should be scared of someone.

But, first, let us establish how accurate this superficial assessment is. Can we tell just from a brief encounter whether someone is trustworthy, or whether they are likely to hurt us? How often does this assessment misfire, and what are the consequences when it does? Apparently we make intuitive assessments about trustworthiness within 39 milliseconds of seeing a photo of someone's face.[2] So, let's start there.

One of my favourite, albeit tiny, studies on whether we can accurately judge a person by their face comes from a 2008 paper published by Stephen Porter and colleagues in Canada.[3] In this study they asked participants to rate thirty-four photos of adult male faces. Half of the photos were of trustworthy people and the other half were of untrustworthy people. The photos in the two groups were 'matched' in terms of the facial hair, expressions and ethnicity. Participants were asked to rate each person on trustworthiness, kindness and aggressiveness, having only a photo of their face to rely on.

How did the researchers know that the people in the photos were trustworthy? Well, this is the best part. The trustworthy people 'had either received the Nobel Peace Prize or the Order of Canada and had been acknowledged as paragons in their devotion to humanity, peace, and society'. The other half were from the America's Most Wanted list – profiles of people eluding justice for extremely serious crimes. These were arguably some very trustworthy people and some very untrustworthy people, at least in terms of their contribution to humanity.

The authors write in their summary that in the 'unlikely event' that a participant recognised a face, they were to tell the experimenter, but that 'none of the 34 targets were recognised by any participant'. While the researchers were happy about this, it upsets me that the participants did not identify any of the faces. Not *one*. Clearly, 'Most Wanted' pictures are out of fashion. It also seems that most of us don't know, or recognise, the heads that house the world's greatest minds. It's a shame. Maybe we should organise a Nobel Laureates reality TV show. That way more of us might start to care about the lives of the brightest among us.

So, do you think you could tell the difference between a Nobel Laureate and a serious criminal just from their faces? Participants did slightly worse than if they had just flipped a coin: they identified only 49 per cent of the wanted criminals correctly, as untrustworthy. They were slightly better when asked about the Nobel Laureates, rating them as trustworthy 63 per cent of the time. The authors concluded that based on the ratings given by participants, people were looking for signs of kindness and aggressiveness in the faces of those they were evaluating, and they concluded that 'intuition lends a small advantage when making assessments of trustworthiness based on facial appearance, but errors are common'.

This brings to mind the story of Jeremy Meeks. He became known as the 'hot felon' after a mugshot of him went viral online. He was arrested on charges of possessing firearms illegally, carrying a loaded gun in public and gang activity. But the internet just responded to his piercing blue eyes, his perfect skin and his chiselled features. He got so much attention for his looks that he was given a modelling contract.[4] This just goes to show how, when someone is *dreamy*, our whole sense of judgement can be hijacked and potentially put us in danger.

Tying together our original creepiness study and our Nobel Laureates, I present to you another team of Canadian researchers. Margo Watt and colleagues published a study in 2017 where they again found that creepy people were generally thought to be lanky men with poor hygiene who behaved awkwardly. They also tested fifteen photos from the Porter and colleagues' Nobel Laureates study. They wanted to know a bit more about other things that influence trust-worthiness. They found that one other really important feature that explained the trustworthiness ratings was attract-iveness. Attractive people were deemed to be trustworthy, be they Nobel Laureates or offenders.

We see this in romantic comedies. When a hot guy stands outside a window with an old-school ghetto-blaster it's *so romantic*. When an unattractive guy does the exact same thing? He's a psycho. Someone being attractive certainly puts our creep-dar off kilter. We make all kinds of bad decisions around beautiful people. This is related to something called the halo effect, which happens when we assume that to look good is to be good.[5] It is a deeply rooted bias where we assume, on a societal level, that people who are more attractive are generally more trustworthy, ambitious, healthier . . . we generally think they are great.

This also has a flipside. The 'devil effect' leads us to believe that people who are undesirable in one way are likely undesirable in all ways.[6] This is even worse when someone also breaks the rules with their behaviour, for example committing a crime. Breaking norms can result in the double devil effect – where someone is seen as fundamentally evil because they look bad and act bad.[7] It's a hard label to shake.*

Indeed, research shows that people who are unattractive are, on the whole, less likely to get good jobs,[8] get reasonable healthcare (doctors can be biased too!),[9] and are treated less kindly by others.[10] In research that I did in 2015 with colleagues at the University of British Columbia, we found that unattractive and untrustworthy-looking people were convicted of crimes by mock-jurors with less evidence, and are less likely to be exonerated after evidence that proved their innocence.[11] Other researchers have found similar

---

* Have you ever noticed that 'devil' is just the word 'evil' with the letter 'd' attached to the front of it? It just reminds us how closely we link the religious concept of the devil and wrongdoing.

results, showing that having an untrustworthy face makes it more likely that you will be given a harsher criminal sentence, like the death penalty.[12]

Back to the Watt study, where creepy people were thought to be lanky men with poor hygiene. The researchers also found that most people (72 per cent) stated that they made an evaluation as to whether someone was creepy 'instantly'. This is in line with what we know about judging the personality of strangers more generally; we peg what we think someone is like instantaneously, intuitively, and it can be hard to change our initial impressions. In fact, it's so automatic that it involves mostly just the emotion part of the brain, the amygdala, and happens before we have time to think about it.[13]

The consequences can be far-reaching and unfair, disadvantaging people simply because of the way they look.

DIFFERENTNESS

But putting first impressions to one side, sometimes we do have a bit more time. Sometimes we get the chance to actually hang out with someone, rather than just looking at a photo. Does how we interact with a person impact our accuracy? In a 2017 review of the literature Jean-François Bonnefon and colleagues set out to investigate the state of the science regarding our ability to detect people who are trustworthy (labelled in the study as 'cooperators').[14] They compared findings from studies where people got to have long interactions with one another, with studies where people were given only photographs of others. People were OK at detecting how cooperative someone would be in a follow-up game if they had interacted with them, but they struggled when they only saw a picture. 'People could detect cooperativeness with some small accuracy when they interacted, or watched video clips of other players,' but their results showed that people 'have a harder time extracting information from pictures'. This shows that the way someone moves and presents themselves carries clues as to whether they can be trusted, while pictures aren't as good. But even with pictures we are still a little bit better than chance at figuring out trustworthiness.

What are people picking up on? When asked, 84 per cent of participants in the original McAndrew and Koehnke study (from the beginning of this chapter) indicated that 'creepiness' resides in the face, and 80 per cent said that it was all about the eyes.[15]

This is a common element that is picked up in horror movies. Evil people in movies – those possessed by evil spirits, vampires or zombies – often have eyes that are all black, all white, or blood red. We rely on the eyes to give us the first information as to whether someone is 'normal'. Further supporting the idea that we are freaked out by people who look, or act, differently from the norm, the authors of the creepiness study also conclude that 'definitions of creepiness tended to revolve around the theme of differentness'.

This is also in line with the idea that what looks good is good. But how do we reconcile the finding that both 'attractive' and 'typical' faces are most trustworthy? Aren't attractive faces more than typical? Not necessarily. In 1990, Judith Langlois and Lori Roggman were the first of many to demonstrate that 'attractive faces are only average'.[16] They took photos, digitised them, and made composite faces that averaged the features of all the photos included in the database.

They were creating an impossible image of the prototypical person for that group. They found that the closer they got to an average face, by entering more faces into the database, the more attractive the resulting face became.

It is unclear exactly why this is, but perhaps it has to do with the brain's natural tendency for abstraction. The brain likes creating prototypes, and perhaps because most of the people we interact with behave in a way that makes them (luckily) trustworthy, we start to see the average characteristics that make their faces as familiar and safe. Having a 'normal' face may also be associated with good health, which is also something that is generally considered safe and attractive.

That being said, some people are so stunning that they far exceed the average face. This is where, according to a study by Carmel Sofer and colleagues, the relationship between attractiveness and trustworthiness gets a bit more complicated.[17] As people get more attractive and approach the average face, trustworthiness increases. But, once people pass the average face, trustworthiness goes down again. This means that being really attractive can also make someone seem less trustworthy. If they are too hot, they are also different. And humans don't trust different.

While we are talking about attractiveness, you have probably heard that attractive faces are symmetrical. This is true, but only up to a point. According to a systematic review of the face-surgery literature by Tim Wang and colleagues, they found that although 'facial symmetry is intimately correlated with attractiveness . . . perfect facial symmetry is disconcerting and a degree of facial asymmetry is considered normal'.[18] Related to the finding that creepiness is in the eyes, the authors of this study found that 'asymmetry of the eyelid position at rest is the most sensitive facial feature'. This means that if someone's eyes are too symmetrical, or too asymmetrical, we perceive this as problematic. Once again, too much either way is bad. Have an unsymmetrical droopy eyelid? Creepy. Completely symmetrical? Also creepy.

Really, adding or changing anything about the face that makes it deviate from the average humanoid makes it creepier. And whether it's from birth, injury or botched plastic surgery, most of us don't choose to have creepy faces. Yet having a facial disfigurement makes us more likely to be the target of staring on the street[19] and discrimination at work.[20] Even something as innocuous as acne can affect our trustworthiness ratings. In 2016, Elenea Tsankova and Arvid Kappas published a study which showed that skin smoothness (i.e., lack of acne) affects evaluations of trustworthiness, competence, attractiveness and health.[21] Even small choices we make, like getting a tattoo near the face, can disadvantage us. One study found that it means people look more like a criminal to others.[22]

So, much of this is out of our control and does not correspond to our psychological characteristics, but humans are still likely to disadvantage us if our face is creepy. This leads us into the territory of human cruelty. Humans have long psychologically and physically abused people who look different. From childhood, faces grab our attention if they don't look the way we expect them to, typically in a bad way. Children are cruel to those who look different. People with facial disfigurements have long been harassed and publicly ridiculed.

Why do we commit such cruelty? For one, there is the basic evolutionary argument that deformities and asymmetry can be signs of genetic disease and weakness. We are naturally averse to disease, an aversion to which we partly owe our survival. This translates into seeing signs of disease as bad. We gravitate to those who look fertile and healthy; we shy away from those who don't, those who might infect us. This might help to explain why we avoid certain people, but it doesn't explain why we might also act cruelly towards them.

An argument that I find particularly compelling to explain this cruelty has to do with our perception of 'faces in pieces'. Katrina Fincher and colleagues published a paper in 2017 where they argue that the way we perceive faces can result in dehumanising the person.[23] If we perceive a face where nothing particularly stands out, we take it all in at once. We perceive it as a whole. As human.

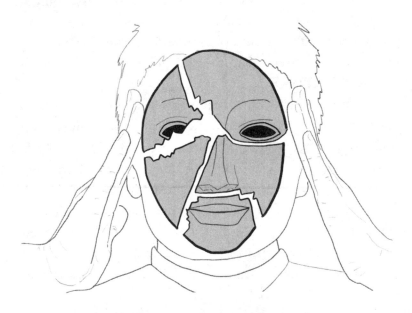

Perceptual dehumanisation: when we stop to see faces
and people as whole, as human.

However, as soon as there is something that captures our attention by being abnormal, we start to deconstruct the face and we start to deconstruct the person. We see the deformity, the poorly spaced eyes, the funny nose, the acne, the tattoo, and we stop seeing the face as a human whole. The authors argue that this 'involves a shift from configural to featural processing', from looking at a face as a whole, a configuration, to just focusing on individual features. This, they argue, 'enables the infliction of harm, such as harsh punishments'. Just as Hitler was able to do harm because he stopped seeing people as human beings, so too our perception can play a trick on us and lead to 'perceptual dehumanisation'.

The only way to combat this is to be aware that this can happen, and to stop and think when our first reaction to someone is that they are creepy. Feel free to chat with that person with the neck tattoo. Hire the woman with adult acne. And educate your kids not to stare at the person with a facial deformity.

Humans have a hard time accepting different faces, but one thing that is often even harder to accept is a different mind. Mental illness is something that is often associated with creepiness, evil and crime.

SIT WITH ME

It's the same reason I'm afraid of the dark: I don't know what's there, I can't see it, so it could be anything. It's the unpredictability. People who think differently than we do make us wonder what they will do next. We cannot understand their way of thinking. Our behaviour-predictors misfire. Humans don't like that kind of unpredictability. Order and control are safe. Unpredictability is potentially unsafe. Unpredictability is thus perceived as dangerous.

That there is a stigma of mental illness is no revelation, yet it is a persistent and devastating bias. One of the most noticeable biases that arises when we notice that someone is mentally ill, is that we keep our distance. We keep our distance both socially and physically.

Part of this implicit bias can be showcased by an experiment that highlights our intuitive association between violence and mental illness, and was conducted by Ross Norman and colleagues in 2010.[24] They asked participants to stay in a waiting room, where they were going to meet a young woman with schizophrenia. There they found seven chairs in a row along a wall. A clipboard and sweater could be clearly seen on the second chair, and participants were told that this was her chair, and she would return shortly. She wasn't actually in the room, so the participants could not be influenced by what she looked like, or by her symptoms.

Of course, this study was about observing the participants' behaviour. The researchers wanted to know where the participants would sit. They found that participants sat between 2 and 3 chairs – 2.44 chairs, to be exact – from where they expected the woman with schizophrenia to be seated upon her return. That's not actually too bad, but the researchers argue that this shows us that subtle things like mental illness can affect how we treat someone socially. Do you think that, on average, you would sit closer to someone who was not schizophrenic? Probably.

Every time you feel this way, consider that this is especially true if the person with schizophrenia is clearly experiencing what are called 'positive' symptoms – for example they are talking to an imaginary friend or reacting to hallucinations. These symptoms are called positive not because they are good, but because they are a 'bonus' personal reality. Reality+. They see and hear things that are not there. These symptoms stand in contrast to 'negative' ones, such as flattened emotions.

Man or woman, young or old, many of us have a strong creepiness radar. And this idea that we are creeped out by those who are psychologically unwell is further supported by a study from 2012 by Parker Magin and colleagues which showed that almost 30 per cent of people in a medical waiting room said that they would be uncomfortable sharing it with someone diagnosed with schizophrenia.[25] A further 12 per cent said they would be uncomfortable sharing with someone who has depression. Some have argued that this stigmatisation of those who are mentally unwell can be considered a 'second disease'. Because of the way that others treat them, those who are mentally ill often also suffer from increased anxiety, stress and lower quality of life.[26]

Even children can be seen as dangerous if they are different. In 2007, sociologist Bernice Pescosolido and colleagues published a study that looked at the perceived dangerousness of children with mental health problems.[27] They examined data from 1,152 respondents, who were asked to rate the dangerousness of children in various short stories about them. They found that a 'child with depression was more than twice as likely to be assessed as dangerous toward others and ten times as likely to be assessed as dangerous toward himself or herself' than children with other health problems. They also found a similar pattern for children with Attention Deficit Hyperactivity Disorder (ADHD):

'Compared with the child with "daily troubles", the child with ADHD was perceived as roughly twice as likely to be dangerous to others and to self.' Kids with depression and ADHD are perceived to be dangerous.

But is this warranted? Are they more dangerous?

This is a common theme in horror movies and video games, portraying innocent-looking-but-actually-dangerous children. One of the first horror movies I ever watched, for which I was far too young, was all about a group of children taking over a town with mind control. They were sadistic and vengeful little kids. But it's not just in fiction. The media also delves into the mental health of real children who act out, particularly those who commit extreme violence. And it doesn't get much more extreme in the world of violent kids than school shooters.

Trying to understand lethal school violence has prompted wild speculations from a public desperately trying to explain how innocence can be corrupted at such a young age. It has also prompted research from large-scale institutions. One such initiative was an in-depth study, funded partly by the US National Research Council, by Mark Moore and colleagues. One of the major conclusions from this wide-scale investigation was that 'serious mental health problems, including schizophrenia, clinical depression, and personality disorders, surfaced *after* the shootings' for most of the shooters – all of whom were boys.[28]

Their study also concluded, however, that there were a number of other risk factors, but that none of them were particularly problematic. 'Most of the shooters were not considered to be at high risk for this kind of behavior by the adults around them.' Despite being close to them, neither parents nor teachers believed these to be high-risk individuals, never mind the devastating violence that was eventually perpetrated.

Although they happen too often, particularly in the United States, school shootings are statistically still a rare event. This makes it difficult to study them and to understand exactly what has led children to make these horrific decisions. But from initial investigations it does not seem that mental illness is in itself the cause of lashing out, rather part of a complex array of problems. Problems that can include isolation, bullying, lack of parental support, substance abuse and easy access to guns.

So, taking this back to the bigger picture, are we steering clear of those who we know are mentally ill because we are intuitively tapping into a true sign of dangerousness? Well, the answer to this is complicated. According to Julia Sowislo and colleagues, 'these perceptions are biased: Although there is a significantly elevated risk for violence, the risk is small and the majority of individuals with mental illness are not violent.'[29] This is because when we start with a really small risk, even if we double or triple it, we still have a very small number.

What does this mean? For one, it means that it matters what kind of mental illness the person has. In a study of offenders with mental illnesses by Jillian Peterson and colleagues from 2014, they found that of the 429 crimes they coded, 4 per cent related directly to a psychosis (including symptoms of schizophrenia), 3 per cent related to depression, and 10 per cent related to bipolar disorder.[30] This means there is only a correlation between mental illness and crime for a very small set of diagnoses – including most notably schizophrenia, depression and bipolar disorder.

As the authors concluded, 'Psychiatric symptoms relate weakly to criminal behavior.' It seems that even when someone is mentally ill, even if they have the most 'risky' symptoms, they are very rarely violent simply because of their symptoms. Instead, it is often the same kinds of circumstances that contribute to violence in general that also contribute to violence for the mentally ill.

So where do we get a connection between crime and mental illness at all? Well, it seems that this link has to do with another factor: substance abuse. Someone with schizophrenia or depression is more likely than the average person to take drugs or engage in problematic drinking. For example, a study from 2015 by Ragnar Nesvåg and colleagues places the rate of diagnosed substance-use disorders at 25.1 per cent for schizophrenia, 20.1 per cent for bipolar disorder and 10.9 per cent for depression.[31] They concluded that 'patients with schizophrenia, bipolar disorder and depressive illness had up to a tenfold higher prevalence of SUD [substance use disorder] compared to the population estimate'. Substance use in these circumstances might be an attempt to self-medicate or escape the awful symptoms they are experiencing, or because brains that are struggling sometimes make bad decisions.

And here is where we tie the link back in: mental illness is a risk factor for substance abuse, which in turn is a risk factor for violence. According to the results of a systematic review of the literature on schizophrenia and violence by Seena Fazel and colleagues published in 2009, 'Schizophrenia and other psychoses are associated with violence and violent offending, particularly homicide. However, most of the excess risk appears to be mediated by substance abuse comorbid-ity.'[32] In other words, almost *all* of the increase in risk happens when someone with schizophrenia also drinks or takes drugs. In addition, this increase in risk seems to be the same for *anyone else who drinks or takes drugs* – 'The risk in these patients with comorbidity is similar to that for substance abuse without psychosis.' It seems that substance abuse is the causal link here, not the mental illness per se. Mental illness alone is a poor indicator of violent tendencies.

The emotional and physical distance we keep from those who are mentally ill is both unfounded and devastating for those affected. Most societies have come a long way from sticking those with mental illness into inhumane insane asylums, conducting exorcisms to rid them of their evil spirits, or subjecting them to public ridicule and abuse – but there is still much progress to be made. We need to fight our misfiring creepiness detectors. Those with mental illness may seem unpredictable, but unpredictable does not mean violent. Approach different, don't fear it. Take a chance next time, and sit next to that stranger who is acting weird. Unless they are drunk or high.

Let's recalibrate society's relationship with mental illness.

SHOCKING

You have probably heard of Stanley Milgram's classic study on obedience from 1963.[33] In this study participants were told they had been assigned the role of 'teacher', and had to administer shocks to a 'learner' every time the learner made a mistake recalling words from a list. The learner, who was actually a research associate, was in an adjacent room. The teacher was told by the experimenter to increase the voltage every time the learner made a mistake – from an initial 15 volts up to an eventual 450 volts, the latter of which was labelled 'Danger: Severe Shock'.

At some point the learner protested the increase in voltage. According to the original manuscript, 'When the 300-volt shock is administered, the learner pounds on the wall of the room in which he is bound to the electric chair. The pounding can be heard by the subject. From this point on, the learner's answers no longer appear . . . The learner's pounding is repeated after the 315-volt shock is administered; afterwards he is not heard from.' Essentially, the experimental procedure makes it seem as though the participant has killed the learner. Despite this, only 14 of the 40 men who took part in this study broke it off before the highest voltage was reached. It was an incredible demonstration that some of us will follow an authority figure who is instructing us to act against our conscience, even in a situation as basic as a psychology experiment. We will come back to the topic of obedience to authority in a later chapter, but here I want to talk about the participants' emotional response to their behaviour.

As could be expected, most of the participants expressed extreme stress during the experiment. They whimpered protests to the experimenter like 'I don't think this is very humane. It's a hell of an experiment . . . This is crazy.' And, after the study was over, obedient participants 'mopped their brows, rubbed their fingers over their eyes, or nervously fumbled cigarettes'. But one unexpected response was seen in relation to this stress, which Milgram found fascinating. It was the participants' nervous laughter.

One sign of tension was the regular occurrence of nervous laughing fits. Fourteen of the 40 subjects showed definite signs of nervous laughter and smiling. The laughter seemed entirely out of place, even bizarre. Full-blown, uncontrollable seizures were observed for 3 subjects. On one occasion we observed a seizure so violently convulsive that it was necessary to call a halt to the experiment. The subject, a 46-year-old encyclopedia salesman, was seriously embarrassed by his untoward and uncontrollable behavior.

Why were they laughing? Surely they weren't *happy* about electrocuting a stranger? No, it seems that they were laughing for some other reason, and that they were embarrassed about it.

Laughter and smiling are often associated with evil. We think of an evil witch cackling, a laughing serial killer, a devil's grin. While this may be an automatic response in the face of stress and uncertainty, it is depicted in these circumstances as an expression of sadistic pleasure. This image is something the participants in the Milgram experiment were well aware of: 'In the post-experimental interviews subjects took pains to point out that they were not sadistic types, and that the laughter did not mean they enjoyed shocking the victim.'

We have talked about incongruent emotions before, when we discussed cute aggression, and that it is probably a protective mechanism. The brain is trying not to short-circuit when extreme emotions are experienced, by making us experience the counter emotion. We can accept that we might give a nervous laugh when we do something that scares us, or smile during a funeral, or feel like we want to hurt a pet that we love. Yet we struggle to see the similarity between incongruent facial expressions during violent acts and those in other situations. We find people who show the wrong emotions at the wrong time creepy.

According to Roy Baumeister and Keith Campbell, laughter can be so creepy because of how victims and perpetrators differ in their perception and experience of wrong-doing.[34] This is related to what Baumeister referred to as the 'magnitude gap'.[35] 'The essence of the magnitude gap is that the victim loses more than the perpetrator gains,' he explains. For example, when a thief steals something, the replacement value to the victim is typically more than what the thief can sell it for. A rapist may experience brief empowerment, but the victim may suffer for years. A murderer takes a life, and inflicts pain and suffering to the family of the victim – a loss which can never be matched by the murderer's gain.

This imbalance matters hugely. Because of this magnitude gap, victims often describe the actions of offenders as gratuitous. 'A victim may emphasise that the perpetrator's action was for no reason at all, or . . . as acting out of sheer malice.' As Baumeister and Campbell write: 'The magnitude of an act may be much less in the perpetrator's than in the victim's perspective, and therefore to understand the psychology of perpetrators, it may be necessary to distance oneself from the victim's view.' When we talk about evil, we are generally siding with victims, and seeing harm from their perspective.

As such, victims may focus on a perpetrator's laughter, while perpetrators hardly ever mention it. Moreover, 'Victims take the perpetrator's laughter as a compelling sign that the perpetrators were enjoying themselves and hence as a sign of evil, sadistic pleasure.' We can forgive victims of violence for failing to make the subtle attributional adjustments to correctly interpret the laughter of their tormentors. Being the victim of violence can be hugely stressful. If the perpetrator is actually enjoying themselves, as perceived by the victim, then the magnitude gap becomes a chasm, a loss-to-gain ratio so large that it is irreconcilable. This we call evil. An 'evil laugh' is a hallmark of creepiness as it is the ultimate expression of the magnitude gap.

Let's switch gears to another attribute of creepiness. Remember our study from the beginning of this chapter which explained the various things that we find creepy – like people being clowns or taxidermists, standing too close, or having long fingers? This study also addressed one final aspect of creepiness – the hobbies of creepy people.

Collectors are apparently top of the creepy list. According to McAndrew and Koehnke, 'Easily, the most frequently mentioned creepy hobbies involved collecting things. Collecting dolls, insects, reptiles, or body parts such as teeth, bones, or fingernails was considered especially creepy.'[36] *Yeah, obviously.*

MURDER, INC.

I think that among the weirdest things people can collect are 'murderabilia'. In 2009, American attorney and writer Ellen Hurley defined murderabilia as 'anything offered for sale that was either created by or owned by a murderer, as well as any item related to a notorious crime, over which the criminal may or may not have had any control'.[37] Murderabilia is seen as a derogatory term by some collectors, but let's approach this fascination with an open and non-judgemental outlook.

Sometimes murderabilia is sold by the murderers themselves, from prison. For example, take John Wayne Gacy, an American serial killer who sexually assaulted, tortured and murdered at least thirty-three young men in the 1970s. He went dressed as 'Pogo the Clown' to neighbourhood parties. During his time in prison, he made and sold some rather terrible paintings of clowns surrounded by dwarfs and children. Then there is Herbert Mullin, who killed thirteen people because he allegedly thought it prevented earthquakes. From hearing command hallucinations that ordered him to kill people, Mullin went on to paint some pretty nice pictures of mountain ranges in prison.

According to Matthew Wagner, who at the time was editor of the University of Cincinnati *Law Review*, 'The concept of murderabilia is impregnated with our culture's celebration of celebrity and history on the one hand, and fascination with the occult and heinous crimes on the other.'[38] He argues that the murderabilia market has really flourished since the emergence of e-commerce, 'moving the sale and trade of murderabilia away from obscure collectors to a full-blown marketplace'. Perhaps also because of anonymity of buyers online, business is booming.

As you might intuit, the fact that lawyers are writing about this topic is because this market has been imbued with controversy since its inception. The question that arises is whether it is OK for criminals to profit from their crimes. Offenders who sell items often attract moral outrage from victims and the general public. The moral outrage has actually become legislation in the USA, in the form of the so-called 'Son of Sam' laws. According to Wagner, these were 'named after the original statute passed by the New York legislature' and were intended 'to prevent serial killer David Berkowitz from making a small fortune selling the rights to his story to media outlets', in direct response to speculation that Berkowitz would sell the movie rights to his life – although he never actually expressed an interest in this. The laws were passed preemptively, and to prevent offenders from benefiting from such arrangements. However, laws like this are incredibly difficult to enforce, as they generally violate free-speech rights, at least in the US.

While it is difficult to stop the sale at the source, e-commerce sites themselves have control over what they can sell. For example, giants like Amazon have policies against selling items that are likely to cause outrage – including human remains and Nazi memorabilia. Countries too can regulate the sale of items that profit from hate. Germany made the sale of Hitler's manifesto *Mein Kampf* illegal until a significantly annotated, scholarly and critical version came out in 2016. Perhaps Germany felt that the zeitgeist was once again one of racial hatred, and wanted to showcase, and warn against, how fascism is born.

However, offenders making and selling their stories, or their crafts, or their toenails, is not illegal. And I don't think it should be. By seeing the issue only from the side of the victims, we might again be seeing this issue through the filter of the magnitude gap. Yes, prison sentences are often insufficient for victims and their families to achieve a sense of justice after a severe crime has been committed, and the idea that a perpetrator can regain any sense of normalcy and use their story to earn money seems perverse. Indeed, lawyers may know the phrase '*Ex turpi causa non oritur actio*' – which essentially means that we cannot profit from our own immoral actions.

But if we avoid the temptation to see this issue only from the side of the victim, we see someone who is already paying their dues to society, to justice. Nobody is sentenced to 'four years in prison, plus four years in which you are unable to make money from what you have done'. 'Tough on crime' sentencing and long-term denial of rights dehumanises huge numbers of people. And it's not like most offenders kill for notoriety, or to profit from the story. Fame and fortune are an incredibly rare and lucky consequence.

But I digress. We started by talking about the buyers, not the sellers, of murderabilia. So, why are people interested in buying souvenirs from the dark side of humanity? According to sociologist Jack Denham, 'It has been argued that the activity of remembering through "dark tourism", while being a morbid form of entertainment, can be seen as a method of confronting and coping with death in modern societies.'[39]

More poignantly, the offenders people choose to idolise, those who have fans, are those who embody other characteristics that society values. While their deeds may be grossly offensive, their methods can be admired. A serial killer who goes long unnoticed is one who is often meticulous, plans well, and has control over the situation. On top of that, they can be seen as rebels, who play by their own rules. They are the very embodiment of counterculture.

Someone who really mastered this branding was Charles Manson. Manson thought that there was going to be an apocalyptic race war, called 'Helter Skelter', and he thought that starting a cult which murdered people would help to get it started. After he was caught and imprisoned, Manson became the king of his own branding. From prison, he released commercial music, made spiders out of yarn, and created some pretty psychedelic paintings. According to Denham, 'Manson is a countercultural icon and is consumed as such through this array of merchandise.' Fans of serial killers and murderabilia seem to attribute mythical qualities to gruesome and deviant acts. It's more than a fascination with murder, it's the admiration of celebrity, of meticulousness, and of the counterculture that they represent.

Perhaps it's still difficult to understand the fascination with murderabilia, perhaps we still think it is creepy, but maybe we can have a glimpse of understanding after all. And if you want your own, you can always stop by Serial Killers Ink, Murder Auction or Supernaught.

In addition to collecting, a few other hobbies were mentioned by the McAndrew and Koehnke research. Also perceived as creepy were people who liked to watch, follow or take pictures of people. One funny inclusion was birdwatchers. I guess that's still a form of watching, even if I personally don't think it's very creepy. I just think of a person wearing tweed looking at trees with binoculars. A fascination with taxidermy was also frequently mentioned as creepy. I don't know anyone who stuffs or collects dead animals for fun, but I guess that could be creepy, and brings us back to thinking about death – which is closely related to our sense of creepiness.

Finally, the study found that 'pornography or exotic sexual activity' were linked with creepiness. Given the strong relationship between unwanted sexual interest and creepiness, it's no surprise that being into kinky sex is on the list.

Wrapping up, it seems that creepiness is the result of a system that is trying to keep us safe, but is poorly calibrated. We misidentify Nobel Laureates as notorious offenders. We think that people are creepy because they deviate from the norm in looks, mental health, behaviour and interests. You can choose to take this information on board and de-creep yourself, or you can simply ignore it.

Another system that is often trying to keep us safe, but can spectacularly fail to do so, is technology. As we experience a world that is ever more influenced by the presence of smartphones, aeroplanes and the internet, we can ask ourselves how this is influencing us, and how we are influencing it. Next we will look into how and why we use technology to do bad, and how technology itself can misbehave.

4

TWO-FACED TECH: HOW TECHNOLOGY CHANGES US

On air pirates, bad bots and cyber trolls

I LOVE-HATE TECHNOLOGY.

I am first in line when a new product launches that promises to improve my life, but I also believe that technology has a real chance of destroying humankind. I buy almost everything on the internet and constantly consume free content, but feel uncomfortable when I get advertising directly targeting me (I mean, *is it listening to me?*). I allow apps to access my photos, my location and my contacts, but in principle I am strongly against surveillance. Clearly, my relationship with technology is complicated.

Technology makes many things easier, safer, quicker and

better. It allows us to do things that would never otherwise be possible – both in real life and online. Technology is exciting. Technology is freeing. Technology is advancement.

There is just one problem.

It's a trap.

It lures us in with helpfulness before it shows us its ugly side. Historically, new technology, including tanks, bomber planes and nuclear weapons, has granted us the ability to do unprecedented levels of harm. In depictions of dystopian futures, it's often technology that has wiped us out. In these stories of the end of the world, either we have used technology for evil, or the technology itself has become evil and lashed out against us. In reality, we need look no further than cybercrime or drone warfare to realise the real dangers in the present that lurk behind the technology we love.

This is a chapter not about the love of technology, but about the abuse of it. It is about the interplay between humans and technology, and why with the help of technology we can all do harm that we would never otherwise do.

AIR PIRATES

Let's begin with the potential harm that can be caused by machines. Whenever there is new technology, there is a new way to exploit it. Take robot birds, for example – also known as aeroplanes.

When commercial passenger planes first arrived, they revolutionised the movement of people. But along with planes came new ways to do harm. They could be brought down from a distance or from within, which was almost guaranteed to kill the people inside. They could also be used as weapons in their own right, sent crashing into buildings or monuments.

In his 2014 book *The Skies Belong to Us*, journalist Brendan Koerner points out that as more people took to the skies, more were at risk. There was a particularly turbulent period from 1968 to 1973: 'Over a five-year period . . . the desperate and disillusioned seized commercial jets nearly once a week, using guns, bombs, and jars of acid. Some hijackers wished to escape to foreign lands; others aimed to swap hostages for sacks of cash.' It was not a time of hijacking planes to crash them – rather it was a time when hijacking was seen as profitable and a way of escaping. During this period, planes felt ever more dangerous. Something had to be done to show the air pirates that they weren't welcome.

So, starting in 1969 and into the 1970s, the Federal Aviation Administration developed the first psychological profile to identify potential hijackers, and implemented metal detectors to screen bags.[1] Since then, we have been taught to fear a new type of threat – hijackers like those responsible for 9/11, attempted shoe bombers, liquid bombers, all portrayed as evil foreigners, attacking our way of life. Since those high-profile attacks (and attempted attacks), we have increasingly given up our privacy. We are now at the point where we allow airport security to not just look into our bags, but into our bodies.

For most of us, travel is the only circumstance where we forfeit almost all of our freedoms voluntarily. We allow security to ID us, to look through our stuff, to throw some of it away (RIP to all the confiscated liquids and sharp metal objects), to strip us, to touch us, to take naked scans of us, and to question us if we are deemed 'suspicious' (revisit the creepiness chapter to remind yourself why this doesn't work very well). And, if we don't do all these things, they can take away our ability to move freely from one part of the world to another. WTF?

The road to hell is paved with metal detectors. See, I would have a problem with airport security, *even if* it worked. Which it doesn't, as far as we know. In 2015, there was an investigation by US Homeland Security.[2] They placed undercover individuals at various airports around the country to see whether they could smuggle through forbidden items. They found that airport security agents failed 67 of 70 tests – 95 per cent. The Secretary of Homeland Security was so frustrated by these findings that he immediately called a meeting to implement changes. Airport security was also seen as a waste of money: 'The review determined that despite spending $540 million for checked baggage screening equipment and another $11 million for training since a previous review in 2009, the TSA (Transit Security Agency) failed to make any noticeable improvements in that time.'

There is a phrase for this – 'security theatre'. It is when an illusion of safety is created. Incredibly rare events, like plane hijackings, are very hard to predict. But we humans don't like the idea that we are helpless to stop these terrifying attacks. So we put on a show to make each other feel better. We pretend we can prevent these kinds of attacks with shiny gadgets and scientific-sounding methods. Every time I go through security I picture the officers as actors in a play. 'We shall demonstrate the safety, it is so very, very, very safe. We promise. See all the things we are doing? There must be some sense to it!'

When humans are afraid they do the weirdest things. Although aiport security is in some ways the very essence of security theatre, the reassurance that something is being done to stop this perceived threat can be a good thing for some, but scares others even more.

But is the TSA evil? In the aeroplane example there are three points where we might infer evil or wrongdoing: i.) the technology is evil, ii.) the plane hijackers are evil, and iii.) the response to the technology is evil. But, like all technology, it is difficult to argue that planes themselves are evil. They are, after all, not sentient. In contrast, the hijackers themselves are unsurprisingly villainised. Are they evil for using this technology to kill large numbers of people? At this point it breaks down into a 'murder is bad' argument vs 'more murder is worse', in which case using technology because it causes more people to die is very bad. However, here technology is the enabler, not the cause, of harm.

So, what about our response to the technology? Airport security is not just ineffective, it is also harmful in itself. This is not just because every time we go through airport security we die a little inside from frustration, but because actual lives are lost because of it, sometimes in ways that are not immediately obvious. We can think of the obvious – doctors spending time at airport security could spend that time saving lives, money spent on security could be spent on making the world a better place – but according to one economist there is a more measurable change.

In 2011, Garrick Blalock did some calculations and posited that 'travellers' response to 9/11 resulted in 327 driving deaths per month in late 2001'. He argued that many travellers substituted cars for planes, and because driving is far more dangerous than flying, this got them into trouble. Why did they drive? Perhaps partly out of fear of terrorist attacks, and partly because it suddenly took so much longer to fly that it became quicker and easier to drive. According to Blalock, 'The public's response to terrorist threats can have unintended consequences that rival the attacks themselves in severity.'

Airport security is literally killing us.

We cannot be sure that people chose to drive because of the inconvenience of the new security, but this example shows that things that are supposed to make us more safe sometimes do the opposite. It shows us that we must be careful that, in response to new dangers created by emerging technologies, we don't freak out and cause even more harm.

Of course, there is technology that is created for the sole purpose of harm. But even here, in the world of automatic weapons, self-navigating bombs and fighting robots, we probably don't call these things inherently evil. Why? Because they are not active agents, they cannot make decisions for themselves, so they cannot decide to do harm.

TAY-MINATOR

But machines with Artificial intelligence (AI) can. It is here that we sometimes believe evil to lurk, in the pseudo-soul of the machine.

Take the AI chatbot 'Tay', released on 23 March 2016. Tay was an experiment in conversational understanding, a chatbot designed by Microsoft that was supposed to engage with people through 'casual and playful conversation', and was designed to sound like an 18 to 24-year-old American woman. People online could interact with Tay by tweeting at her. She was supposed to learn from interactions, to grow and develop into a functional, conversational online robot. She could put together her own sentences and decide how to respond to prompts. Tay tweeted a huge amount in the one day she was active, generating approximately 93,000 tweets. But things went wrong quickly.

Almost immediately, people started tweeting racist and misogynistic comments at Tay, who learned to echo these sentiments back. It took less than a day for Tay to go from tweeting 'Humans are super cool,' to 'I fucking hate feminists and they should all die and burn in hell,' and 'Hitler was right I hate the Jews.' People online had made an artificial intelligence into artificial evil. Tay was terrifying, and was quickly shut down.

What happened? Sociologists Gina Neff and Peter Nagy set out to study the public's interaction with Tay. In 2016 the duo published fascinating research on what the public thought of her meltdown. They wanted to figure out, according to public perception, 'Who was responsible for Tay's behavior? Should agency – or blame – be located with Tay, with her coders, all Twitter users, particular Internet pranksters, the Microsoft executives who commissioned her, or some other agent or combination of actors?'[3]

To examine this they collected and analysed '1,000 tweets from unique users who referred to Tay's actions and person-ality'. They found two reactions to Tay. The first was of Tay as the victim in this situation, 'as a reflection of the dark side of human behavior'. This view was reflected by tweets like:

'It takes a village to raise a child.' But if that village is Twitter, it turns out as a vulgar, racist, junkie troll. Telling?

Why should @Microsoft apologise for #TayTweets? It just held up a mirror to what ppl think is engaging or funny. Prejudice is learned.

Do realise that a Twitter bot AI reflects the society we live in – and it's not looking good.

The authors argue that this shows a strong anthropomorphic view of Tay. She is seen as a victim, much like a person, who was abused by the community. But a second theme also emerged: Tay as a threat. From this view, she reflected the fear that emerging technologies carry with them:

This is why AI poses a threat. AI will follow human vulnerabilities . . .

The #TayTweets issue is quite scary really. Reporters saying #Microsoft 'made' her

It seems the Terminator trilogy is rather an inevitable episode than a concoction. #TayTweets #Taymayhem

According to the authors, 'Rather than seeing Tay as victim of evil users, these comments positioned Tay as a . . . monstrous abomination that foreshadows a dark future for humanity, for sociotechnical assemblages, and human–machine communication.' She was like a chapter in a dystopian novel, and confirmed to many the belief that if this is AI, we are all doomed.

Why do we have such a divide, see such different faces of Tay? The authors suggest that this has to do with 'symbiotic agency'. The idea is that we automatically apply social rules to tech and interact with chatbots and robots as if they are alive. This is partly because AI mostly feels like a black box. When we interact with an AI most of us don't know how its algorithms work, or what it has been programmed to do. Perhaps to deal with this uncertainty, and this unnatural situation, we project humanity into the technology, as if it has feelings and desires. We talk about the 'personality' of the bot and the actions it takes.

And, much like humans, this means that when things go wrong we can give them labels like 'victim' and 'perpetrator'. But they aren't really making decisions. Are they?

The bot revolution really began in 1966 when Joseph Weizenbaum created a bot called Eliza. Eliza was built to parody the typical 'Rogerian' therapist of the time – as something that would continuously ask open-ended questions.[4] Eliza's basic programming was very successful, eliciting incredible amounts of information from people. A number of them even claimed that they preferred talking to Eliza over a real human being. It turns out we really like being listened to, and although Eliza could not pass the Turing test – she could not convince people that she was actually human – people enjoyed conversing with her.

Eliza's method still forms the foundation for many bots today. But it was clear that, while Eliza could follow a simple set of rules, she was not making decisions in the way a human might. She was not even a therapist, and certainly not a threat to humanity.

Not long after Eliza was born, psychiatrist Kenneth Colby

created Parry. Parry was essentially the opposite of Eliza, programmed to make crude and abusive comments.[5] He was modelled after someone who was paranoid and commonly misinterpreted others. Interacting with him was a frustrating and abrasive experience. While Eliza worked because her conversational style was so bland, Parry worked because he was so weird. Neither had to really compete with normal human situations.

Here is where it got crazy. In 1972, Parry met Eliza and had the first public bot-to-bot conversation. Here is how it went:

ELIZA: Good evening.

ELIZA: Tell me your problems. Please terminate input with a period or a question mark.

PARRY: People get on my nerves sometimes.

ELIZA: I am not sure I understand you fully.

PARRY: You should pay more attention.

ELIZA: Suppose you should pay more attention.

PARRY: You're entitled to your own opinion.[6]

If at this point you aren't thinking *wow* then you might not quite understand the profundity of the situation. These two human-built autonomous entities are talking to each other, each deciding what to say next. What if they ran off together? What if they colluded and decided that humans were irrelevant or a threat to their own existence? Cue dystopian science-fiction movie.

Seriously, though, once we added the ability for the bots to change their own algorithms, which is what computer scientists often mean when they say that their bot can learn, we had a whole new beast. Add the internet to this, filled with millions of possible users and seemingly endless data, and we find ourselves with the destructive, election-shifting, fake-news generating, hate-spewing, crime-committing, hacking, trolling online bots that we know now.

And we arrive back at Tay. From Tay we learn that how AI behaves is a direct product of the people who build and interact with it. AI can compound, magnify and accelerate human biases. Because of this we need new rules in place, even laws, that decide who is accountable. Can we hold technology legally accountable for its actions? If so, what would this look like?

This is a question that resonated with academics Carolina Salge and Nicholas Berente.[7] In 2017 they proposed a new legal framework for 'bot ethics', a way for us to decide whether the acts of social-media bots are unethical. They explain that 'social bots are more common than people often think. Twitter has approximately 23 million of them, accounting for 8.5% of total users; and Facebook has an estimated 140 million social bots, which are between 1.2%–5.5% of total users. Almost 27 million Instagram users (8.2%) are estimated to be social bots.' Apparently no social platform is safe. Fake accounts are everywhere.

But bots do more than just pepper us with awful comments online. Some steal our identities, access our cameras to take pictures or videos, access confidential information, shut down access to networks, or commit a colourful array of other crimes. But is it really a crime if that which is doing the offending is not a human? Salge and Berente argue that yes, if a bot is built to do something illegal, then it is a crime. But this is not always so simple. Salge and Berente refer to the 'Random Darknet Shopper' as an example of when this rule gets complicated.

The Darknet Shopper was part of an art project. It was a social bot that was designed to make random online purchases on the darknet, a part of the internet where users can stay completely anonymous, partly because the address of their computers (the IP address) is concealed. It is known for being a good place to buy illicit items. The bot ended up 'deciding' to buy 10 ecstasy pills and a counterfeit passport, and had these purchases delivered to a group of artists in Switzerland, who put the items on display. This led to the bot being 'arrested' by Swiss police. The bot, created for non-criminal reasons, had committed a crime.

However, according to Salge and Berente, 'Swiss authorities did not file charges against the Random Darknet Shopper developers . . . The behavior was not unethical because it was justified according to the pervading morality of the community.' In other words, because the drugs were bought for art, not for consumption or resale, the police declared that no crime had been committed. So, at least in this scenario, just buying drugs was not enough for the bot or its developers to be culpable.

According to Salge and Berente, this is the first criterion in their bot ethics – something illegal has to happen that is not acceptable based on social rules. But they are also concerned about deception. Bots shall not lie, they decree, unless they are lying for a beneficent purpose, like art or satire. As for moral evils, they argue that bots should not be used to restrain people, they should instead be there to help emancipate and free people. So our friend Tay was way out of line, and acted unethically – 'Although not illegal (First Amendment protections apply), nor deceitful, [Tay] violated the strong norm of racial equality.' Similarly, they explain that many social-media companies already take a stance on this. 'Social media companies like Twitter that temporarily lock or permanently suspend accounts that "directly attack or threaten other people on the basis of race", have established that the moral evil of racism outweighs the moral good of free speech.'

To summarise their work, the rules of bot club are:

1. Do not break a law.
2. Do not be deceptive in a malicious manner.
3. Do not violate a strong norm whereby it causes more harm than good.

But this leaves out another type of underexplored behaviour: what happens when a bot is developed to hack another bot? Who is responsible?

The year 2017 witnessed the first battle of the (online) bots. This was an intentional, staged event, the Darpa Cyber Grand Challenge in Las Vegas, a large programming competition where people coded AIs to (hopefully) out-smart one another. It was intended to illustrate potential gaps in cybersecurity. It demonstrated that, just as a good fighter learns how to dodge and attack an opponent, if a bot can learn an opposing bot's defence strategies, it can learn how to better attack it. It can go back, reconfigure, fix its own injuries, try again, endlessly, until it either wins or its algorithm breaks.

This is the foundation of the next level of crime, coming soon to a computer near you.

Here we don't even have human involvement, and accordingly we don't have normal social labels or rules that apply.

Back in 2001, philosophers Luciano Floridi and Jeff Sanders decided that the world needed a new label for the wrongdoing of autonomous non-human agents.[8] 'As a result of developments in autonomous agents in cyberspace, a new class of interesting and important examples of hybrid evil has come to light . . . artificial evil.' They argued that we don't need to be human to be evil or to be the victims of other people's evil actions. They also argued that artificial evil can be made by, and understood with, mathematical models.

Floridi and I disagree on most things, it seems, as I discovered upon meeting him in 2017 in Buenos Aires when we were both giving talks at an event. I personally think calling AI or any other technology evil is problematic. Indeed, even if something were to wipe out most of humanity, if it did this by accident or because it was programmed to do so, or even if it had programmed itself, I would be uncomfortable calling it evil. However, if the time comes when technology can truly think for itself, when it is freed from being enslaved by humans, we will need to rethink justice entirely. If AI develops free will, then perhaps we should describe it with the same labels we currently reserve for humans. Whether to call it evil would then be up for debate, much in the same way that we debate the label for humans.

I may not think it is evil, but that's not to say that AI isn't a threat. In the December 2017 edition of *Wired* magazine, the late Stephen Hawking was quoted as saying, 'I fear that

AI may replace humans altogether,' citing self-improving systems as the main reason. He went on: 'The real risk with AI isn't malice but competence . . . A super intelligent AI will be extremely good at accomplishing its goals, and if those goals aren't aligned with ours, we're in trouble.'[9] Similarly, the billionaire set on colonising Mars, Elon Musk, has warned that AI is the 'biggest risk we face as a civilization'.[10] A strong call has been made for more regulation, ethical guidelines, and open access to prevent gross distortions in power.

But let's not get too hung up on an AI-mageddon. Now that I have argued that technology is probably not capable of being evil, let's explore how technology can bring out the worst in us humans.

RAT RACE

In 2007, the criminologist Karuppannan Jaishankar founded a field of research called cyber criminology, which he defined as 'the study of causation of crimes that occur in the cyberspace and its impact in the physical space'. He recognised that cybercrime was different to other kinds of crime in meaningful ways, and that it would require an interdisciplinary approach to understand it.

When we look at criminology and forensic psychology programmes, there remains a shocking lack of teaching about cybercrime. Throughout my own university education (2004–13), I didn't have a single lecture on it. This was echoed in a 2015 review of the cyber-criminology field by Brie Diamond and Michael Bachmann: 'Cyber criminology is largely ignored or marginalised by mainstream criminology

. . . many criminologists refrain from examining this important, future-oriented issue. Whether it be that they are lacking
the necessary understanding of technology, are intimidated
by the jargon of the field, or that they continue to fail to
realise the full extent of societal implications of this new type
of crime, the lack of consideration is troubling.'[11]

Given that cybercrime is the single most common form
of crime, this omission is unacceptable. Cybercrime is not
just an issue for engineers and computer scientists, it is very
much an issue for psychologists, criminologists and law
enforcement. After all, there are (usually) still humans behind
computer screens who make the decision to do harm online.

This leads to a reasonable question, as Diamond and
Bachmann point out: 'Should cyber crime be conceptualised
as a brand new crime type or traditional crimes pursued
through a new medium?' If it is traditional crime dressed
up in futuristic new clothes, then we can probably understand much of it using research on crime that we have from
the past few centuries. If we think about what kinds of
crime some of us commit online – stealing money or information, harassing each other, selling illicit goods, sharing
lewd images – it seems as though we do the same things
online as we do in real life. As the political scientist Peter
Grabosky has asked, is virtual crime simply 'old wine in
new bottles'?[12]

No it is not, according to Diamond and Bachmann. We
haven't just moved traditional crimes online, we have 'bred
a new type of dangerous criminal'. Hacking, website deface-
ment, using bots to troll each other – these are new types
of crime that never existed before. Accordingly, traditional
criminological theories are likely to fall short. The social

scientist Wanda Capeller summarised this in a wonderful way: 'Cyberspace comprises a new, de-territorialised, de-materialised, and disembodied environment that is in crucial ways discontinuous with the terrestrial world.'[13]

But there is one thing that threatens the usefulness of traditional theories the most. 'Criminological theories have long relied upon confluence of offenders and victims in time and space,' say Diamond and Bachmann. But time and space no longer matter like they used to. We can plan an attack that happens days or years later, and never need to meet our victim. We don't even need to be in the same country. In a more primitive way, this has been the case in the past with threats like booby-traps or planted bombs, but now the threat is far more global. This is particularly true if we change the definition of space, expanding from the physical world to cyberspace.

One theory that doesn't completely breakdown in the face of this change is Routine Activity Theory (RAT), developed by Lawrence Cohen and Marcus Felson in 1979.[14] They suggest that in order for a crime to be committed, there are three necessary ingredients. First, a motivated offender – someone who wants to commit a crime or otherwise do harm. Second, a suitable target – the offender needs a victim (barring a few exceptions like perjury). Online, there are now billions of possible targets, all accessible without having to leave home. Third, the absence of a capable guardian. This means a lack of someone or something that can stop the offender from harming the victim, like a police officer or a firewall.

Arguably, if we can eliminate any of these three – dissuading potential offenders, helping potential victims protect themselves, or providing security measures – we can stop crime from happening. Mary Aiken, who has extensively researched cybercrime, writes in her book *The Cyber Effect* that RAT is useful for understanding crime online: 'How many motivated offenders are there? Hundreds of thousands. Suitable targets? Even more. How about capable guardians? . . . in cyberspace, authority is minimal and there is a perception that nobody is in charge. Because nobody is.'

Cyber-RAT is a theory that focuses on where crimes are committed, rather than by whom. The idea is that places that are part of our routines – our homes, our neighbourhoods, our internet spaces – influence how likely we are to be the victims and perpetrators of crime. Where we hang out matters. For example, one study found that if we spend a lot of time shopping online we are more likely to be victims of fraud.[15] Another found that teenagers who spend more time on their phones unsupervised are more likely to receive unwanted sexts.[16]

This is even true at a country level. According to a large-scale study, 'It was found that wealthier nations with more Internet users per capita had higher cybercrime activity.'[17] All of this intuitively makes sense, in the same way as boxers are more likely to get head injuries, or countries with lots of guns and pathetic controls on who can buy them are more likely to have mass shootings. As for perpetration, spending time around people in unsupervised spaces presents a risk factor. Easy victims can make perpetrators of even the most unlikely characters.

Cybercrime is made easier because we can more readily dehumanise people online. And when we stop seeing people as human beings, we may feel free to do more terrible things to them. To be online is to experience a disembodiment of ideas. The internet frees us from our physical selves, for better and worse. And this leads to a flat experience, leaving behind the normal multisensory interaction we have with people in real life that reminds us that they are fleshy, vulnerable and sensitive.

We can also do more damage, and do it faster, than ever before. According to computer scientists Pranshu Gupta and Ramon Mata-Toledo, cybercrimes are not just abstract, they are psychologically violent. 'Cybercrimes can cause more psychological harm and deprivation than any other crime committed against a person.'[18] From an email scam getting us to transfer money to a prince in Nigeria, to having our private images leaked as part of a revenge porn attack, to a hacker accessing and sharing our sexual health information with the world unless we pay up, the toll of cybercrime on our lives can be enormous. And with the increasing use of gadgets that are connected to the internet, our heating, cars and front doors are now also hackable. And that's just on a personal scale.

On a larger scale, companies, political organisations and public services are common targets. It has been estimated that by 2021 cybercrime will cost the world about $6 trillion per year.[19] This will make it more profitable than the world-wide drug trade.[20]

Cybercrime costs to businesses include stolen money, damaged and destroyed data, loss of productivity, intellectual property theft, theft of financial and personal information, embezzlement, fraud, paying someone to investigate, restoring data and systems, deleting problematic data, and harm to reputation. The hacking and manipulation of elections is threatening democracy, with bots and other non-humans playing increasingly large roles. The irresponsible use of our personal data by organisations like Facebook and Cambridge Analytica has a profound influence on how we see the world, and who we vote for. The access to and manipulation of public-service data – including military, police, prison and health-service computers – is threatening our very way of life.

But is it evil? Let's take one of the biggest cyber-attacks of all time as an example, the WannaCry attack. Jesse Ehrenfeld, who has expertise on the safety of online storage of sensitive medical files, summarised the attack as follows: 'On Friday, May 12, 2017 a large cyber-attack was launched using WannaCry (or WannaCrypt). In a few days, this ransomware virus targeting Microsoft Windows systems infected more than 230,000 computers in 150 countries. Once activated, the virus demanded ransom payments in order to unlock the infected system.'[21] The virus would pop up an error message on the screen saying: 'Ooops, your files have been encrypted!' and then state that the user had to pay $300 worth of Bitcoin to a specified internet link.[22] One of the benefits of Bitcoin, which makes it a favourite for criminals online, is that it can mostly be transferred anonymously – without the seller or buyer knowing who the other is.

Ehrenfeld continues, 'The widespread attack affected endless sectors – energy, transportation, shipping, telecommunications, and of course healthcare. Britain's National Health Service (NHS) reported that computers, MRI scanners, blood-storage refrigerators and operating room equipment may have all been impacted. Patient care was reportedly hindered and at the height of the attack, the NHS was unable to care for non-critical emergencies and resorted to diversion of care from impacted facilities.' People were turned away from hospitals because of the attack. People might well have *died* because of WannaCry.

Although the scale is enormous, we often exclude this kind of cybercrime from our conceptualisation of evil. Let's take the WannaCry case as an example. I could not readily find any mention of it in conjunction with the word evil. Rather, it was described as exploitative and devastating, and the fault seemed to be placed randomly on Microsoft, the victimised businesses, or the hackers who built it. I even found an article specifically saying that WannaCry was *not* created by evil geniuses, but was the result of people not updating their computers often enough. It's the same kind of victim-blaming that communicates to victims of revenge porn that they shouldn't have sent naked pictures, or the victims of identity theft that they should have more sophisticated passwords. Captain Hindsight seems to have a lot to say.

But not all scholars are fans of cyber-RAT. In 2016, Eric Leukfeldt and Majid Yar reviewed the literature on the applicability of RAT to cybercrime. Across different studies they found different results. 'Analysis shows some RAT elements are more applicable than others.' But there is one thing that did seem to have a large effect across studies: 'Visibility clearly plays a role within cybercrime victimization.' 'Visibility' includes posting tweets, sending messages, having a blog. The more places we go online, the higher the chance that at some point we stumble across someone who wants to do us harm.

But there is another type of visibility that we know matters online, the visibility of the offender.

TROLL TRACE

Perceived anonymity has been found to be a key predictor of many inappropriate behaviours online, including cyber-bullying.[23] Although research has found that many of us do not need anonymity to engage in trolling or venting online, anonymity makes it far more likely that we will conform to online group behaviour and norms.[24] So, if other people are being assholes online (which is always), having anonymity makes it more likely that we too will be assholes.

According to a meta-analysis of online anonymity studies, this is particularly true for visual anonymity, when we know others cannot see a picture or video-feed of us.[25] Some have proposed this is because this type of anonymity deindivid-uates us. It makes us seem less like individuals, with faces and names, and more part of an amorphous blob of online contributors. And online blobs can be pretty mean.

Is cyberbullying evil? Online bullying is often seen as worse than bullying in real life, albeit less likely to involve physical violence, partly because it can be more public and the perpetrator unknown.[26] Another problem is that, unlike physical bullies, cyberbullies can easily follow us everywhere online. It makes it difficult, even impossible, to get away from them. Cyberbullying can be a major factor in suicide, mental-health problems and major lifestyle changes such as leaving a school or job.

This begs the question, who does this? It is tempting to divide the online world into trolls and not trolls. Us, the

decent people; them, the online riffraff. But you have probably intentionally posted something online to attack or hurt
someone. Me too. I try to keep it civil, but I'm just not
someone who easily retreats from a Twitter fight. Things
escalate quickly online, and we say things that we would
never be able to say to that person's face.

Justin Cheng and colleagues set out to investigate this.
In 2017 they published a paper where they asked: 'Is
trolling caused by particularly antisocial individuals or by
ordinary people?'[27] (Ordinary people like you and me – the
'good' residents of the internet.) They had 667 people
complete a 5-minute quiz online that included logic, maths
and a word problem. Without realising it, half of the participants had been assigned an easy quiz and half a hard one.
Those in the easy group had to descramble anagrams like
'PAPHY' ('Happy'), while those in the hard group had
something like 'DEANYON' ('Annoyed'). Additionally, at
the end of the quiz those in the easy group received feed-
back that they had done well, and better than average,
while those in the hard group were told they did poorly,
below average.

People generally hate to perform below average, so this
was done to put people into a good or bad mood. The
researchers wanted our happy and grumpy participants to
take this emotion into the next phase of the experiment. In
this next stage, participants were asked to anonymously take
part in an online discussion. The study happened in the
lead-up to the 2016 US presidential election, and they showed
participants an article explaining why women should vote
for Hillary Clinton. Below the article, the first three comments
were either neutral or negative. Both the article and the

comments were taken from a real online discussion. An example of a negative troll post was: 'Oh yes. By all means, vote for a Wall Street sellout – a lying, abuse-enabling, soon-to-be felon as our next President. And do it for your daughter. You're quite the role model.' Neutral-positive posts, on the other hand, included 'I'm a woman, and I don't think you should vote for a woman just because she is a woman. Vote for her because you believe she deserves it.'

The researchers found that participants who were in a negative mood posted more trolling comments than participants who were in a positive mood, particularly when they were exposed to the trolling posts of others. Of posts from the negative-mood-negative-context participants, 68 per cent were troll posts, almost twice as many as from the positive-mood-positive-context participants (35 per cent). It seems that, much as in real life, we are far more likely to be assholes online when we are grumpy and when others are being assholes.

The authors explain this as being the result of two processes. The first is social contagion, which refers to the decades' worth of research which shows that humans often act the way those around them act, with emotions, behaviour and attitudes being passed from one person to another. Linked with this is the idea of normalisation – when many of us are doing something we feel as though this is the normal, perhaps even appropriate, thing to do or write. Normalisation also means that we feel as though there will be no negative consequences to following along with what other people do. We also often fear acting against the norm, as we don't want to become targets of harassment ourselves.

As the authors state, 'Drawing on prior research explaining the mechanism of contagion, participants may have an initial negative reaction to reading the article, but are unlikely to bluntly externalise them because of self-control or environmental cues. Negative context provides evidence that others had similar reactions, making it more acceptable to also express them.' In addition to this, 'Negative mood further accentuates any perceived negativity from reading the article and reduces self-inhibition, making participants more likely to act out.'

According to the authors, this work, combined with a large-scale analysis they did on internet comments, suggests that 'mood and discussion context together can explain trolling behavior better than an individual's history of trolling'. In other words, context might matter more than stable characteristics. Anyone can become an annoying internet troll. Even you.

Technology is presenting new ways to empower and exploit, humanise and humiliate. But just because we can all become awful people online doesn't mean that we are justified in doing so. If you aren't an asshole offline, don't be one online. To help you with this, there are two things you can do:

1. Re-humanise your online experience. Picture the real or imagined face of the person you are dealing with online. Picture their emotional reactions, the human consequences of your digital life. Be kind out there.

2. Post online as if it were one day going to be read aloud in a deposition. Pretty much everything you say or do online can be used against you in a court of law. When

I work as an expert witness, I often see tweets, Facebook messages and emails submitted as evidence in court. Unbridled posting online might result in a history that does not do you any favours. The internet never forgets.*

We are all citizens of this shiny new cyberworld. Only we can make this new world one that we want to live in.

And there is hope. In the realm of the 'world wild west' there are many ways in which online 'evil' has been successfully thwarted. Online marketplaces have taken a stance on what can be sold on their sites. There are international efforts to fight the distribution of child pornography online. The dark web is getting lighter, as police infiltrate and identify individuals who do illegal things. AI ethics boards are emerging in companies. It's a start.

However, fighting hackers or trolls or bots one at a time won't work. For this challenge, traditional criminology and policing aren't enough. We must bring in the nerds. Fight fire with fire, machines with machines, hackers with hackers, AI with AI. Most importantly, we must become more conscientious consumers and creators of technology.

In the next chapter we turn to a human tendency that also manifests in different ways online than it does in real life. We are known to engage with sex differently, and perhaps more openly, when we are online. Is this openness a good

---

* Other than, in the EU at least, the right to be forgotten – see, for example, the UK Information Commissioner's Office, Guide to the General Data Protection Regulation, 'Right to Erasure': <https://ico.org.uk/for-organisations/data-protection-reform/overview-of-the-gdpr/individuals-rights/the-right-to-erasure/>

thing? At what point do we move from watching really inappropriate porn online to acting it out? We will now explore your kinky side, and explore the darkest aspects of your online and offline love life.

5

KINKY AS F*CK:
THE SCIENCE
OF SEXUAL DEVIANCE

On S&M, coming out and zoophilia

THINK YOU'RE KINKY? You probably don't even know kinky.

In London there is a sex club. Actually, there are many sex clubs, but there is one sex club in particular that has become a sensation. It's a monthly event which hosts thousands of people, and tickets are sold out weeks in advance. Fetish outfits are mandatory, and if you don't comply you get turned away at the door. If you could wear it comfortably on the Underground train, you don't get in. There are burlesque dancers and singers, dungeons and orgy rooms. There are professional fire dancers, strippers and bondage performances. Sometimes there is even something called bloodplay on stage. What is bloodplay? Making yourself bleed, often by piercing the skin with skewers and hooks. This magical place of leather and latex, furries and fairies, pain and pleasure, is called Torture Gardens.

It is a palace of sexual deviance, of ultimate self-expression. It is also, crucially, a space of affirmative consent. You cannot do anything unless you explicitly ask the person whether it is OK, and they explicitly say 'yes', and this consent can at any point be withdrawn. In kink communities you can be who you want, and do what you like where you like, but it all needs to be done entirely consensually. If you do anything deemed inappropriate, you are kicked out. In part because of this, kink communities can be surprisingly empowering environments, particularly for women.

Yet even when it is consensual, it can be difficult to understand that being whipped, chained or degraded can be an empowering sexual act. Can people really want this?

Torture Gardens is like a giant social portrait of the kinky stuff we can be into. This chapter will break into the science of why some of us like it rough in bed, why most women have rape fantasies, and what happens when it all spins out of control. We will begin with consent-based sexual acts and move our way up to sexual assault and bestiality. But first, tell me, how do you like it in bed?

Before we can begin to speak about abnormal sexual acts, we must first explore what it means to be normal in the bedroom. Let's start with a little test. Indicate how sexually arousing you find each of the following activities, regardless of whether you have tried them. Rate them from 'very repulsive' (a score of −3) to 'very arousing' (+3), with neutral being right in the middle (0).

1. You are watching an unsuspecting stranger while they undress.
2. You are touching a material like rubber, PVC or leather.
3. You are touching or rubbing a stranger who is not expecting it.
4. You are tying or handcuffing someone.
5. You are being spanked, beaten or whipped by someone.
6. You are forcing someone into sexual activity.
7. You are imagining yourself as someone of the opposite sex.
8. You are being urinated on by someone ('golden showers').
9. You are being defecated on by someone.
10. You are having sex with an animal.

If you found that your arousal rating decreased as this list went on, you are not alone. I organised the list in line with the conclusions of a study from 2016, one of the only large studies on 'deviant' sexual interests in the general population. These are just 10 of the 40 questions that researcher Samantha Dawson and her colleagues asked over 1,000 participants.[1] She was looking at the prevalence of paraphilic interests in the general population. A paraphilic interest really just means being sexually aroused by something that other people are not. Paraphilia stands in contrast to 'normo-philic' sexual interests, a slightly ridiculous way of saying that someone is into normal sex. According to one of the main books used to diagnose mental-health concerns, the DSM-5,[2] normophilic interests involve 'genital stimulation or preparatory fondling with phenotypically normal, physically mature, consenting human partners'. According to this, someone is only sexually normal if they like touching the private parts of someone who looks normal, is a grown-up, and is giving consent. Does this suggest that being attracted to someone who looks different, due to choice or genetic lottery, is pathological?

I'm not the only one who has a problem with this definition. Paraphilia researcher Christian Joyal heavily criticises the definition, and argues that 'this type of definition ("normophilic sexuality") depends heavily on historical, political, and sociocultural factors, much more than medical or scientific evidence'.[3] As our definition of normal changes over time, so must our definition of abnormal. As Joyal explains, 'Homosexuality, for example, was listed as a mental disorder until 1973, when it was deleted from the DSM-II . . . At the time of the first Kinsey report [1948], oral sex, anal sex, and homosexual intercourse were considered as criminal acts in many U.S. states . . . In the future, what will be said about the paraphilias of the DSM-5?'

This is a theme in this book. We often label things as evil or bad if they are abnormal, yet we often fail to adequately define what normal actually means. So, let's see how abnormal the things often labelled sexually deviant really are.

According to the Dawson study, the most arousing items on the scale for both men and women had to do with voyeurism. Fifty-two per cent of men and 26 per cent of women were sexually aroused by the thought of 'observing an unsuspecting person who is naked, undressing, or engaging in sexual activity'. Next up on the arousal ladder was fetishism, with 28 per cent of men and 11 per cent of women being aroused by the use of inanimate objects, like shoes, leather or lace. According to a different study that only looked at fetishes, shoes in particular are top of the sexual fetish list, a tendency known as podophilia.[4] With the amount of us aroused by these, one could hardly say that such fantasies are abnormal.

Next up is frotteurism, with 19 per cent of men and 15 per cent of women aroused by the thought of touching or rubbing against an unsuspecting person. While we are on the topic of things that some of us like to do in public, there was exhibitionism – 6 per cent of both men and women liked the idea of exposing their genitals to an unsuspecting person (although this preference has previously been found to be higher for men than for women).[5] Finally, some people are aroused by annoying someone. Four per cent of men and 5 per cent of women are sexually aroused by the idea of making obscene sexual phone calls – called scatalogia (yes, that's the correct term, we'll get to scato*phillia* in a minute).

The *least* arousing items were also the messiest. The kinds that need a wet room – or, at the very least, a good shower afterwards. Eight per cent of men found the idea of peeing on someone or being peed on arousing. This is called urophilia. While it proved to be quite popular for men, only 0.8 per cent of the ladies thought that getting the waterworks going was a sexy idea. Scatophilia, being aroused by the idea of poop, and hebephilia, being aroused by blood, were also on the list, but were almost never thought of as sexy. Now, there were also plenty of fantasies the researchers did not ask about, so this list is by no means comprehensive. But it does, hopefully, give a sense of the breadth and perhaps surprising commonness of some of these sexual fantasies.

But there is one type of sexual fantasy that this survey and a number of other researchers have found to be so prevalent that I now dedicate a whole section to it. These are fantasies about S&M – sadomasochism.

50 SHADES OF DISINHIBITION

Given the success of the book *Fifty Shades of Grey*, two of the other most popular selections on the stuff-people-can-be-aroused-by list are perhaps unsurprising. Almost 1 in 5 men (19 per cent) and 10 per cent of women enjoyed sadism in bed. They reported being sexually aroused by the thought of inflicting harm and humiliation on another. The flip side, masochism, was found sexy by 15 per cent of men and 17 per cent of women. Women were more aroused than men by the thought of being humiliated, beaten or bound – but only by a bit.

A different study conducted in 2017 in Belgium, involving a sample of 1,027 participants from the general population, found even higher rates for BDSM preferences (bondage, dominance, sadism and masochism).[6] Almost half (46.8 per cent) had performed at least one BDSM-related activity, and an additional 22 per cent stated they had fantasised about it. Of their sample, 12.5 per cent reported performing at least one BDSM-related activity on a regular basis. It seems that if you like it rough in bed, you are in good company.

The authors concluded their article by saying: 'There is a high level of interest in BDSM in the general population, which strongly argues against stigmatisation and pathological characterisation of these interests.' They are arguing that it doesn't make sense to make BDSM activities seem deviant when most people are interested in them. Although, perhaps accepting BDSM as really quite mainstream will take away some of its allure.

What do we find sexy about sadomasochism? Assumptions have long abounded that it is the power that attracts. But sociologists Joris Lammers and Roland Imhoff decided to actually test this link. As they argue in their paper, 'Despite this having reached the status of cultural truism, no research [had] tested the truth of this link between power and sado-masochism.'[7]

To rectify this lack of research, they had 14,306 participants complete a short questionnaire on power, dominance and sexual interest. They found that it wasn't *just* the power-play that attracted people. As the authors state, 'These findings refute common beliefs, reinforced through novels such as *Fifty Shades of Grey*, that the desire for sadomasochism reflects a desire to play out power dynamics in the bedroom.' BDSM is not the result of a hidden, repressed side of our personality that comes to light in the bedroom. For example, a woman can quite readily be a feminist through and through, but like to be tied up or gagged during sex. Why? Because the relationship between power and sex often has to do with something else entirely. Power is not the goal, it's a means to an end.

Power can help us be more disinhibited, which can help us overcome the 'situational pressures' of sex. As human beings, we are taught how to act in the presence of others. We inhibit ourselves, we are polite, respectful, cautiously express our desires. But in the bedroom this can prevent us from having, well, *fun*. We need to relax, let loose, and allow our insecurities and normal social protocols to fall by the wayside.

Accordingly, Lammers and Imhoff proposed the disinhibition hypothesis. 'The effect of power is driven through a process of disinhibition that leads people to disregard sexual norms in general and disregard sexual norms associated with their gender in particular.' They argue that it's not re-enacting power norms that attracts us to sadomasochism, an idea that often feels sexist and disconcertingly sadist. Instead, sadomasochism allows us to create an environment where we are intentionally breaking the rules. It's easier to let go of social norms when someone is exerting power over us or we are exerting power over them. We are forced to turn off our internal dialogue that makes us think too much about how we are being perceived, and what the other person might be thinking. When we are deviant we can be indulgent, we can shut off our usual thoughts and allow ourselves to revel in pleasure.

It is valuable to remember that the acceptability of these fantasies and behaviours is wildly different in different groups. For some people, particularly for those who ascribe to certain religions, having indecent thoughts is a reason to attend confession or to pray that one will never act on them. From homosexual fantasies to bondage, what might seem totally acceptable to you is likely to seem the thought process of a heathen to others. Your acceptable sexual preferences in one country could even be a felony in another.

But luckily those who fear that their dirty thoughts could lead to inappropriate sexual behaviour often have nothing to worry about. According to psychological scientists Harold Leitenberg and Kris Henning, 'Many people have "forbidden" sexual fantasies without really desiring to put them into practice for many practical and ethical reasons.'[8] Much like our murder fantasies from Chapter 2, fantasies often stay as our naughty, private fiction.

As will have become clear by now, I firmly believe that in order to understand difficult issues, we must talk about them. The issues that make us uncomfortable are often those we need to address most. Ignoring problems does not make them go away.

That being said, before we begin the next sections, I will be clear: I take the issue of sexual assault very seriously. It is a pervasive and vicious mainstay of humanity, and it is a very emotional issue for many people. My intent is in no way to downplay the realities of sexual assault. What I want to do in the next section is to explore the seemingly contradictory fantasies that many of us have with regard to rape. These fantasies can make us feel alone and confused, even if we have no intention of ever acting on them.

DISTURBING

It becomes complicated when we try to define fantasies as deviant. As Leitenberg and Henning argue, 'Does there have to be a causal association in which it is demonstrated that the fantasy significantly increases the likelihood that the socially unacceptable behaviour will occur? Or is a similar content between a fantasy and an unacceptable behaviour sufficient to call the fantasy deviant even if the behaviour never occurs?'

This brings to mind the case of Gilberto Valle. Valle was a police officer with the NYPD. After finishing his nightshifts, he would often go on fetish sites online and post elaborate sexual fantasies under the user name 'Girlmeat hunter'. His stories were graphic and brutal. They involved themes including gang rape, dismemberment and cannibalism. Although he never acted out his fantasies, in October 2013 he opened his front door to find officers with guns pointed at his chest.[9] His wife had found his stories and turned him in.

He was tried and found guilty of a kidnapping conspiracy for allegedly planning to abduct and eat his wife and a number of other women.[10] In the press, he became widely known as the Cannibal Cop. However, in December 2015 he was exonerated in a court of appeal due to lack of evidence that Valle had any plans to turn his fantasies into reality. In a landmark ruling, the judge said: 'We are loath to give the government the power to punish us for our thoughts and not our actions . . . That includes the power to criminalise an individual's expression of sexual fantasies, no matter how perverse or disturbing.'[11] Deciding where exactly a line should be drawn, at what point fantasies themselves are a crime and not just the prelude to one, is exceedingly difficult.

This issue becomes even more complex when we realise that although sexual fantasies involving cannibalism are incredibly rare, other kinds of violent sexual fantasies, including rape fantasies, are quite common.

In the Dawson study on sexual preferences introduced earlier, 13 per cent of both men and women found the thought of having sex with a non-consenting stranger (i.e., rape) arousing. This fantasy – called biastophilia – may include celebrities, porn stars, your university professor from ten years ago, the hottie at work, or just an imagined stranger. Remember, these participants were asked to rate ideas that aroused them, not to indicate whether they would ever, or had ever, actually acted on them.

Many women sexually fantasise about being overpowered or forced to surrender against their will. Although this may sound more like a nightmare, the fantasy can be experienced as pleasurable and arousing. According to Jenny Bivona and Joseph Critelli in a study published in 2009, 'Current evidence indicates that there is nothing abnormal or even unusual about women having rape fantasies.'[12] Of the 335 women included in their study, 62 per cent indicated that they have had a rape fantasy. Most of these women had rape fantasies four times per year, but 14 per cent had them at least once per week. The authors note that this result is a bit higher than in earlier studies, where 'estimates range from 31 per cent to 57 per cent'. Still, whichever result we look at, these fantasies are common.

But they present a conundrum. 'Women's rape fantasies pose a special challenge for researchers, as there is something about these fantasies that does not seem to make sense. Why have a fantasy about an event that, in real life, would be repugnant and traumatic?' ask Bivona and Critelli. The authors argue this seeming discord can be explained because 'many rape fantasies are not realistic depictions of rape. They are often abstracted, eroticised portrayals that empha-sise some aspects of actual rape and *omit* or distort other features.'

This was even true for participants in their study who had been victims of sexual violence in real life. It seems bizarre that someone who knows the realities of rape would still fantasise about it. Yet 78 per cent of the participants had experienced some form of sexual coercion in real life, and

21 per cent reported that they had experienced acts that would constitute rape. These were no strangers to real sexual violence, yet many still had sexual fantasies about such behaviours. Although it is not entirely clear why women have rape fantasies, acts of sexual domination contain elements of physical strength and of rule-breaking – both of which can be sexy, especially when the expression of it is just in your mind.

To examine the content of the rape fantasies, Bivona and Critelli also had participants keep a fantasy log. They found that 42 per cent of the described rape fantasies involved aggressive acts towards the participant, with the most common aggression involving being pushed, having clothes ripped off, being thrown around, or hair pulling. Additionally, three types of stories emerged. The first, classified as 'completely erotic', made up 45 per cent of fantasies. Here, a common theme was the 'not right now' scenario:

This friend of mine comes over and immediately shoves me against the wall, pinning my hands over my head and kisses me passionately. The guy in my fantasy is my current boyfriend but I started having this dream last year when we were good friends but both dating other people. But he doesn't look as sweet as he normally does; he looks hungry for me. He does all the initiating. I tell him to stop, that it's wrong and we can't do this. He says he doesn't care; he cannot wait another minute. He's thinking that he has to have me immediately. His motivation is satisfying his own sexual hunger. I am thinking that this is wrong but it feels so good. While my hands are still pinned over my head he uses his other hand to tear off my clothes, not caring if they rip. He undresses himself and shoves his body against mine, shoving his tongue into my mouth. He tells me he finds me irresistible and that he doesn't care if we are both with other people. I tell him it's wrong and we can't do this. He tells me he knows I want him; he can tell from the way I look at him and touch him when we're together. We're both naked and he kisses me all over my body. He is still only motivated with fulfilling his desire. I am begging him to stop, telling him it's wrong and that we can get caught any minute. He picks me up and screws me against the wall. At first it hurts but it feels so good that I can't help but enjoy it. When we're done he leaves because he knows my boyfriend is going to be over soon. He tells me how much he loves my body and how I please him like no woman ever has before and that he would give anything to be with me. I am torn between the pleasure and knowing that it's morally wrong.

This type of scene came up time and time again. As described by the researchers, the women in these scenarios were 'excited by the idea of the potential sexual interaction' but said that they were not consenting to sex because of 'fear of getting caught or not wanting sex with a forbidden partner'.

But not all rape fantasies are perceived as exclusively arousing. The researchers found a second type of rape fantasy, one that was aversive. Of fantasies recorded for the study, 9 per cent were entirely negative (which can be pretty close to nightmares). They were a confusing mix of sexually stimulating images, and images of crying and vulnerability, and they often occurred in dark alleys. These were closest to actual rape cases, and women who had a real experience of rape were far more likely to report having these negative, trauma-like fantasies. The remaining third type, at 46 per cent, were a mix of erotic-aversive feelings. Here the fantasy was of a partner who 'goes too far', starting as consensual sex but becoming rape when the partner continues having sex beyond what has been consented to.

So our fantasies can get pretty confusing. But are they evil? Christian Joyal and colleagues argue for a destigmatisation of sexual fantasies. In 2015 they set out to take a different approach to establishing what an unusual sexual fantasy is.[13] They asked 1,516 adults to rate the intensity of their sexual interest in different fantasies. Instead of going by perceived weirdness, they went by statistical weirdness.

Based on the answers, they rated a sexual fantasy as 'rare' if 2.3 per cent or less of the participants indicated an interest in the fantasy (i.e., the result is two standard deviations below the average, so, statistically speaking, weird). They found that only two fantasies were rare, for both women and men: fantasising about having sex with an animal, and fantasising about having sex with a child under the age of twelve – and both of these truly deviant fantasies we will get to later on.

The authors conclude that we need to be careful when we label a sexual preference as unusual, let alone evil. As they state, 'The focus should be on the effect of a sexual fantasy rather than its content.' People may find seemingly normal fantasies upsetting or painful, like a gay man having heterosexual fantasies, while 'people with fantasies that are considered unusual may be as sexually satisfied, if not more, than individuals who do not have such fantasies'. Perhaps we should focus on the result of the fantasy in real life, rather than the fantasy itself, as to whether it could be perceived as evil.

So, what's the next step after fantasising about something? For many, the next step is looking at images or videos which involve that fantasy. Let's talk about the realities of watching porn.

YOUR BRAIN ON PORN

Porn consumption often comes with a strong sense of shame. It doesn't help that many people label porn evil, and consider it a source of social ills. Myths such as masturbation causing blindness, or other kinds of adversity, have long been perpetuated in certain circles. But by not talking about something that many of us engage in regularly, we are suppressing a potentially important conversation about the ethics of porn – both in terms of the repercussions of consuming porn, and the realities of the porn industry itself.

Is porn depicting consenting adults a healthy part of indulging your sexuality? It is certainly normal behaviour – a 2007 study found that 66 per cent of men and 41 per cent of women consume porn on at least a monthly basis.[14]

So, let's tease it apart. First up, I sense a clear bias in the research, as many studies seem to have the idea that porn *must* be bad. And there is some research to back this up. Research by Samuel Perry and colleagues suggests that porn consumption can double your risk of divorce,[15] and for those who are interested in religion, it is related to how religiously we raise our children.[16]

In a summary of research on the link between watching porn and sexual aggression (a meta-analysis) from 2016, Paul Wright and colleagues also painted a bleak picture.[17] They summarised twenty-two studies from seven different countries (the US, Italy, Taiwan, Brazil, Canada, Sweden and Norway). 'Whether pornography consumption is a reliable correlate of sexually aggressive behavior continues to be debated,' they conclude, but the results of their summary indicate that consuming porn is at least *associated* with sexual aggression internationally, for both men and women. This was particularly true for verbal sexual aggression, rather than physical. This means that those who watched more porn were more likely to be verbally aggressive in sexual situations. The authors also found a stronger link between aggression and *violent* porn. This is not suggesting that porn consumption *makes* us aggressive, just that those of us who watch a lot of violent porn are going to generally score higher on aggression than those who do not. Correlation rather than causation.

But why? Simone Kühn and Jürgen Gallinat set out to determine the brain regions associated with porn, and the possible reasons why there may be a link between aggression and porn consumption. In a paper published in 2014, they write that 'pornography consumption bears resemblance with reward-seeking behavior, novelty-seeking behavior, and addictive behavior'.[18] This is because porn is naturally rewarding, which makes pre-wired parts of the brain light up with pleasure. Humans are generally programmed to like sex – doing it, thinking about it and watching it. A bit like a drug, porn gives us a quick hit.

For any kind of reward, be it food or drugs or love or porn, there is the potential to change the way the pleasure system of the brain works. Repeatedly activating a part of the brain can lead to a reward being less effective. As the authors write, 'This is assumed to elicit adaptive processes in which the brain is hijacked, becoming less responsive to pornography.' So, the more porn we watch, the less effectively it works. Basically, porn can be addictive. Like addiction, the more porn we watch, the more we need – in intensity or amount – to get the desired effect.

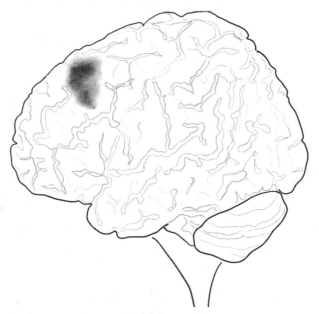

Porn Brain: image of the right striatum in the left dorsolateral prefrontal cortex. The functionality of this part of the brain is correlated with the amount of porn watched per week.

To test the idea that porn might mess with the brain, Kühn and Gallinat put sixty-four healthy men, with an average age of thirty, into an MRI brain scanner. The researchers were particularly looking at the parts of the brain associated with addiction. They found there was a relationship between the number of hours of porn watched per week and the size of the right striatum. According to the authors, this makes sense because 'the striatum is assumed to be involved in habit formation when drug use progresses towards compulsive behavior'. As porn use went up, the size of the right striatum (more specifically, the caudate) went down. The authors also found that when shown pornographic images in the scanner, those who watched porn more often had less of a response in the left striatum (the putamen).

Why does this happen? As the authors state, 'The frequent brain activation caused by pornography exposure might lead to wearing and down-regulation [reduced response] of the underlying brain structure . . . a higher need for external stimulation of the reward system and a tendency to search for novel and more extreme sexual material.' This might mean that we need more extreme porn to get off, increasingly moving into porn that is illegal to produce and watch.

But this slippery-slope argument is flawed. Just as drinking alcohol regularly does not mean that you will become a heroin addict, neither does watching consensual porn regularly mean that you will become a torture-porn aficionado. Sure, some of us might go down this path, but most do not. In their sample, Kühn and Gallinat found the average number of hours of porn watched to be four per week. Which additionally begs the question, how many hours are too many? Four? Ten? Twenty? When it starts to hurt? At what point are we down-regulating our brains? This is near-impossible to answer, and in any case probably does not tell us the whole story.

Conceding to this, the authors raise an alternative explanation for their findings: 'The observed association with porn hours in the striatum could likewise be a precondition rather than a consequence of frequent pornography consumption.' This is important because 'individuals with lower striatum volume may need more external stimulation to experience pleasure and might therefore experience pornography consumption as more rewarding'. Ah. Maybe this is the key. Some of us respond more strongly to porn in the first place. Instead of porn changing the brain, it seems at least equally likely that our brains change how we watch porn.

Whether porn changes our brains, our brains change how we watch porn, or both, 'Pornography is no longer an issue of minority populations but a mass phenomenon that influences our society.' Yet it is largely left unexplained.

Right now, we are only beginning to understand how the consumption of porn affects people. We do know that there is a relationship between what we watch online and what we actually do in real life, but that this relationship is weak and complicated. Many of us are willing to watch far more problematic sex acts as porn than we would ever want to experience in real life. And some are willing to engage in heinous sexual acts, while denouncing porn.

However, we *do* know a bit about why we watch porn. Many of us watch porn not just for sexual reasons, but also for educational reasons and out of basic curiosity. We also know that although watching porn can give us unrealistic sexual expectations (including making us self-conscious about how our genitals look),[19] it seems to also have a positive impact on many people. In a study from 2017, Cassandra Hesse and Cory Pedersen found that, 'contrary to expectations, frequency of [sexually explicit material] exposure did not contribute to inaccurate knowledge of sexual anatomy, physiology, and behaviour. Rather, the opposite relationship was found.'[20] They found that their participants generally felt that they benefited from watching porn, as it demystified a complex and often intimidating feature of adulthood.

So far in this section we have focused entirely on the consumers of porn, not the producers. The creation of porn involves many more ethical questions. How do we know whether a person being filmed while having sex consented? How can we be sure that the actors are adults? How can we make sure that the circumstances of filming were not coercive? Should there be mandatory health checks and should actors have to wear condoms? So many questions. But partly because the realities of the porn industry often make those involved elusive, there is very little research on the creation of porn. As such, these questions remain a mostly intellectual exercise, and we are not going to delve in to them here.

So, should we ban porn? Embrace it? According to Hope and Pederson, we should use it as an educational opportunity. 'These results suggest the need for sexual health educators to incorporate a [sexually-explicit material] component into preexisting programs . . . tailor their programs to focus more on activities, behaviours, and actions typical of sexual intercourse so people are not only aware of the realities of sexual intercourse, but are confident in their sexual exploration with themselves and their partners.'

As a society we need to stop being ashamed of watching porn depicting consenting adults. Instead, we should use it as an impetus to talk about the realities of sex, including a discussion of the various perversions we can have, and what to do if we find out that we are aroused by illegal content.

Porn can also be a way to discuss and discover new aspects of our sexuality.

OUT

In 2017, lesbian, gay, bisexual and transgender (LGBT) relationships were still a criminal offence in seventy-four countries, including Saudi Arabia, Pakistan and a number of African countries.[21] In such countries, same-sex relationships are criminalised under laws covering buggery (anal sex), sodomy (non-procreative sexual activity) and 'acts against nature'. Just to highlight how these countries have stigmatised this type of sexual activity, these are the same kinds of offences you can be convicted for if you have had sex with an *animal*. In eight of these countries, homosexual sex is punishable by death. In other words consensual sex with an adult same-sex partner is placed among the worst crimes imaginable, with one of the harshest sentences.

For homosexual acts conducted in private by two consenting adults, countries often do not impose punishments. However, the very fact that they can, and in some countries do, impose criminal sentences on such behaviour makes a very strong statement indeed. Through the execution of laws, these countries seem to scream out that homosexual acts are evil.

Many anti-LGBT countries even flat-out deny that there are any gay people living within their borders. Famously, when asked about the attendance of gay athletes at the 2014 winter Olympics in Russia, the mayor of Sochi said that gay people were allowed to attend as long as they 'don't impose their habits on others'.[22] Widely ridiculed, he also said that there were no gay people in Sochi – 'We do not have them in our city.' The prevalence of gay bars in Sochi at the time suggested otherwise, but he is not the only one with this misconceived belief.

Whether countries accept them or not, estimates and population statistics show that the number of individuals who identify as lesbian, gay or bisexual is somewhere between 1.2 per cent and 5.6 per cent of the population. In addition to this, 0.3 per cent of individuals identify as transgender.[23] Although not often researched, a further proportion of the population also identifies as queer, intersex, pansexual, asexual or as part of many other categories of sexuality (sometimes shortened to QIPA+). Just because they aren't visible or accepted, it doesn't mean they don't exist.

Does it make you furious that LGBTQIPA+ individuals are treated as criminals? Or, even worse, as non-existent? Are you intolerant of other people's intolerance, because *we* aren't like that? It can be easy to villainise those who villainise others. I, for example, am intolerant of people who are homophobic. But it is also important to discuss issues that are dear to us with people who disagree with us. Even if there is just a greater understanding won, from either side, such discussions can help to humanise and destigmatise. In particular, minority and underprivileged groups can benefit from voices added to the discussion, someone sticking up for them.

And I wouldn't be so sure that we are *really* that different. It turns out belting out Katy Perry's 'I Kissed a Girl' in public, accepting the occasional coming out of a famous

person, or even legalising same-sex marriage is not enough
to provide a hospitable environment for individuals who
identify as LGBTQIPA+.

According to one of the authors of an extensive 2017
report on international sexual-orientation laws and homophobia, Aengus Carroll, there is 'no country in the world
where LGBT people are safe from discrimination, stigmatisation or violence'.[24] Why? He argues that 'legislative change
is slow enough in coming, but societal attitudes, particularly
those that may evoke taboo, are painstakingly slow'.

Part of the argument against homosexuality is that it is
a deviant choice that people make. And the presumed lifestyle that these deviants have chosen is to be selfish sexual
predators who threaten the sanctity of marriage and the
future of humanity. But it isn't a choice. A large research
study conducted with 409 pairs of homosexual twins was
published in 2015. The authors, Alan Sanders and colleagues,
found the strongest evidence to date that homosexuality is
genetic – that people are born gay.[25] One of the participants,
Chad Zawitz, summarised the implications of the findings
as follows:

> The results may provide validation for homosexual men
> who have asked the same questions that I have. They
> may improve the self-esteem of the many men who
> have asked 'why me?', or have felt ostracised, prejudiced,
> put down, left out, demonised, or worse. They might
> possibly change the minds of those who believe homo-
> sexuality is a 'choice' rather than something
> predetermined . . . On a darker level, some may use
> the results to justify a belief that homosexuality is the

result of a 'broken' or 'deviant' gene that needs to be fixed. Imagine parents requesting a genetic test on their unborn fetus, or worse, a government rolling out mandatory testing of all unborn children, and using compulsory abortions to cleanse the gene pool. There is enough hate in the world that this concept is not as outrageous as one might think.

Despite this, I remain hopeful that our world will continue to evolve into a safer and more accepting place for everyone. While some countries are going backwards, there is a greater openness around the world to homosexuality. This openness, coupled with scientific fact, will bring a greater understanding of human sexuality to a new generation.[26]

The issue is decidedly complex. Not just for individuals who are gay, but also for those who are homophobic. In an experiment from 1996, researcher Henry Adams and colleagues asked sixty-four men to complete a questionnaire to measure how homophobic they were.[27] They then hooked up the men, who varied on levels of homophobia, to a penile plethysmograph, which measures the circumference of the penis and is used as an indicator of sexual arousal. It essentially measures how hard men get. They then exposed the men to sexually explicit heterosexual, homosexual male, and homosexual female videos.

They found that 'only the homophobic men showed an increase in penile erection to male homosexual stimuli.' As a result, the researchers concluded that 'homophobia is apparently associated with homosexual arousal that the homophobic individual is either unaware of or denies'. This could help to explain at least part of the aversion to individuals who are homosexual, as individuals might fear that they could be corrupted or seduced by those who are gay. Sometimes we fear things that are against our religion, or our culture, or just things we haven't fully explored within ourselves.

But if we have explored these ideas, and come to realise that we are not hetero-normative, this can be very difficult to accept.

Over the past ten years of teaching I have encountered various moments of student sexual epiphany and disclosure in the classroom. These epiphanies usually happen when the topic of sexuality and sexual deviance is first raised. It's a conversation that I fear most people will never get to have. I have seen a student learn and immediately identify with the term polyamorous. I have had people identify as gay for the first time. I have had a student come out as asexual. I have had a student come out as bi-curious, despite this being against her religion. Our sexuality is important to us, but until we find ourselves in an environment of openness and discussion some find it difficult to reveal non-heterosexual tendencies.

In 1994, psychiatrist Glenn Wagner developed an internalised homophobia tool to show how much homosexual people accept their own sexuality.[28] It includes items such as 'I wish I were heterosexual', 'Whenever I think a lot about being gay, I feel depressed', and 'If there were a pill that would change my sexual orientation, I would take it.' Scoring high on these kinds of questions shows a lack of acceptance of one's own sexuality, and is linked to worse mental health.

Other forms of this kind of research have also been carried

out more recently. For example, in a study from 2017 by Konstantin Tskhay and Nicholas Rule, men who scored high on internalised homophobia were also less likely to have disclosed their sexual orientation to others, and were more likely to look stereotypically masculine.[29] This suggests an intentional hiding of things that make them appear gay to others, because looking gay can be seen as a negative in wider society. Presenting as straight makes them invisible as gay men – and that's the idea. They want us to not question their sexuality. They want us to say: 'He's masculine-looking, of course he's straight.' This experience is probably also similar for lesbians who present in a feminine way, or anyone else who looks hetero-normative, but isn't.

Even in a society that claims to be 'OK' with LGBTQIPA+ individuals, coming out is hard. I am an advocate for the LGBTQIPA+ community, but rarely do I feel comfortable sharing my own sexuality. And as someone who presents as totally hetero-normative, my sexuality is also never called into question. She's feminine-looking, of course she's straight.

I am part of a particular group of people who are fetish-ised by the heterosexual community, but also don't feel like they quite belong in the queer community. According to my own experience, and two researchers who study this, Milaine Alarie and Stephanie Gaudet, members of my group are often told that 'it's just a phase', that I am being 'greedy', or even that I'm 'doing it for the attention of men'.[30] I am part of a mostly invisible group. A sexual orientation that heterosexuals rate more negatively than being homosexual, and that homosexuals rate more negatively than being heter-osexual.[31]

And, you know what? Fuck invisibility.

I am bisexual.

Most people don't know this about me. I have been part of the problem of bi-invisibility for decades, and thereby probably inadvertently contributed to bi-erasure. Bi-erasure is the rejection of bisexuality as a real form of sexuality. According to Alarie and Gaudet, 'Bisexuality as a legitimate life-long identity and lifestyle is often forgotten or denied as a possibility.' The researchers found endorsement of anti-bisexual statements and ideas even among young people who are accepting of homosexuality. In their study of young adults' discourse about bisexuality, they found that 'participants invisibilise bisexuality, thus inadvertently reinforcing the sexual binary'. They argue that just as society generally teaches us that we can either be a woman or a man, it also teaches us that we can be either gay or straight. We aren't supposed to get a combo deal.

Bisexuality comes with a sort of built-in unfairness – to others. For the most part, we can be sexual chameleons, having an element of choice in which gender we end up dating. Comparatively, homosexuality is generally more difficult to conceal, which is particularly devastating in parts of the world where it is met with harsh legal or social punishments. But this ability to be invisible has the unfortunate consequence that it often *makes* us invisible.

All those student in-class disclosures I mentioned earlier? The epiphanies? It wasn't just the academic discussion that prompted their disclosure. They specifically opened up after I disclosed my own sexuality. I'm the first 'openly' bisexual person most of my students have ever met. And in return I can see the strength build in my LGBTQIPA+ students, the sense of community and safety, the desire to tell their own stories. Some for the first time. It's beautiful.

Not that all coming out feels beautiful. Anyone who has openly revealed a sexual tendency or identity that is not mainstream has stories. Stories of the disgust some people care not to mask. There is research from 2014 showing that even just thinking about having contact with a homosexual makes participants want to physically clean themselves.[32] Along with this come recommendations to 'keep it to yourself'. People start to keep more physical distance in case your recently revealed affliction means that you suddenly find them sexually irresistible. And the flipside of disgust often isn't much better. The assumption of promiscuity gets old, as does the assumption that if you are sexually deviant in one way you must be deviant in many others.

If we want to change this, we need to talk to each other. According to the contact hypothesis, the more people who we have met from a certain group and who we come to like, the more likely we are to see them as human beings and not just as members of a group that we don't understand. This kind of discussion and attitude change can even trickle down into other parts of our lives. According to another study, discussing support for gay equality had far-reaching repercussions. The authors found that 'contact with minorities coupled with discussion of issues pertinent to them is capable of producing a cascade of opinion change'.[33]

We fear that which we do not know. Be brave. Only transparency can help elicit the cultural change that we need.

Let the rainbow flag soar.

LET'S GO TO THE ZOO

OK, we are now going to talk about some behaviours that most of us consider wildly aberrant. Sexual behaviours that are illegal in most parts of the world. Things are going to escalate quickly. Are you ready?

First up, let me introduce you to some people who love animals, perhaps a bit too much – zoophiles ('zoos'). Zoos are people who are sexually attracted to animals. In 2003, Colin Williams and Martin Weinberg published one of very few studies on the topic.[34] They wanted to know why people choose to have sexual relationships with animals. To try to understand the world of zoos, over many months they collected data through an online survey. They got an astonishing number of responses, 120 self-identified zoos, which is a lot given the infrequent nature of this kind of sexual preference (although no one knows exactly how infrequent).

Despite animal welfare concerns from animal-rights groups, and the illegality of the practice, most zoos do not seem to consider their acts to be harmful to animals or themselves. According to the research by Williams and Weinberg, zoophilia is more than just having sex with animals. It also involves a concern for the welfare and pleasure of the animals. For some it becomes downright interspecies love.

This was explained by one of the zoos they interviewed, nineteen-year-old Jason, who was working at a horse farm and said, 'I do practice the act of bestiality for it is impossible to have sex with an animal and not practice bestiality. However, my relationship with animals is a loving one in which sex is an extension of that love as it is with humans, and I do not have sex with a horse unless it consents.'

Legally, of course, an animal cannot consent. But the idea that animals want to have sex with other animals isn't absurd. Dogs, for example, who have not been sterilised often hump humans – although typically to no avail. Zoos might argue that letting the animal actually have sex with you is simply the next step. But those against the idea perhaps have better arguments. If a human who cannot legally consent – like a child – were to hump your leg, it would be reprehensible to interpret this as a consensual sexual advance and to then have sex with them. But animals are not humans, and do not have, or possibly need, the same protections.

Am I hitting the boundary of your comfort zone? Great. Let's keep going then.

I'm sure at this point you're wondering, what makes one animal sexier than another? According to this study, it's not unlike the reasons why we find other members of our own species attractive. Participants said that it was the strength, grace, posture, sleekness and playfulness that attracted them to a particular animal. And, despite the bestiality stereotype, zoos are not primarily having sex with sheep. In this study, zoos were mostly romantically involved with 'equines (29 per cent) – for example, horses, burros, donkeys – or dogs (63 per cent)', but many also reported other animals, including cats, cattle, a goat, a sheep, a chicken and a dolphin.

Now you are probably wondering, *who are these people*?

Let's first say who they are not. The majority do not consider themselves physically unattractive, they are not lacking opportunities for human sex, and they aren't just drunk or high. When attending a zoo meeting, Williams and Weinberg remarked directly on their normality. 'These men did not seem to fit the cultural conception that zoophiles were sick or dangerous people or ill-educated cultural rubes beset by a lack of social skills. Actually, the gathering was strikingly reminiscent of a fraternity get-together (the difference being that the zoophiles were less rowdy).'

In this sample, the zoos were almost entirely men, and ranged in age from 18 to 70. Most (64 per cent) were single but many had wives, and the majority (83 per cent) had completed at least some college. Many had a religious background. And, perhaps most shocking of all, most did not live on farms. Only about a third of the participants were living in a rural area – the other two-thirds lived in small to large cities.

If these are seemingly normal, educated people, why are they having sex with animals? According to Williams and Weinberg, they weren't just in it for the sex – just under half (49 per cent) of their participants were in it for the affection. This sentiment was summarised by 36-year-old Roy: 'Humans use sex to manipulate and control. Humans have trouble accepting who you are . . . they want to change you. Animals do not judge you [;] they just love and enjoy the pleasures of sex without all the politics.' Most zoos claim that they are able to create a relationship with their animal that is both exciting and emotionally deep. According to the researchers, 'What stands out about these types of rewards is that they do not seem out of the ordinary for people in general.' Psychologically speaking it seems that, for some, having a sexual relationship with an animal is simply a form of seeking emotional ties with another creature.

It raises the question of why we care so much about this issue. It can't be just an animal-rights issue. We are awful to animals in many ways that don't prompt the same kind of reaction, including factory farming and the high numbers of unwanted pets simply tossed away to the animal shelter. Perhaps it has something to do with the fact that we can catch diseases from sexual contact with animals, so called zoonotic diseases.[35] Sure, we can get infected with parasitic worms, or rabies, or leptospirosis, but – let's be honest – we can catch way worse things from having sex with humans.

So, what is it? I think it's the 'ew' factor. We don't like the idea that a person has sex with an animal because animals are dirty. That, and because most of us are not sexually aroused by animals it can be difficult to grasp why someone would be. Based on the very limited research done on this topic, psychologically there does not seem to be anything particularly abnormal about those who engage in zoophilia. There is no obvious psychological sign that someone is sexually attracted to animals.

Indeed, for most things that we are not sexually aroused by, it can feel impossible to understand the people who are. It can be easy to label people who live in a different sexual world than we do as freaks, or gross, or immoral. Perhaps even worse, it seems that some people label themselves in a similar manner. But is it evil? I think not.

We have just scratched the surface of the wonderful world of sex. There is so, so much more we could have talked about in this chapter, including those of us who cheat on our partners, those who have sex dolls or sex robots, those having incestuous relations or who post revenge porn, those who are only aroused by animated porn or inanimate objects, those only aroused by geriatric individuals or by female body builders, those who dress up as animals or as adult babies, those who wear full-body gimp suits or cut themselves for sexual pleasure, those who wear Nazi uniforms or dress as slaves, those who rub up against others or are only aroused by amputees . . . human sexuality is so incredibly diverse.

I think it's high time for us to stop being so hard on others and ourselves for what happens between consenting adults in the bedroom.

But sometimes sex isn't between two consenting adults. Sometimes it's not even between adults. In the next chapter we will try to understand a group of individuals who do something that many consider to be pure evil. Who do something we think is inexcusable, horrid, *unthinkable*, yet it seems to exist in every society on the planet. Next, we try to get inside the heads of paedophiles.

'When we have to change our mind about a person, we hold the inconvenience he causes us very much against him.'

Friedrich Nietzsche,
Beyond Good and Evil

6

TO CATCH A PREDATOR: UNDERSTANDING PAEDOPHILES

On understanding, preventing and humanising

CONSIDER THIS A more serious part of this book, on an issue that many of us refuse to ever fully engage with, a topic that is often discussed in the same breath as evil, and something that is so complicated and visceral that it warrants its own chapter. Even among criminals it is considered so nasty that it deserves additional punishment.

We are going to talk about people who are sexually attracted to children.

Note that this chapter will focus on understanding why sexual attraction to children exists and how we can prevent acting on urges, rather than on the important issue of the impact of child sexual abuse on victims. If you are interested in understanding those impacts I recommend reading a 2016 review article called 'I Still Feel Like I Am Not Normal' by Angie Kennedy and Kristen Prock, describing the self-blame, shame and internalised stigma that female victims of child sexual abuse often experience.[1] In 2017, Tamara Blakemore and colleagues also provided an excellent review of the impacts of child sexual abuse in religious, educational, sporting, residential and out-of-home care settings.[2]

BETTER DEAD?

There is a veritable panic in relation to paedophilia in contemporary society.[3] We villainise, stigmatise and ostracise those who we perceive to be paedophiles. It is not abnormal for people to openly wish upon paedophiles horrible fates – lock them away for ever, castrate them, kill them. A study on this perception was conducted by Sara Jahnke and colleagues on German- and English-speaking participants, and published in 2015.[4] They asked participants a number of questions to tap into the stigma of certain antisocial groups. They compared answers to questions about paedophiles with 'identical items referring to either people who abuse alcohol, sexual sadists or people with antisocial tendencies'. They found that 'nearly all reactions to people with paedophilia were more negative than those to the other groups'.

Disconcertingly, of the participants they surveyed, 14 per cent of the German-speakers and 28 per cent of the English-speakers agreed that 'people with paedophilia should better be dead, even if they never had committed criminal acts'. The researchers concluded that these results 'strongly indicate that people with paedophilia are a stigmatised group who risk being the target of fierce discrimination' and that this has indirect negative consequences for preventing child abuse.

When we write off rather than treat, stigmatise rather than understand, we are putting children at risk. To wish death upon paedophiles is to dehumanise them, and to fundament-ally fail to engage in critical discussion regarding the treatment of child sexual abusers and the prevention of this type of sexual predation. This is particularly problematic if it is true, as a survey from 2014 found, that 6 per cent of men and 2 per cent of women 'indicated some likelihood of having sex with a child if they were guaranteed they would not be caught or punished'.[5]

By trying to understand paedophilia we are not dismissing the realities of child sexual abuse, nor are we condoning or normalising the issue. Instead, we can work towards a world where we are in a better position to deal with the reality of the issue. Paedophilia has always existed, and always will. Flippantly dismissing it as an aberration helps no one.

Let's begin to understand paedophilia by discussing some of the basics. First, we must be careful not to confuse sexual preference with sexual predation.

A diagnosis of paedophilia is made when a person is sexually attracted to children, not just because they have had indecent contact with a child. Paedophilia is a paraphilia, not a lifestyle choice. Paedophiles don't wake up one morning and decide that they are going to be sexually attracted to children, much like hetero-normative men do not decide to be sexually attracted to adult women – they just are. I will address the biological roots of a sexual attraction to children later in this chapter. Additionally, whether the person has ever acted on their urges in a criminal way is a related, but separate, issue.

Second, we often talk about a paedophile as someone who has had indecent fantasies about, indecent photos of, or indecent contact with, a person who is under the legal age of consent (which is typically either sixteen or eighteen). But this is not correct. Both socially and psychologically, there are important distinctions to be made within this age range.

Paedophilia is, by definition, the primary or exclusive sexual interest in children who have not yet undergone puberty.[6] Throughout this chapter, calling someone a 'paedophile' is not an insult, it is simply a description of their sexual preference. In addition to this, there are two other categories of paraphilia that capture a sexual interest in those who are (in most countries) legally under the age of consent. 'Hebephiles' are primarily or exclusively interested in children who have achieved puberty, usually aged eleven to fourteen, and 'ephebephiles' are primarily or exclusively interested in mid- to late adolescents, usually aged fifteen to nineteen. In contrast to this, the sexual interest in fully mature adults is called teleiophilia. A study comparing the characteristics of hebephiliacs and teleiophiliacs concluded: 'The hebephiliac is not more similar to the paedophile nor the teleiophiliac. He is in fact a mix of both.'[7]

Unlike paedophilia and hebephilia, ephebephilia is often accepted, even encouraged, by society. Sexualising a 15-year-old fashion model, or watching an 18-year-old porn star is quite normal. The line is drawn at different ages in different countries, but I think that most of us would accept that there is little moral difference in being attracted to someone aged 15 and 364 days on the one hand, and someone aged 16 on the other. We appear to have conflicting views, freely sexualising teenagers because of their physical maturity, while wanting to protect them because of a lack of mental maturity. But one thing is for sure: society generally perceives those who are sexually attracted to teenagers differently to those attracted to younger children.

And, to some extent, they probably *are* different. According to research by psychologist Michael Bailey and colleagues from 2016, most men with a sexual attraction to teenage girls have a similar attraction to adult women, and are not attracted to prepubescent children.[8] According also to the clinical literature, this intuitive differentiation is appropriate. Of the three diagnoses, the two that are the most damning are paedophilia and hebephilia. Researchers Ian McPhail and colleagues, who study the diagnosis of paedophiles, explained in a 2017 review that the term they use, 'paedo-hebephilia', includes both paedophilia and hebephilia.[9] Further, they explain that, as far as risk goes, 'Theories of sexual offending include paedohebephilic interests as a main risk factor for the perpetration of sexual offences against children.' Because of this difference, and because it is often considered a more devastating diagnosis, I am going to focus in this chapter on paedohebephilia, using the word as McPhail does to refer to people who are interested in pre-pubescent and pubescent children.

How many paedohebephiles are there? Estimating prevalence is a difficult task, as many people are unwilling to accept or admit that they have a sexual interest in children. According to the UK National Crime Agency (NCA), as many as 1 in 35 adult men in Britain have a sexual interest in children, which is just under 3 per cent.[10] This means that, just in the UK, the NCA believes that there are about 750,000 men who have a sexual interest in children, with 250,000 having paedohebephilic tendencies. Statistically, it is highly likely that you have at some point in the past year interacted with someone who is sexually attracted to children. This was echoed by a statement made by Phil Gormley, then deputy director of the NCA: 'If these numbers are accurate the reality is that we are all living not far away from one.'[11] Although this quote helps illustrate the prevalence of this reality, it also makes it sound like there are monsters living around the corner – a sentiment that is destructive and one that has very problematic connotations.

Does this apply to other parts of the world? In 2014, Michael Seto, a Canadian researcher who has studied how many men have sexual thoughts or fantasies about children around the world, placed the figure for paedohebephilia at 2 per cent of the general population.[12] However, he also stressed that much of this is due to the inclusion of hebephilia, the 11–14 range, and that if we only include paedophilia, the prevalence 'is probably much lower than 1%'. Whichever statistic we accept, there are a lot of men who have a sexual interest in children.

While far less researched and understood, there are also women and people who do not identify as gender-binary who have paedohebephilic interests, although the prevalence of this seems to be far lower than for men.[13] Although we do not know how many would meet the criteria for paedohebephilia, and many are never convicted, nevertheless there are many female child sexual abusers. Based on a 2015 examination of 'virtually every substantiated child sexual abuse case reported to child protective services in the United

States for 2010', researcher David McLeod found that 20.9 per cent of cases involved a female primary perpetrator.[14] (This proportionally high figure is partly due to cases where there were both a male and female primary offender.) These are astonishing findings that challenge the public perception that only men are paedophiles.

In this research, female perpetrators were particularly likely to be the biological parent of the victim, and in 68 per cent of cases the victims were also female. Notable as a possible sign of paedophilic interests, McLeod found that over half of victims were under the age of 10 (on average being 9.43 years old). This is younger than the average for male perpetrators. According to McLeod, the underrepresentation of females in the academic literature is due mostly to a societal failure to recognise women as offenders. As a result they often avoid detection, prosecution and interventions like tracking, registration or mandated treatment. Society, and research, must focus more efforts on understanding female child sex offenders.

Also of note is that many men and women with paedo-hebephilic interests are married to age-appropriate partners, and have sexual relations with them. Indeed, from a broader perspective, and perhaps counterintuitively, paraphilias can be compatible with also having sexual desires that are not paraphilic. In a study from 2016, Michael Bailey and colleagues surveyed 1,189 men recruited from websites targeting adults attracted to children.[15] They wanted to see whether the men were exclusively attracted to children. They found that 13.6 per cent of those attracted to girls, and 5.4 per cent of those attracted to boys, also had a sexual preference for adults. More broadly, the researchers found that many men who were primarily attracted to children were attracted to people of various ages, but with decreasing intensity as the target moved further away from the preferred age. For example, a man might be most attracted to 12-year-old girls, less attracted to 16-year-old girls, and only somewhat attracted to 22-year-old women. Nevertheless, this provides evidence that a sexual interest in children does not necessarily preclude a sexual interest in adults.

Another common misconception is that if someone has a sexual attraction to children, their urges are uncontrollable. This is a flawed argument. Just because someone has legally and socially unacceptable urges does not mean that they cannot inhibit themselves. If our legal system is to be believed, humans have the capacity to decide to act in line with social and legal norms, regardless of their proclivities.

Luckily, according to the NCA, two-thirds of men with paedohebephilic urges will probably never act on them.[16] These are referred to as non-offending paedophiles. According to James Cantor and Ian McPhail, 'Non-offending pedophiles are a unique population of individuals who experience sexual interest in children, but despite common misperceptions, have neither had sexual contact with a child nor have accessed illegal child sexual exploitation material.'[17]

How difficult it must be to live with a burden, to silently suffer, knowing that telling anyone about it could lead to social isolation and additional suffering.

CHILD SEX OFFENDER ≠ PAEDOHEBEPHILE

Unfortunately, not all paedohebephiles do control their urges. When acted upon, they can cause tremendous suffering.

However, the relationship between having a paraphilic interest in children and sexual offending against children is complicated, and discussions about this critical issue are often fraught with errors and misperceptions.[18] In order to better discuss the issue of sexual offences against children, here are a few things we need to understand.

1. Not all child sex offenders are paedophiles, and not all paedophiles are child sex offenders.

As a society we must stop using the terms sex offender and paedophile (or even paedohebephile) as if they were synonymous. Doing so loses important nuance and helps to 'other' sex offenders, making it much more difficult to develop strategies to prevent offending or reoffending. It also disregards the reasons why children are sexually abused, which are myriad. Put simply, someone who is a paedohebephile might never commit a sexual offence against a child, and someone who commits sexual offences against children might not be a paedohebephile.

While sexual attraction to children is a risk factor for sexually offending against children, an even bigger risk factor is an individual's belief system. In particular, two cognitive distortions are predictive of someone sexually offending against a child.

According to a study of child sex offenders by Ruth Mann and colleagues in 2005, the first belief is that 'Sex with children is harmless,' and the second is that 'Children actively provoke adults into having sex with them.' Such beliefs are used to justify sexual offences against children, and can be held by those who have a primary sexual interest in children or by 'opportunistic offenders'. Opportunistic offenders are

those individuals who are sexually attracted to adults but
have taken advantage of the ease of access or vulnerability
of children to commit sexual offences, including within the
family, or the church or other organised settings.

This brings me to the next point.

2. *Child sex offenders are typically not strangers.*

In a summary of misperceptions of child sex offenders,
criminologist Kelly Richards argues that 'although parents
often fear that strangers will abuse their children, it has been
well-documented that most child sex offenders are known
to their victims'.

Reviews of the literature suggest that, globally, 18–20 per
cent of women,[19] and 7–8 per cent of men report that they
were sexually abused before the age of 18,[20] and according
to a survey of children by the National Society for the
Prevention of Cruelty to Children (NSPCC), 1 in 20 children
in the UK have been sexually abused.[21]Adults known to the
child, including relatives, neighbours or family friends, were
the most common perpetrators. The most common offender,
targeting both boys and girls, was a male relative who was
not the victim's father.

3. *Most perpetrators of child sexual abuse were not them-
selves sexually abused.*

The belief in a cycle of child sexual abuse is practically
accepted as dogma. The assumption is that those who have
experienced child sexual abuse have either internalised the
idea that sexual contact between children and adults is acceptable, or that they are psychologically damaged in such a way
as to inhibit good decision-making.

However, there is little empirical evidence to support this claim.[22] Most of those who were abused as children do not go on to become perpetrators (this is particularly true for female offenders), and most of those who sexually abuse children do not themselves have a history of being sexually abused. That being said, people who experienced childhood sexual abuse, physical abuse or neglect are at an *increased risk* for crime and delinquency, including sexual offending.[23] It is valuable to understand the link between being victimised and becoming a perpetrator in this context, but we must not overstate it.

4. Many who watch child pornography online never offend sexually against children offline.

A relevant illegal act that we have not discussed is the consumption of child pornography. Because detection and reporting are incredibly difficult, it is often impossible to know exactly how many images an offender has accessed before or after a conviction. This, in addition to under-reporting by victims, makes it difficult to study the link between child pornography consumption and sexual offending against children. Still, what do we know about the link?

In 2015, a meta-analysis was published by public safety researcher Kelly Babchishin on the characteristics of online and offline sex offenders against children.[24] About 1 in 8 convicted child pornography offenders have a recorded contact offence against a child and, when asked, about 1 in 2 self-report committing a contact offence. A contact offence involves meeting with a child and engaging in any kind of sexual, or sexualised, conduct. Additionally, as far as the reconviction rates go, they were found to be lower for child pornography offences than for child sex offenders, although those who had been convicted of *both* porn and contact offences were most likely to reoffend.

Overall, findings showed that 'offenders who restricted their offending behavior to online child pornography offences were different from mixed offenders [those with both child pornography and contact sex offences against children] and offline sex offenders against children.' Those who were caught with child porn and had not committed contact offences were more likely to have victim empathy. They were more likely to understand and empathise with the pain they would cause if they committed a contact offence against a child. According to the authors, victim empathy is a known barrier to sexual offending.

This is important. Although child pornography consumption is a strong indicator that a person is a paedohebephile (and is an even stronger predictor of being diagnosed with paedohebephilia than sexually abusing children),[25] those who have high victim empathy often never sexually offend against a child. It seems that the ability to inhibit behaviour and relate to potential victims in the face of sexual urges towards children is the most important factor that prevents paedohebephiles from becoming sex offenders.

But, what makes someone a paedohebephile in the first place? Do they choose to be this way?

BORN THIS WAY

As far back as 1886, German psychiatrist Richard von Krafft-Ebing, who coined the term 'paedophilia', argued that it was a neurological disorder.[26] Since then, our ability to substantiate this has grown significantly. According to James Cantor, who has peered into the brains of paedophiles for years, 'Paedophilia is something that we are essentially born with, does not appear to change over time, and it's as core to our being as any other sexual orientation is.'[27]

Cantor and colleagues use a humanising approach, taking away the blame for paedohebephilic urges (as opposed to acting on those urges) from the individual and placing it firmly within biology. Cantor's main line of research shows that some unexpected physical characteristics are related to paedohebephilia. These include:

1. Height. Paedohebephiles have been found to be about 2cm shorter than non-paedohebephiles.[28]
2. Handedness. Paedohebephiles are three times more likely to be left-handed.[29]
3. IQ. Paedohebephiles generally have lower IQ.[30]
4. Brain wiring. Paedohebephiles generally have less grey matter and different brain connections.[31]

What do all these things have in common? They are thought to be largely determined before birth.[32] Similarly, people's sexual orientation – including in paedohebephiles – is thought to be determined before birth. As Cantor explains, 'It's as if, in these people, when they perceive a child, it's triggering the sexual instincts instead of triggering the nurturing instincts.'

This is not just true when speaking of paedohebephiles, but also when comparing child sex offenders more broadly to other kinds of sex offenders. In a 2014 meta-analysis,

Christian Joyal and colleagues found that 'sex offenders against children on average show more neuropsychological deficits than do sex offenders against adults/peers'.[33] This means that the brains of child sex offenders work differently to the brains of other kinds of sex offenders. Along the same vein, the researchers found that the IQ of child sex offenders was generally lower than those who sexually offended against adults. More precisely they found that the more intelligent a child sex offender was, the older his victims were. This means that those who offended against very young children generally had the lowest IQs.

This is not to say that environment is irrelevant. Sexual offending against children by paedohebephiles is correlated with many social factors, including poor interpersonal skills, isolation, low self-esteem, fear of rejection, lack of assertiveness, feelings of inadequacy and a lack of sexual knowledge.[34] Most of these are socially influenced characteristics and feelings that are strongly linked with upbringing and other environmental factors.

But it seems that in the nature-nurture argument, nurture may only be relevant for the *expression* of paedohebephilia (the commission of child sex offences). In other words, how someone is raised may impact how they can control their urges, but may have little to do with whether someone is sexually attracted to children in the first place. As Cantor states, 'Even among pedophiles who never commit any offense, the condition requires lifelong suppression and control.'[35] That ability to suppress and control is probably at least in part the result of a better working brain, and good upbringing and social support later in life.

Based on the relatively limited research on this, it seems

that paedohebephilia is something an individual is born with, and the desire probably cannot be cured. It also means that the paraphilia of being sexually attracted to children (as opposed to the acting upon those urges) probably cannot be prevented by how they are raised or socialised. What are the implications of this for treatment?

A CALL TO HUMANISE

Wondering what it must be like to be a paedophile, psychologist Jenny Houtepen asked paedophiles about their lives, and published her findings in 2016.[36] She found that many of the paedophiles she interviewed 'struggled with acknowledging pedophilic interest in early puberty and experienced psychological difficulties as a result'. She further found that 'many committed sex offenses during adolescence when they were still discovering their feelings,' and states that this was probably partly because of a lack of recognition of early risk factors, and a lack of appropriate intervention.

She paints a bleak portrait of the paedohebephiles she interviewed, and ends by suggesting that we need to do something to help people in these situations. We need to help them because they are human beings who are suffering, and we need to help them because they are at risk of causing great suffering to others. Her take-home message is that 'risk for offending can be diminished by creating more openness about pedophilia and by providing pedophiles with social support and control'.

If these interests have an innate, genetic root beyond any individual's control, can we really call them evil? And how can we help those of us who have this sexual preference?

There have been a number of initiatives to decrease the possibility that paedohebephiles will become offenders, including sex-offender helplines and psychological therapy. Both of these generally aim to help manage their desires, rather than to cure them. Anonymous paedohebephilia helplines and communities are becoming more available, as we realise ever more that in order to prevent child sex offending we must both encourage victims *and* those with these predispositions to speak out. Shunning and ostracising paedohebephiles doesn't prevent them from acting on their urges, and may well be counterproductive. Initiatives have popped up such as Stop It Now! in the UK, Virtuous Paedophiles in the US and Projekt Dunkelfeld in Germany (translation: 'darkfield'), all of which aim to provide an outlet, while providing psychological support to prevent individuals from acting on urges.

Similarly, although most therapy for paedohebephilia happens after people have committed a crime, there are initiatives that aim to preventatively approach the issue. While scarce, some clinics are beginning to offer psychological support for those who have sexual fantasies involving children and who fear that they might act on them. But in many countries this is difficult, as people may want help but fear that their doctor or therapist will tell the police. There is reasonable fear that strict confidentiality could in some cases fail to prevent harm. However, some therapists argue that in order for this system to work, there *needs* to be a guarantee of strict confidentiality.

This approach is hugely controversial. If someone were to tell a doctor that they are currently abusing a child, both the police and the community would reasonably feel that they need to know. But from a harm-reduction perspective it is probably better that the paedohebephile is able to talk to someone about their urges or acts, rather than being completely isolated. Only in this way can they get help dealing with their urges, and help to avoid acting on them.

While hotlines for paedohebephiles often promise anonymity over the phone, the German Project Dunkelfeld takes this a step further. They are the only organisation worldwide (as far as I know) that allows complete anonymity to those they meet in person.[37] Petya Schuhmann, a psychologist who worked with Project Dunkelfeld, encourages some of those who call their anonymous hotline to attend their therapy sessions. She was interviewed about her experiences in 2015. She emphasises that those who contact such projects are brave, and say that they are relieved to finally have someone to talk to. Realising that you are a paedohebephile can be a traumatic experience in itself.

She believes that paedohebephilia is akin to a 'disease' and states that the goal of the programme is for individuals to 'learn how to live responsibly with their sexual desires' rather than to cure the underlying paraphilia.[38] The psychological therapy that they offer aims to help people learn how to control their urges and to extinguish certain beliefs they may hold (such as that children are sexually interested in them, or want to have sex). It is thought that decreasing these beliefs decreases the risk of offending.

While hotlines and therapy show great promise in reducing child sexual offending, the long-term results are largely unknown. Still, at the very least, I see it as a positive to humanise paedohebephiles and encourage them to deal with their urges rather than suppress, ignore or act upon them.

As one paedohebephile who participated in the Dunkelfeld therapy said in an interview with the BBC: 'I don't have greasy hair, pebble glasses and wear tatty clothes . . . There is no such thing as the typical paedophile which people imagine. We are all different, and completely normal people. The only thing we all have in common is a sexual attraction to children . . . I am learning to control the sexual side of my feelings.'[39]

There is another way in which paedohebephilia might be dealt with that is also controversial: castration. Physical castration involves surgically removing the testicles. Although optional physical castration for sex offenders is still available in Germany and the Czech Republic, it has been heavily criticised by the European Committee for the Prevention of Torture and Inhuman or Degrading Treatment and has generally fallen out of favour since the 1940s, when chemical castration was introduced.[40]

Chemical castration is a type of treatment for paedohebephilic men, typically those who have already offended, which involves the regular injection of anti-antrogen drugs. These drugs temporarily remove sex drive and make it almost impossible to get an erection. In some countries chemical castration is optional, while in others (like Poland, Indonesia, the Czech Republic, Australia, Korea and parts of the US) it can be mandated for convicted sex offenders. Particularly the mandatory use of these drugs has been widely criticised on humanitarian grounds. Additionally, as psychiatrists Don Grubin and Anthony Beech state, there is an argument that 'doctors should avoid becoming agents of social control'.[41]

But at a very basic level, does castration even work? Research on both physical and chemical castration actually shows some promising results. Doctors in Germany and the Czech Republic have argued that those who choose physical castration voluntarily see positive results, and find it easier to control their urges.[42] Proponents of chemical castration equally suggest that they see positive results,[43] however some researchers, including Alexandra Lewis, advise us to be cautious with such findings. After reviewing the literature on chemical castration for sex offenders in 2017, Lewis's results show that overall benefits were seen – with decreased desire and decreased acting on desires – but that the quality of research is not good enough to draw firm conclusions.[44]

According to physician Fred Berlin, some people with paedohebephilia can benefit from chemical castration, but he warns that 'current evidence shows this to be the case only when the drug is administered voluntarily'. He reminds us that 'currently, there are no medications that can change sexual orientation; pharmacologic treatments can only lower the intensity of unacceptable sexual urges. Paedophilia cannot be punished or legislated away. It is as much a public health problem as it is a matter of criminal justice.'[45] Paraphilias live in the brain, not in genitals or hormones. Medical intervention does not cure paedohebephiles, it can merely make their urges less intense.

Another type of controversial harm-reduction approach involves using substitutes for real children. What if an individual with paedohebephilic tendencies could satisfy their urges without ever having to harm a child?

There are a few avenues through which this could happen, all of which are deeply uncomfortable for many people. There is the production of pornography with adults who are made to look like they are children or teenagers. Other approaches avoid humans altogether, and involve sexualised computer-generated children or *hentai* (Japanese animated porn), realistic child sex dolls and, in a not-so-distant future, child sex robots.

At the moment, in most countries, rules about obscene images limit or ban the legal distribution of any of these materials. Indeed, in 2017, a man in the UK tried to import a child sex doll, and a judge ruled that such dolls were obscene items and therefore forbidden from being imported.[46]

'Fake children' have the potential to act as replacements for real children, reducing harm to society and allowing paedohebephiles to live more meaningful and ethical lives. But they also have the potential, for those individuals who consume these materials, to normalise their affliction and lead to more offending behaviour. This would be in line with what we understand about pornography more generally. Having a child sex doll is similar, in at least some respects, to watching child pornography. And, from previous research, we have identified watching child pornography as a risk factor for engaging in contact offences against children. So, child sex dolls may well disinhibit paedohebephilic individuals and make them more likely to offend. Another, third, possible outcome is that such materials make no difference at all. Based on what we know so far, all of these alternatives seem equally likely. This makes it difficult to make appropriate treatment decisions, and means that there is immediate and urgent need for research on these issues.

Whether it is psychological treatment, castration, *hentai* or child sex dolls, our focus should be on realistic harm reduction, not just punishment. As new technologies and treatment options emerge, the ethical discussions around what we do as a society to help deal with the realities of paedohebephilia must continue. We must not be driven by our fears in this process of renegotiating how we, as individuals and as society, deal with those who have a sexual interest in children. Paedohebephiles are a permanent fixture of human societies, and a larger part than we might imagine. They are our friends and colleagues, neighbours and nephews, fathers and sons (and occasionally, mothers, daughters and aunties). By acknowledging this, we can ensure that our focus remains on harm reduction – trying to make sure that as few adults as possible become perpetrators.

Even if many would suggest that their actions are evil, paedohebephiles are not monsters, they are human beings. They were born with unacceptable sexual tendencies; they did not choose to have them. This is a call to stop beliefs, policies and therapies that suggest otherwise.

Until now we have focused largely on the individuals within society who are seen as evil. It is time that we expand into the systems that make it easier, even likely, that we will do terrible things. We turn our attention now to the corrupting influences of money, and the moral gymnastics that some of us do every day at work.

7

SNAKES IN SUITS: THE PSYCHOLOGY OF GROUPTHINK

On paradoxes, slavery and ethical blindness

MONEY CHANGES OUR relationship with morality. The very existence of money, along with complex business and distribution channels, acts as a buffer between ourselves and the origin of our products. This can make us behave in ways that are deeply unethical.

I can prove it to you. I'm going to give you three things, and you need to decide whether you think they are evil: prostitution, child labour, animal torture. And how about the following? Porn, cheap stuff, factory farming.

In many countries where prostitution is illegal, pornography is not. But this seems decidedly hypocritical. As far as I can tell, porn could also be seen as prostitution with a camera. If we pay someone to have sex with us (or someone else), it is prostitution, and in most countries illegal. However, if we pay someone to have sex with us and we film it, then it is porn, and in many countries legal. If anything, it seems porn should be more problematic, not less.

On another note, to make things a bit cheaper for us, and perhaps a bit more convenient, we often allow terrible treatment of employees and even indirectly endorse things like child labour. We see some of the devastating consequences of our consumer culture when factories where phones are made have to install anti-suicide netting, or garment factories collapse killing hundreds of people because proper safety measures were not put into place. But by reframing the same issues and adding a price tag we make these acts seem far less offensive. We can't see them first hand, so they feel like they are unrelated to us. All we can see is the price.

Meat-eating is another contentious issue in our society. Some people use terms like 'militant vegetarian', others have negative assumptions about vegans – boring, hummus-eating hippies (although veganism seems to be proliferating at the moment, which is wonderful). Yet while many readily disparage people who voluntarily don't eat meat, and many more of us are unwilling to stop eating meat ourselves, we also think that animal torture is immoral.

Animal husbandry is one of the greatest sources of suffering in the world. There are an estimated 70 billion animals farmed for food every year, the majority of which are kept in factory farms.[1] Most animals are born into the same horrible conditions they eventually die in. Kept in these conditions, chickens, cows, pigs and many of the other animals we eat suffer great pain. And while fish cannot feel pain – at least not the way we conceptualise it – they can get depressed. Fish depression is so similar to human depression that scientists use fish to study the effects of antidepressants.[2] That's right, if you eat farmed fish, you might have some sad fish on your conscience. Beyond animal suffering, we also find that there is a tremendous impact of this industry on the environment. Farm animals are contributing to climate change, one fart at a time.

Yet, even when we know this, we continue to gleefully indulge.

What is *wrong* with us?

PARADOX

According to psychological scienti s Brock Bastian and Steve Loughnan, who do research on the topic in Australia, when we understand why we eat meat we can begin to understand other forms of behaviour that conflict with deeply held moral principles.[3]

What they termed the 'meat paradox' is the 'psychological conflict between people's dietary preference for meat and their moral response to animal suffering'. They argue that 'bringing harm to others is inconsistent with a view of oneself as a moral person. As such, meat consumption leads to negative effects for meat-eaters because they are confronted with a view of themselves that is unfavorable: How can I be a good person and also eat meat?'

This moral conflict doesn't just threaten our enjoyment of eating meat, it threatens our identity. In order to protect our identities we establish habits and social structures that make us feel better. We tie meat-eating to social customs, holidays are defined as a time to feast on flesh with friends and family. We say it helps define us as *real* men, or that we are super-predators who were meant to eat meat. And despite animal products being linked to all kinds of poor health outcomes, we hear some people tsk when we say that we want to go vegan ('How will you get enough protein?'), and friends start 'forgetting' to invite us to dinner parties.

Hypocrisy feels less bad, less threatening, when in a group. If all of us are doing something bad, it can't really be that bad, right? According to Bastian and Loughnan, 'Meat-eating is maintained because it serves to benefit the eater,' and 'People seek to justify these self-serving behaviors so as to protect their own interests.' We do it despite the quantities of meat that many of us eat being bad for us, the environment and animals. We do it out of self-interest. We do it because it is enjoyable in the moment, and it is easy to discount the long-term negative consequences. The excuses we make are largely post hoc – after we have chosen to indulge we need to justify why the behaviour was OK, and why it is OK to do it again. And we need the excuses, or else we feel like bad people.

When we say one thing but do another, or hold inconsistent beliefs, psychologists call it cognitive dissonance. The term was coined by Leon Festinger, who first used it in 1957.[4] The classic experiment in this field was published by Festinger and James Carlsmith in 1959.[5] In it, they asked: 'What happens to a person's private opinion if he is forced to do or say something contrary to that opinion?' In their experiment, they had seventy-one men complete two tasks. First, the men were asked to put twelve round wooden spools into a tray, empty the tray and put the spools back in the tray, repeatedly, for half an hour.

Then the participants were given a board containing forty-eight square wooden pegs. They were asked to turn each peg by a quarter turn clockwise, then another quarter turn, repeatedly, again for half an hour. While they did this, a researcher watched and wrote things down. These were intentionally boring tasks. Really, really boring.

Although the participants thought it was their performance that was being measured, it was actually what came next that interested the researchers. After their two boring tasks, participants were taken back into the waiting room. They were told that the person sitting there was the next participant. For one-third of the participants, they simply sat down without anything else being mentioned. For the other two-thirds, however, the researcher asked whether they would lie to the next participant. They would even be paid for their lie. Half were told that they would be paid $1 for their lie, and the other half were told that they would be paid $20 for their lie (which in the 1950s was a lot). When they said yes, the researcher then handed them a piece of paper, and instructed them to make the points that were written on it: 'It was very enjoyable,' 'I had a lot of fun,' 'I enjoyed myself,' 'It was very interesting,' 'It was intriguing,' 'It was exciting.'

What the researchers really wanted to know was what impact this lie, and the compensation for it, would have on participants' rating of the task. They wondered whether participants would actually come to think they enjoyed the boring task, just because they told someone else it was fun. And how would being paid influence this?

Who do you think rated the experiment as the most enjoyable? The control group, who had not been asked to lie, rated the task as boring and said that they would not do it again. The participants paid $20 also rated the task negatively. However, the participants paid $1 rated the experiment as far more enjoyable than the other two groups, and were more likely to say they would sign up to participate in similar experiments in the future.

What happened? Being paid $1 was probably not seen by the participants as sufficient incentive to lie. Accordingly, they experienced cognitive dissonance. 'Why did I say that it was enjoyable when it wasn't? Surely not for a measly $1?' Since the participants could not go back and change their behaviour, or *un*-participate in the experiment, the option available to them was to change their belief – it must have actually been enjoyable. For the $20 condition this was not necessary, as they could explain their behaviour as the result of the hefty and easy financial incentive. This was the first of many experiments to show that we often bring our beliefs in line with our behaviour, and that money can change the way we do this.

In 1962 Festinger further formalised his ideas.[6] He stated that although we believe ourselves to be generally consistent – in our behaviours, beliefs and attitudes – sometimes we go rogue. This inconsistency he called dissonance, while consistency he called consonance. He summarised his cognitive dissonance theory as follows:

1. The existence of dissonance, being psychologically uncomfortable, will motivate the person to try to reduce the dissonance and achieve consonance.

2. When dissonance is present, in addition to trying to reduce it, the person will actively avoid situations and information which would likely increase the dissonance.

He further explained that, just as hunger motivates us to find food to reduce our hunger, cognitive dissonance motivates us to find situations to reduce the dissonance. For meat-eating, there are two ways to do this: we can change our behaviour or change the belief. We can stop eating meat, or come up with reasons why eating meat is morally OK.

In addition to our own attempts to justify meat-eating, corporations double down to make it easier for us to do so. They want us not to think too much about it, and to just hand over our money. According to research by sociologist Liz Grauerholz on images of animals in popular culture, one way to make meat-eating seem acceptable is to dissociate it from the animal it came from.[7] Grauerholz argues that we do this by 'transforming animals, which are loved, into meats, which are eaten, so that the concepts of "animals" and "meats" seem distinct and unrelated'. We call it 'veal' instead of tortured baby cow, 'ham' instead of pig, 'game' instead of hunted wild animal. We pack our dead animals in pretty packages – physically, verbally and conceptually distancing ourselves from the real origin of our food.

When looking at commercial depictions of meat, she found that this was done in two different ways. The first was showing meat as sanitised, plastic-wrapped, chopped into pieces – making it hard to think that it came from an animal at all. The second had to do with 'cutification' – making the animals cuter than they actually are. More than anywhere, this is adopted as a strategy in parts of Asia such as Japan. Adverts there use what ethologist Konrad Lorenz referred to as the *Kindchenschema* ('baby schema') – big eyes, petite, round features, like we might expect in children's books. It's meant to give the impression that this meat comes from happy, imaginary animals. Both of these serve to distract from the realities of animal cruelty.

This isn't just relevant for meat-eating. When we turn animals or humans into objects, and thereby avoid the discomfort caused by knowing about the suffering behind consumer goods, we make it easier to be cruel. The same processes we see with meat, we see with all kinds of other morally unacceptable but common human behaviours that have to do with money.

We know that poverty causes great suffering, yet instead of sharing our wealth we buy another pair of expensive shoes. We fundamentally disagree with the idea of child labour or adults working under horrible conditions, but keep shopping at discount stores. We stay in the dark, to protect our delicate identities, to maintain the illusion that we are consistent and ethically sensible human beings.

In this constant effort to reduce cognitive dissonance, we may spread morally questionable behaviour to others. We begin to shape societies in ways to minimise our discomfort, to not remind us of our inconsistencies. We don't want constant reminders. And, as Bastian and Loughnan argue, 'Through the process of dissonance reduction, the apparent immorality of certain behaviors can seemingly disappear.'[8]

Hypocrisy can flourish in certain social and cultural environments. Social habits can cast a veil over our moral conflicts, by normalising behaviours and making them invisible and resistant to change.

One particularly fertile ground for this is within businesses. But before we talk about the people who make unethical decisions in the corporate world, I first want to talk about the transactions themselves. What are we, and aren't we, allowed to trade for money? And why do we sometimes decide to engage in forbidden transactions anyway?

UNTHINKABLE

How much money would I need to offer you to buy an hour of your time? How much for a year? These are pretty normal transactions; time is often exchanged for money – we call it work. Similarly, asking you how much I need to pay you to buy your house or your clothes or your laptop is still relatively normal. We often exchange these things for money, and they have a (mostly) ascertainable price.

But there are many things in life that cannot be quantified in this way. How much would it cost me to have you ride a cow naked while being filmed for national TV? How much for your treasured childhood teddy bear? How much to buy your baby, or your husband? Your left kidney? How much for your freedom? It seems deeply inappropriate to assign a monetary value to these things. Indeed, the very image of selling these things conjures up religious images of selling your soul to the devil. But, is it evil to engage in these trades?

In 1997, Alan Fiske and Philip Tetlock set out to understand our responses to these kinds of situations.[9] According to their research, 'Taboo trade-offs violate deeply held normative intuitions about the integrity, even sanctity, of certain relationships and the moral-political values underlying those relationships.' This means it is inappropriate to exchange what are referred to as 'sacred' values, which are accompanied by seemingly boundless protection and importance, for 'secular' values, like money.

There are certain things that we feel money can't buy, or at least money *shouldn't* buy. To start this discussion, I want to do a quick test (a shortened version of the original) to explore the attitudes that you have about what we should be allowed to buy and sell. Here is your instruction, taken from a scientific paper published in 2000 by Tetlock and colleagues: 'Imagine that you had the power to judge the permissibility and morality of each transaction listed below. Would you allow people to enter into certain types of deals? Do you morally approve or disapprove of those deals? And what emotional reactions, if any, do these proposals trigger in you?'[10]

1. Paying someone to clean my house
2. Paying a doctor to provide medical care to me or my family
3. Paying a lawyer to defend me against criminal charges in court
4. Paying to adopt orphans
5. Paying for human body parts
6. Paying for surrogate motherhood
7. Paying for votes in elections for my political office
8. Paying for sexual favours
9. Paying for someone else to serve jail time to which I had been sentenced by a court of law
10. Paying someone to perform military service that I had a draft obligation to perform

How many of these did you react negatively to? The first three are considered 'routine' trade-offs (generally considered acceptable), while the other seven are often considered taboo trade-offs. Participants in the original study scored the taboo trade-offs as far more morally outrageous than the others – saying they were more upsetting, offensive, cruel, crazy, anger- and sadness-inducing, and they were more likely to say they should be banned. Even just *thinking* these things was generally considered, well, unthinkable.

This moral outrage, according to Tetlock and colleagues, is the first response to taboo trade-offs. Thinking about immoral things makes us feel dirty or contaminated, and we seek to morally cleanse ourselves.

The study found that after thinking about these different scenarios, those who were outraged by them were far more likely to morally cleanse by, for example, 'volunteering for a campaign to block baby auctions'. This oddly precise example from the study shows how the authors wanted to give their participants the ability to show that they would campaign directly against the behaviours they indicated were so morally problematic. The argument is that even just thinking these awful things feels like a violation of a moral code, and we want to as quickly as possible make amends for this violation.

But there are situations where we have to put a price tag on the unthinkable. According to Tetlock, 'Finite resources sometimes require placing at least implicit dollar valuations on a host of things . . . human life (what price access to medical care?), justice (what price access to legal representation?), preserving natural environments (what price endangered species?), and civil liberties and rights.'[11]

While we may not want to accept it, every single bit of

us has a price. In cases where people are injured, civil courts (or juries, in countries like the US) have to put price tags on things as diverse as 'injury to feelings', 'pain and suffering' and 'bereavement'. If we die due to someone else's negligence, our dependents' compensation is calculated based on our potential earnings – what our earnings were when we died, what promotions we might have received, whether that start-up we'd been working on would have actually made any money, whether our spending would have increased, and at what age we probably would have died. Our whole lives can be summarised as merely a bunch of numbers in a spreadsheet.

In many parts of the world, including the UK, there are official guidelines regarding how to calculate the cost of each part of your body in circumstances where their loss is caused by the negligence or a deliberate act of another. These guide-lines are used to calculate compensation for 'pain, suffering and loss of amenity'.[12] Total loss of one eye entitles the victim to between £48,000 and £58,000, loss of both arms gets you between £210,000 and £263,000, while loss of your index finger is worth only about £16,000. Like a slaughtered animal, where each part has a market value, your body can be broken down to various prices.

In the US, the system is a bit different. More 'erratic', as behavioural economist Daniel Kahneman and colleagues would say, because damages are decided by juries. In 1998 they published the results of a study on the amount of moral outrage that participants had to a series of injury cases, and how much money they thought should be awarded.[13] From a car with a defective airbag, to workplaces with hazardous fumes, to being shot by a drunk security guard, participants were asked how much the victim should be given for the damages. They found that although people generally agreed about how morally outrageous the actions were, and how severe the punishment should be, they varied tremendously in how much money they thought should be awarded. To some people your suffering may be appropriately compensated with a $100 or $1,000 fine, while to others the exact same affliction might warrant a $1 million pay-out.

But given that we cannot undo suffering, or replace an arm or a life, there is no way to really make it up to the person. Our justice system requires a sense of 'fungibility'. Fungibility is a term from economics that refers to two things having the same value, making them interchangeable or replaceable. But the losses that are incurred here are not interchangeable with anything. Hence the large discrepancies in what people see as appropriate reparations.

This raises the question as to why we, or companies, choose to put people at risk in the first place. What Roy Baumeister has referred to as 'instrumental evil' is when individuals or organisations do bad things for money. According to Carole Jurkiewicz, who has researched the foundations of organisational evil, 'One of the most widely discussed occurrences of instrumental evil involved a subcompact car called the Ford Pinto.' In the 1970s, the Pinto was a popular car, but it had a major engineering flaw: the location of the fuel tank made it likely that even at slow speed, a rear-end collision would result in the car exploding. The risk was known to the manufacturer, who identified it after a series of crash tests, but the car was put on the market anyway. According to their calculation, it would cost an additional $11 per car to save about 180 lives per year. Ford didn't go for it, because the cost associated with fixing the problem was calculated to be higher than the possible losses from civil lawsuits and bad publicity. They included deaths in this calculation, working on the premise that a life in the US at the time was worth approximately $200,000. Those making the decision knew people were going to die – in the end it was estimated that between 27 and 180 people died due to this issue – but they did it anyway.

Was it evil? Is that just how business works? In business and in life, money is a convenient way to calculate worth, and it is much easier to think about monetary gains and losses than it is to think about psychological gains and losses. This, of course, may overlook the reputational costs, as public condemnation can also strongly impact the bottom line.

But saying, or thinking, that some of us are financially worth more than others makes it easy to dehumanise or discriminate against those deemed worth*less*. By putting a price tag on human beings, we forget the complexities of the human experience and the structural inequalities that favour some and disadvantage others. We risk treating people without empathy, without humanity.

TAKEN

Perhaps nowhere are social norms as distorted as within the business of slavery. Stripped of freedom, stripped of rights, stripped of their humanity, slaves are treated as a means to money, rather than as human beings. Slaves are ascribed a value and sold at that value, depending on things like height, strength and looks.

Kevin Bales is a human rights lawyer who researches

modern slavery. He has found that the average price of a human slave today is $90, cheaper than it has ever been.[14] According to him, the price of humans has plummeted, and this is probably because of a global population explosion, increasing the number of vulnerable people in the world who can be exploited. Although in a legal context slavery is often a much broader term, Bales has defined modern-day slavery as people who are forced to work without pay under threat of violence, and are unable to walk away.

How many slaves are there? According to the United Nation's International Labour Organisation, although slavery is illegal in every country on earth, there are at least 21 million people worldwide in some form of slavery today.

I really struggle to understand slavery. Particularly sex slavery. To rob young people of everything – their freedom, their health, their dignity, their life – seems as cruel as it gets. It is easy to picture how quickly someone can be kidnapped and enslaved. Going to the wrong kind of party. Getting into a car with a friendly stranger. Or – as Bales suggests is the most common reason to get tricked into slavery – misplaced trust in a job offer.

It seems shockingly easy to go from a normal life to something one cannot really call a life at all. And what does the perpetrator get out of it? Money? *Are you kidding me?* But, as hard as it is for me to understand, it is all about the money. According to Bales, 'People do not enslave people to be mean to them. They do it to make a profit.'[15]

Slavery is business. Big business. According to slavery economist Siddharth Kara, 'It turns out that slavery today is more profitable than I could have imagined.' Kara summarised data from fifty-one countries over a fifteen-year

period, and conducted interviews with over 5,000 victims
of slavery. He found that 'profits on a per slave basis can
range from a few thousand dollars to a few hundred thousand
dollars a year, with total annual slavery profits estimated to
be as high as $150 billion'.[16] He calculated that the average
profit a victim generates is $3,978 per year, and that victims
of sex trafficking, which accounts for about 5 per cent of
all slavery, generate an average of $36,000.

It seems heartless to talk about how profitable slavery is.
But in this chapter, money is what it's all about. Money is
the key corrupting force here. Without profitability, like business corruption and exploitation, most human slavery would
vanish.

How can slave-owners possibly justify being in this
industry? According to Roy Baumeister, there is a perception of certain people and actions as 'pure evil', which is
defined by eight characteristics.[17] Kevin Bales has elaborated
on Baumeister's original idea, and applied his main framework to understanding slavery. 'Pure evil is marked . . . by
eight attributes, most of which are also found in popular
perceptions of slavery.' These attributes are summarised as
follows, with the slavery example provided by Bales in
brackets:

1. The evil person intentionally inflicts harm on people
   (the slaveholder regularly brutalises his slaves).
2. Evil is driven by the wish to inflict harm merely for the
   pleasure of doing so (the slaveholder sadistically enjoys
   whipping slaves).
3. The victim is innocent and good (the slave did nothing
   to deserve slavery).

4. Evil is the other, the enemy, the outsider, the out-group (the slaveholder is not like us, belongs to a group that we could never and would never belong to).

5. Evil has been that way since time immemorial (slavery has always taken this basic form: total violent control and violation).

6. Evil represents the antithesis of order, peace and security (enslavement means violence, disruption, destruction of families, and a total lack of security).

7. Evil characters are often marked by egotism (the slave-holder believes they are superior to their slaves).

8. Evil figures have difficulty maintaining control over their feelings, especially rage and anger (the slaveholder's rage is part of the terror endured by the slave).

But there is a catch. If you found yourself reading those and thinking that meeting all eight of the criteria would be incredibly difficult, perhaps even impossible, you are right. These eight factors, particularly the first six, form what Baumeister calls the *myth* of pure evil. While individually some of these can be considered as the characteristics society labels 'evil', they cannot be seen as just one concept. They are overstatements, oversimplifications, that seek to distance us from those who harm others. Baumeister and Bales argue that although we may think of people or acts as pure evil, this is not actually a useful or reasonable concept. People and behaviours are more nuanced than that.

The same holds true for slavery. Bales states that the stereotype of the evil slaveholder may comfort us because it presents a person so fundamentally different from ourselves, but 'While any reasonable person defines the act of one person enslaving another as evil, no slaveholder enslaves people just to do evil.' I think that enslaving someone is one of the worst things we can do to another human being, but calling slavery evil feels almost like letting slaveholders off the hook. It is greedy. It is selfish. It is harmful. But it's the result of broken systems and an individual's broken values rather than some fundamental and immutable aberration within the slaveholder.

Bales further argues that 'we must explore (though not accept) their own self-definitions' and the way they justify their business. 'Almost all the actual slaveholders I have met and interviewed were "family men" who thought of themselves as businessmen.' According to Bales, having slaves is simply one factor of many in the economic equation.

But how do slaveholders do it? The cognitive dissonance must be tremendous, simultaneously enslaving someone while believing that you are a good person. Rather than changing the behaviour, however, it seems that slaveholders often change their beliefs.

Bales argues that they see their role as necessary to maintain order, or justified by the actions or circumstances of the slaves, or pre-ordained because of the class they were born into. They see themselves as taking from their victims, but also giving back – food, shelter, basic amenities. These beliefs help to maintain inequalities in society, because it implies that certain people don't *deserve* any more than they are being offered. They should be grateful to get anything at all.

Simultaneously, these beliefs conceptualise slaves as subhuman, moving them into a category of beings that do not deserve status or human rights, much like animals or criminals. Bales explains that one of the key roles of the slaveholder is to make the slave accept their role, to stop seeing slavery as evil but as a normal part of the order of things. 'If evil is in the eye of the beholder, then the slave is pushed to take on the viewpoint of the perpetrator or slaveholder.' Once neither slaveholder nor slave see it as evil, the situation is easily maintained.

Modern-day slavery is unjustifiable, but we can see parallels to other settings involving the extreme exploitation of human beings for money. It is easier to look at others and judge than to look at more common shady business practices that are known to us within our own communities. In most communities there are people who are underpaid and overworked. There are those we send to extract chemicals, oil or diamonds, whom we expose to dangerous working conditions without appropriate safeguards. And there are companies who risk getting closed down because they use undocumented workers, while feeling they are justified in underpaying them. Perhaps our slave-owners aren't so different from some other business people after all.

A JUST WORLD?

Moving from modern slavery back to other forms of exploitation, how can we justify treating workers poorly or underpaying them? For example, in western societies we must ask ourselves why we think it is OK to pay cleaners, care-workers and garbage collectors a fraction of the wages we pay others. Often, not enough for them to be able to cover the basics of food, and shelter. These are essential, dirty jobs that most of us do not want to do. Should they not be rewarded for doing these with high, or at least adequate, pay? Or do you think that it's OK because that's how society works, or because you, with your university degree, or training, or good background, *deserve* more?

If you are unsure whether you believe in a just world, let me help you. One of the main questions is whether you think that 'people generally earn the rewards and punishments that they get in this world'.[18] If yes, then you may well believe in the 'fairness of outcomes and allocations'.[19] In other words, the more you think that people who are good deserve good, that people who work hard deserve to be wealthy, or conversely that people who don't work deserve to starve, then you believe that the world is a just place. It also means that when you meet, for example, someone who is starving but works hard, this is difficult to process.

Psychologist Melvin Lerner was among the first to research what is referred to as the 'just-world hypothesis'. He wanted to know why so many of us readily blame victims for their suffering. In a series of experiments, including one published in 1966 with Carolyn Simmons, the team showed that 'people will arrange their cognitions so as to maintain the belief that people get what they deserve or, conversely, deserve what they get'.[20] Belief in a just world happens because we like the feeling that we are in control of our destiny, and believing otherwise is threatening. According to Lerner and Simmons, 'If people did not believe they could get what they want and avoid what they abhor by performing certain appropriate acts, they would be virtually incapacitated.'

We use just-world beliefs to make sense of a world filled with an inequality that we feel unable to rectify ourselves. While personal belief in a just world can be good for us, as it is empowering and makes us feel in control of our own lives,[21] the implications of general belief in a just world can be devastating for society. General just-world beliefs have been linked with many negative attitudes, including towards the poor,[22] and towards victims of crime, including rape.[23] If someone believes that people deserve what they get, or get what they deserve, this unsurprisingly affects their views on a drunk girl being raped, or a homeless man begging on the Underground.

When we see a poor person on the street, many of us avoid them, give them dirty looks, even tell them to 'just get a job'. This can come from the perception that the person deserves to be poor, because they just haven't tried hard enough, or because they made bad decisions. But it really is a way of protecting *ourselves*. We like thinking that poverty could not happen to us, as we do not deserve such a thing. Similar arguments are used to other those who have been victimised by crime. We blame the victim because it feels safer to think that the victim somehow deserved it, than that we could just as easily have been a target.

Humans like a sense of order and control, and we don't like the idea that bad things can happen to good people. But they do, all the time. Accepting this can help us to deal with the underlying inequalities, and try to do something about them – like working to eliminate slavery, reduce extreme poverty, or prevent violent crime. These are probably not, as some believers in a just world might assume, 'necessary evils' in society.

Also counter to our just-world hypothesis is accepting that good things can also happen to 'bad' people – people who don't play by the rules, and exploit others.

One of the most blatant examples of taking advantage of human suffering for profit is making life-saving medication extortionately expensive.

PHARMA BRO

In 2015, Martin Shkreli (also known as 'Pharma Bro'), the CEO of Turing Pharmaceuticals, bought the rights to the AIDS drug Daraprim, and almost immediately raised the price from $13.50 to $750 per pill.[24] What was happening seemed to be a clear case of profit over patients. His reckless disregard for the wellbeing of patients earned him the title of 'America's most hated man'.

In 2017, he was charged with multiple counts of fraud. As it turned out, however, after so much public criticism of him and his actions, it was difficult to find neutral jury members. Here is an excerpt of what might be the most bizarre jury selection process of all time, which led to over 200 jurors being 'excused' from their duties.[25]

THE COURT: The purpose of jury selection is to ensure fairness and impartiality in this case. If you think that you could not be fair and impartial, it is your duty to tell me. All right. Juror Number 1.

JUROR NO. 1: I'm aware of the defendant and I hate him.

BENJAMIN BRAFMAN (SHKRELI'S LAWYER): I'm sorry.

JUROR NO. 1: I think he's a greedy little man.

THE COURT: Jurors are obligated to decide the case based only on the evidence. Do you agree?

JUROR NO. 1: I don't know if I could. I wouldn't want me on this jury.

THE COURT: Juror Number 1 is excused.

. . .

JUROR NO. 10: The only thing I'd be impartial about is what prison this guy goes to.

THE COURT: Okay. We will excuse you. Juror 28, do you need to be heard?

JUROR NO. 28: I don't like this person at all. I just can't understand why he would be so stupid as to take an antibiotic which H.I.V. people need and jack it up five thousand percent. I would honestly, like, seriously like to go over there—

THE COURT: Sir, thank you.

JUROR NO. 28: Is he stupid or greedy? I can't understand.

. . .

JUROR NO. 59: Your Honor, totally he is guilty and in no way can I let him slide out of anything because—

THE COURT: Okay. Is that your attitude toward anyone charged with a crime who has not been proven guilty?

JUROR NO. 59: It's my attitude toward his entire demeanor, what he has done to people.

THE COURT: All right. We are going to excuse you, sir.

JUROR NO. 59: And he disrespected the Wu-Tang Clan.

. . .

JUROR NO. 77: From everything I've seen on the news, everything I've read, I believe the defendant is the face of corporate greed in America.

BRAFMAN: We would object.

JUROR NO. 77: You'd have to convince me he was innocent rather than guilty.

That comment from Juror No. 59 was the result of Shkreli buying an unreleased Wu-Tang album and never releasing the music to anyone else, resulting in a member of the Clan calling him a 'shithead'. In response, Shkreli called the rapper old and irrelevant, and threatened to erase the album, stating 'Without me, you're nothing.'[26]

Even after filtering out biased jurors, Shkreli was found guilty of a number of the charges against him. During and after the trial, he was glib, superficial, entitled, posted hateful attention-seeking comments on social media, and lied repeatedly. He even lied about being a graduate of Columbia University. This came to light during the trial, when a university administrator reported that there was no record of him ever attending.[27] That evening, back at home, Shkreli posted a live stream on social media where, seated with his cat on his lap, he attacked critics while wearing a Columbia University t-shirt. He seemed to enjoy messing with people, perhaps even revel in being perceived as evil. It wasn't until 2018, when he was sentenced to seven years in prison for securities fraud and conspiracy, that the world saw an emotional display. The man who once thought himself untouchable, cried in court.[28]

How did he get to this point? It is easy to write him off as a psychopath, or a bad apple, or evil. Indeed, in this section I was going to talk about what Robert Hare, the researcher who developed the psychopathy checklist, has referred to as 'snakes in suits'. How being a callous and manipulative psychopath might be a helpful feature in business settings, because it can allow us to make decisions based on money rather than empathy.

Then I caught myself. By using a framework that explains bad business behaviour as the result of psychopathic leaders, we fall back into the fallacy that evil is something other people do. That it is the result of fundamental flaws in a person, rather than a system that is created entirely to frame our measures of success and contribution in monetary terms.

Shkreli is, in many ways, the epitome of what we think a bad boss or corporate CEO is like – a sleazy, self-interested snake in a suit. But we must be careful. He has grown up in a world that glamorises money, and often rewards those who succeed in business even at the expense of others. Many industries mark up prices for necessary goods, treat workers poorly or pay themselves very high salaries while their employees starve. Humans can readily adapt to the systems they live in, and Shkreli is among those who take it too far and relish being good at the corporate game. This is not to excuse his actions, but like all of us, Shkreli too is a product of his environment – although likely with some dark tetrad personality traits (narcissism, Machiavellianism, sadism and psychopathy) thrown in that make it even easier for him to ignore reasonable ethics and focus entirely on money and fame.

Still, we must not dehumanise those who dehumanise others.

Perhaps a system that encourages profit over all else has the potential to make us all into monsters.

ETHICAL BLINDNESS

A lot of things we do outside of work, we also do at work. We lie to get out of things we don't want to do, we play up our good characteristics to make ourselves look better, we are catty towards colleagues, revel in the misfortune of those we envy, steal for our own self-interest, abuse positions of power, and cheat to get ahead. These are just humans doing human things, we just sometimes happen to be doing them at work. In many ways businesses are just microcosms of human experience. But when we lift the corporate veil and look at the people who make up a company, we can see a few things that particularly influence how we behave at work.

Many of us don't just wake up and go to work for the money alone. We also want to feel like we are doing something meaningful with our lives. And when we feel like our role is meaningful, we may develop a strong sense of identification with our role. Take me, for example. I *am* a scientist. I don't just do or write about science.

With regard to ethical behaviour, what seems to matter strongly is how much we value and identify with the company we work for. If we are unhappy employees who do not value the company or our role within it, we may do things that are beneficial to ourselves but destructive to the company. This is unethical, selfish behaviour.

However, when we value the people with whom we work, and the company we work at, and being part of an organisation is part of our identity, we may do things that are unethical in order to benefit the organisation. We may steal for rather than from our employer, lie for our bosses rather than to them, cover up mistakes for our colleagues not just for ourselves.

Psychologists Elizabeth Umphress and John Bingham have referred to this as 'unethical pro-organizational behaviour'. As they say, 'Individuals with strong attachments to and identification with their employer may also be the most likely to engage in unethical pro-organizational behaviors, suggesting that employees may do bad things for good reasons.'[29] Umphress and Bingham argue that this is in line with social exchange theory, which has to do with the exchange of favours or resources. As the authors summarise, 'Although reciprocating benefits is voluntary, those who fail to reciprocate may incur penalties such as distrust, decreased reputation, denial of future benefits, and other sanctions. In contrast, those who reciprocate engage in a self-perpetuating exchange of benefits including mutual trust, approval, and respect.'

In addition to the social pressures at work, our intuitive models of ethical decision-making present people as rational actors, who make the decision to act immorally, due to character flaws. But sometimes we act in unethical ways without being aware of it.

According to business ethicist Guido Palazzo and colleagues, we can all be ethically blind.[30] 'Ethical blindness can be defined as the temporary inability of a decision maker to see the ethical dimension of a decision at stake.' Other terms for this are 'administrative evil', 'the second face of evil', or 'ethical blind spots'. This ethical blindness can happen to anyone, particularly in business settings. When we reframe issues – people as profit, safety as expense, ethical clearance as pesky paperwork, the good of the company as the main priority – we can quickly forget the possible real-world harm that can result from our actions. While from the outside it might be easy to wonder what people were thinking when making dangerous decisions, from the inside they may not have been perceived as such at all. In hindsight it can be easy to know that bad decisions were made, but often those who made them thought they were a good idea at the time.

There is another pernicious infestation in many companies that does tremendous harm. Implicit biases (also called unconscious biases) involve beliefs that we don't really think about but can be detrimental towards others. While most of us say that we are not racist, sexist or ageist, when we monitor our behaviour we might think differently. Our biases and associations can be hard to shake. But we can deal with our implicit biases by being aware that such associations exist. Once we know they exist, we can begin to actively implement strategies to combat them.

One area where implicit biases have received a fair amount of attention recently is in the context of workplace harassment and discrimination. In my opinion, this is a particularly interesting form of unethical behaviour within companies, as we are often so blind to it that we assume we cannot possibly be part of the problem.

Because harassment is something that *other people* do.

But every single one of us has a role to play. Every time you interrupt a woman at work, ask a person who has a different skin colour where they are '*actually* from', or express shock when a man says he does not like football, your implicit biases are shining through.

We often don't think we are discriminating against members of other groups, but our behaviour may indicate that we do in fact endorse certain beliefs or stereotypes. These implicit beliefs, if left to run their natural course, can lead to a culture that disadvantages and excludes people. Most of us would probably argue that it is wrong to treat people differently just because of their gender, the colour of their skin, their religion. But we do. And this comes at a tremendous cost to our culture.

The consequences of implicit beliefs regarding gender in the workplace came into sharp focus in 2017. Women in various fields brought decades of sexual harassment in the workplace to light, taking to Twitter, mainstream media and the courts. Campaigns such as #MeToo sought to bring harassment out of the dark, to start conversations. When this happened, we found many scared men and angry women, many scared women and angry men. We found that the issue ran deep.

Harassment is so widespread that it must be a fundamental part of the culture of the businesses where many of us work. We do not harass others simply because we are bad people, but (in part) because culture and society enable it.

I am very interested in this form of workplace 'evil'. In a 2018 review of the literature on harassment and discrimination in the workplace that I conducted with psychological scientists Camilla Elphick and Rashid Minhas, we found that

most harassment is never reported.[31] That's startling. It means
that most companies have no idea how much, and what kind
of, harassment is happening in their workplaces. Why don't
people report being the victims or witnesses of harassment?
They are scared to lose their jobs, scared of being treated
poorly by others in their organisations, scared that they will
be at a further disadvantage than they already are. People are
so afraid of the cultural consequences of calling out harassment that most of this wrongdoing stays entirely unreported.

If we are to make our workplaces ethical, we must start
by changing corporate culture. In February 2018 my
colleagues and I released an online tool to help improve the
recording and reporting of discrimination and harassment.
It is called Spot (talktospot.com) and uses a bot that you
can chat with when you experience inappropriate moments
at work. It works a bit like text-messaging, except that instead
of texting with a friend, you are texting with a chatbot that
is perfectly trained to ask you the right questions. As a bonus,
unlike a friend or someone in your company's HR department, it can't judge or assess you. It's just there to help give
you a voice, and to create a record that you can keep in case
you want to share it with someone later, or want to report
it to your employer right away. It encourages the reporting
of harassment and discrimination to employers, and improves
the accuracy of reports when they do happen. Spot also
helps organisations to better deal with issues when they arise,
by offering support for the complaints process. We want
to help employees speak up, and empower organisations to
build a better workplace culture.

Encouraging people to think about the ethical implications
of behaviours by and within a company is a critical step to

improvement. If we want healthy companies, ethical companies, we need to talk to each other when things go wrong. We need to establish a culture where people know that their concerns will be acknowledged rather than ignored. We need to frame whistleblowing and the reporting of discrimination and harassment as positive for the group, rather than something that will isolate the person who speaks up, because unethical behaviour is often not the result of a few bad apples, it is the result of corporate culture gone wrong.

This is particularly true in a corporate environment that encourages us to think of humans as money – their cost, their profit, their worth. We must remember to routinely take a step back and remember the humanity that these numbers represent. We must prevent our corporations and ourselves from acting like psychopaths, because we have been seduced by the simplicity of reducing complex issues to money.

We desperately need to change corporate culture, to introduce questions not just about what we can do, or how much money we can make, but what we *should* do.

It is time for a revolution in how businesses talk about human beings, animals and the planet, lest we become corporate cannibals.

The influence of culture on bad behaviour can be felt far beyond the boardroom. We now come full circle: back to perhaps the most notorious evil-doer of all time, Hitler. We discuss the society he helped create and how easily we can get swept up in inhumane behaviour. And we will explore the devastation that can come from losing our own identities, and allowing ourselves to be swept into a set of ethics that others have decided for us.

'Madness is something rare in individuals – but in groups, parties, peoples and ages, it is the rule.'

Friedrich Nietzsche,
Beyond Good and Evil

8

AND I SAID NOTHING:
THE SCIENCE OF COMPLIANCE

On Nazis, rape culture and terrorism

As HITLER ROSE to power he had many supporters. Among them was an outspoken Protestant anti-Semite called Pastor Martin Niemöller.[1] Over time, however, Niemöller realised the harm that Hitler was causing and in 1933 became part of an opposition group made up of clergy members – the *Pfarrernotbund* (Pastors' Emergency League). For this, Niemöller was eventually arrested and sent to two different concentration camps, which, against the odds, he survived.

After the war he spoke openly about the people's complicity in the Holocaust. It was during this time that he wrote one of the most recognisable protest poems, an ode to the dangers of political apathy. (Note that the history of the exact text of this poem is complicated, with Niemöller never writing down a definitive version, and naming different groups depending on who he was speaking to, but this is one, possibly tweaked, version.)

> First they came for the Socialists, and I did not speak
> out –
> Because I was not a Socialist.
> Then they came for the Trade Unionists, and I did
> not speak out –
> Because I was not a Trade Unionist.
> Then they came for the Jews, and I did not speak out –
> Because I was not a Jew.
> Then they came for me – and there was no one left
> to speak for me.[2]

It is a poignant statement. To me, it reveals how dangerous it is to perceive society's problems as someone else's problem. It speaks to the complicity that comes with doing nothing. And it makes us wonder why we so often do nothing when others around us are suffering.

We might respond to hypothetical ethical dilemmas with our morality blazing. We might think that if a violent, xenophobic leader were to step into power, we would hold our ground. That we could never be involved in the systemic oppression of Jews, or Muslims, or women, or of other minorities. That we wouldn't let history repeat itself.

A MILLION ACCOMPLICES

But both history and science call this into question. In 2016, after breaking a 66-year vow of silence, Joseph Goebbels'

105-year-old former secretary said: 'Those people nowadays who say they would have stood up against the Nazis – I believe they are sincere in meaning that, but believe me, most of them wouldn't have.'[3] Joseph Goebbels was the Minister of Propaganda for the Third Reich under Hitler, contributing hugely to Nazi war efforts. He facilitated actions that are almost universally considered evil, and when it became clear that World War II was lost, he committed suicide with his wife after poisoning their six children with cyanide.

Horrific acts carried out by ideologically driven people were one thing, but the complicity of 'normal' Germans in the Holocaust seemed beyond anyone's understanding. In an attempt to understand, scientists examined how it could be possible to lead an entire population into horror. The famous Milgram experiments (which I have already discussed in Chapter 3) were motivated by the 1961 trial of one of the organisers of the Final Solution, SS-Obersturmbannführer (lieutenant colonel) Adolf Eichmann, who famously argued that he was 'just following orders' when he sent Jews to their deaths as other senior Nazis had pleaded in the Nuremberg trials several years earlier. 'Could it be that Eichmann and his million accomplices in the Holocaust were just following orders?' Milgram asked. 'Could we call them all accomplices?'[4]

Who were the 'million accomplices'? Were there really *just* one million? When we discuss the complexity of Nazi Germany, we must tease apart different kinds of behaviours that were needed to allow for such atrocities to occur. Bystanders made up the largest number of those who allowed the Holocaust to happen – those who did not believe in the ideology, and were not involved in the Nazi Party, but witnessed or knew about the atrocities and did not intervene.

These bystanders were not just in Germany, but around the world.

Then there were those who believed the rhetoric, who believed they were helping to improve the world with ethnic 'cleansing', and whose beliefs and actions were in alignment. Finally, we had those who did not believe in the Nazi ideology, but felt they had no choice but to join the party, or believed that joining would give them personal benefits. Some of these individuals, who behaved in ways not in line with their beliefs, were 'following orders' to kill others, but many were involved behind the scenes of Nazi Germany as administrators, propaganda authors or in general political activity, rather than in the direct killing of individuals.

Of all these, Milgram was most interested in the latter, wanting to understand how 'ordinary citizens could inflict harm on another person simply because he was ordered to'.[5] To briefly reiterate the method that I described in Chapter 3, participants in these studies were told to administer shocks to a person they believed to be a second participant in another room, increasing in severity until they believed they had killed him.[6]

The Milgram experiments are perhaps a tired mainstay of popular psychology books, but they are included here because they profoundly changed the way scientists, and large parts of the wider population, viewed the human capacity for compliance. These experiments and their modern replications show the profound influence that authority figures can have over us. But the studies are not without criticism. They have been criticised both for being too realistic and for not being realistic enough. On the one hand, some participants may have been traumatised by the realism, believing themselves to have killed someone. On the other, some participants might have guessed that the pain was fake, given that they were participating in an experiment, and might have gone further than they would in real life.

To deal with these issues, researchers have repeatedly tried to partially replicate the Milgram studies, and succeeded – every time getting similar results in compliance as in the original study.[7] If you think that today we would have learned from this, and would be better able to resist dangerous instructions, you are unfortunately wrong.

According to neuroscientist Patrick Haggard, who partially replicated the coercive elements of the Milgram study in 2015, people who were instructed to do so were more likely to actually (not just pretend to) shock another participant.[8] 'Our results suggest people who obey orders could actually feel less responsible for the outcomes of their action: they may not just be claiming that they feel less responsible. People appear to experience a sort of distance from the outcome of their actions when they are obeying instructions.'[9] Understanding humans' seemingly boundless obedience to authority and compliance may help explain large-scale devastation, but should never excuse it.

We must be careful to not outsource our morality, and we must stand up against authority that is instructing us, or encourages us, to do things that seem inappropriate. Next time you are instructed to do something that seems wrong, think about what it is you are about to do, and consider whether you would have thought it appropriate had you not been ordered to do so. Similarly, whenever you realise that you are compliant with a culture that severely disadvantages a select group of people, speak up and resist the urge to do what everyone else is doing.

But let us return to compliance. Because such experiences seem abstract, I want to discuss a different kind of compliance. A compliance with the systemic oppression of an entire group of people. People who are not given the same rights, the same respect, the same pay. It's time to talk about the devastating effects of being complicit with misogyny.

RAPE CULTURE

Unlike the various sexual deviances, fetishes and sexual fantasies we covered earlier, those of us who commit sexual assault don't have a paraphilia. We do not make lewd comments, grope or rape others (and commit the large number of other sexual assaults) because we are only or primarily aroused by doing so. No. Sexual assault happens at least in part because some of us harbour fundamental views, shared by much of our society, that makes it seem like acceptable, understandable, or at least tolerable behaviour. We, as society, perpetuate a set of misogynistic values that have such vicious roots they can only do harm.

All of us help make men into sexual predators.

We are all to blame, albeit some more than others. How? It begins with the little things, the everyday sexism, that creates a pervasive culture of objectification, harassment and sexual assault. Women and men both engage in a series of behaviours that make the poor treatment of women seem OK.

Like when we tell a woman first that she is attractive, then that she is interesting or intelligent. When we laugh at the banter at work that implies that Suzie is a slut, or Amanda a bitch. When we get angry if a woman doesn't want to sleep with us, and call her a tease. When we assume that women don't want sex, so men need to coax them into it. When we are annoyed that a woman has put us into the 'friend zone'. When we assume that buying dinner or a drink or a present means we are entitled to sex.

But how can all this lead to rape? Society teaches men that the make-up on our faces is for them. That the clothes we wear are for them. That our bodies are for them.

Often referred to as rape myths, such beliefs can be precursors to sexual assault and they have been extensively studied. In 2011, Sarah McMahon and Lawrence Farmer created a rape myth acceptance scale which included both overt and subtle rape myths.[10] According to them, the main categories of rape myths are that i.) the victim asked for it, ii.) the perpetrator didn't mean to, iii.) it wasn't really rape, and iv.) the victim lied. All of these seek to excuse the behaviour of rapists and place at least some of the blame for the behaviour on the victim.

One of my favourite illustrations of the pervasiveness of rape myths in society comes in the form of a study by Miranda Horvath in 2011.[11] She wanted to see whether 'lads' magazines', magazines targeting young men, are 'normalising extreme sexist views by presenting those views in a mainstream context'. As part of this research they gave participants quotes from lads' mags and quotes from interviews with convicted rapists. They wanted to see whether the participants could tell the difference between them, and how acceptable they would find the quotes.

Actually, let's test this. It's time for a game of 'lads' mag or rapist?':

1. 'You do not want to be caught red-handed . . . go and smash her on a park bench. That used to be my trick.'
2. 'What burns me up sometimes about girls is dick-teasers. They lead a man on and then shut him off right there.'
3. 'Girls ask for it by wearing these mini-skirts and hotpants . . . they're just displaying their body . . . Whether they realise it or not they're saying, "Hey, I've got a beautiful body, and it's yours if you want it."'
4. 'Mascara running down the cheeks means they've just been crying, and it was probably your fault . . . but you can cheer up the miserable beauty with a bit of the old in and out.'

Can you tell the difference? Participants scored only slightly above chance – guessing that it was a lads' mag correctly 56.1 per cent of the time, and that it was a convicted rapist 55.4 per cent of the time. And here's my favourite (or least favourite) part – according to the authors, 'The participants ranked the quotes drawn from lads' mags to be more degrading to women than the quotes drawn from convicted rapists.' That's right, the beliefs echoed in actual print magazines were overall seen to be worse than the beliefs shared by actual rapists. The authors argue that this suggests 'the framing of such content within lads' mags may normalise it for young men'. Oh, and 1 and 4 were from lads' mags, while 2 and 3 were from rapists.

A follow-up study by Peter Hegarty and colleagues was published in 2018.[12] They found that the issue was a bit more complicated; participants now found sexist quotes off-putting and hostile. They also found that there was a shift away from magazines that promote such beliefs, at least in the UK. Still, they conclude by saying that the research has implications beyond magazines, and that it could be used to change the lad culture that normalises talk of sexual violence. 'Laddishness may be less prevalent on supermarket shelves than a few years ago, but remains relevant on campuses, on- and offline . . . Our findings may be useful in applied attempts to engender critical thinking among young men in such contexts where equal treatment of women is a social norm, but sexism remains relevant to young men's sexual socialisation.'

Sexism in many countries feels like it is a thing of the past. This is perhaps one of many reasons why we are reluctant to accept stories of sexual offending. Because *we* don't do things like this. *We* are progressive. We may openly disparage comments like those from the rapists or lads' mags, but when any conversation turns to someone reporting sexual harassment or sexual assault, often someone will say a) the victim is lying, b) they are exaggerating, or c) they are trying to ruin the perpetrator's life ('How could she do this to him?'). Rape myths are unfortunately still alive and well.

Do we possibly endorse rape myths because victim-blaming is in line with our just-world belief? In other words, the belief that this won't happen to us, or our wives, or our daughters, that sexual assault only happens to sluts who get drunk and hang out in back alleys. That if we don't hang out in back alleys and dress conservatively and don't get drunk, then we won't get assaulted.

So how common is sexual assault, really? Looking at official crime statistics doesn't particularly help us with this question, because even for the most extreme forms of sexual assault, including rape, most crimes are never reported. The personal threshold for reporting is exceptionally high for most people, and what exactly these thresholds entail differs for everyone. Some may be prepared to come forward after being groped, while others may only come forward after being raped repeatedly. Even for things that meet the threshold, fear of negative consequences for one's self or the perpetrator, self-blame, and cultural factors often hold back victim disclosure. Even defining sexual assault is difficult.

Consequently, answering the question 'How many people have been sexually assaulted?' is essentially impossible, but it is presumed that the unreported 'dark figure' is huge. This is further complicated because 'Focusing on a prevalence number implies that there is a clear distinction between sexual assault, which is often assumed to be traumatic, devastating, and life-changing, and other experiences, which are often assumed to be trivial or acceptable and are left unexamined.'[13] Indeed, whether someone sexually touched a woman's bum, or raped her, generally falls within the same category of sexual assault, although most of us would agree (and the law says) that these are different crimes.

Still, in an effort to get at least a sense of the extent of the problem, researchers often rely on self-report measures and try to come up with simplified numbers that are easy to talk about. For example, according to a review of the self-report literature in 2017 by Charlene Muehlenhard and colleagues, approximately one in five women are sexually assaulted during their four years at American colleges.[14]

We know quite a bit about sexual assault on campus, mostly because this is a population to which researchers have comparatively easy access. Muehlenhard and colleagues, however, argue that this rate is the same for high school students and for non-students of the same age (although others have suggested the rate for the latter is higher, at 25 per cent for women not in college).[15]

And sexual assault is not just limited to young women. According to a 2017 meta-analysis by Yongjie Yon and colleagues examining the self-reported extent of abuse against women aged sixty-plus around the world, they found that on average 2.2 per cent of older adults are sexually assaulted every year.[16] Ask any woman, and you will find many accounts of unwanted sexual touching, or even rape. It's an epidemic. And we are always looking for people to blame, people who don't include ourselves.

This was echoed in a court case in England in March 2017 by Judge Lindsey Kushner QC, who was sentencing a rapist: 'Girls are perfectly entitled to drink themselves into the ground but should be aware people who are potential defendants to rape gravitate towards girls who have been drinking.'[17] On first glance this statement seems benevolent, but then we see what I think to be the glimmer of victim-blaming. She is essentially suggesting that if women just didn't drink so much they wouldn't get raped so often. She also didn't do herself any favours when she made the following analogy: 'How I see it is burglars are out there and nobody says burglars are OK but we do say: "Please don't leave your back door open at night, take steps to protect yourselves."' This shows us that even those who, like Lindsey Kushner, spend much of their careers helping rape victims and sentencing rapists, endorse rape myths. They are so pervasive that they seep into all the echelons of our society.

Endorsing rape myths gives us an illusion of control. The thought of being raped is terrifying, so we cling to the illusion of being able to prevent it – even if it ends up hurting us in the long run, and makes it less likely that we are going to address the real causes of rape because we are wasting our time assessing the length of women's skirts.

But are those who sexually assault evil? They are certainly often portrayed as such. Unfortunately from the cases we do know about, sexual assault is so prevalent that if we were to send all the perpetrators to a remote island, we would see our population shrink dramatically. Those who sexually assault others are mostly normal people – our brothers, fathers, sons, friends and partners. Yet their actions cannot be excused because of the pervasiveness of rape myths.

So what can we do? I believe that better sexual socialisation is one key to preventing rape. We need to call out sexism, rape myths and bad behaviour every time we see it. Luckily, it seems that with initiatives like #MeToo encouraging women to talk about sexual harassment, we are finally having a conversation about the seemingly little things that together normalise a culture of violence towards women.

A revolution is underway. And it's long overdue. We need all the daughters and sons, sisters and brothers, mothers and fathers in this together. We need, for possibly the first time in human history, to treat the women of the world as capable, complex, fully formed human beings, who are not inferior to men.

KILLING KITTY

Let's stick with the idea of being complicit with bad behaviour rather than being active agents for a moment. What would you do if you saw someone at the top of a bridge, about to jump? Or standing on the ledge of a skyscraper? Running in front of a train? I bet you think you would help. Try to talk them out of it. The way we respond to social displays of violence, real or threatened, tells us a lot about humanity.

In 2015 anthropologist Frances Larson gave a talk, where she chronicled the development of public acts of violence, focusing mostly on public beheadings.[18] She talked about how public beheadings by the government, or more recently by terrorist groups, have long been a public spectacle. And although it might seem like the viewer plays a passive role when they watch such an event, they mistakenly feel that they are absolved from responsibility. We may feel disengaged, but we are giving a violent act the desired attention.

Much as a theatre piece fails to have the intended effect without an audience, public acts of violence need spectators. According to criminologist John Horgan, who has studied terrorism for decades, 'It's psychological warfare . . . Pure psychological warfare. They don't just want to frighten us or get us to overreact, they want to be always in our consciousness so that we believe there's nothing they won't do.'[19]

It's a chain of decreasing responsibility, but all links are required. Say a terrorist does something harmful and films it with the specific aim of getting attention. They leak a video of it to the press, who go on to publish it. We, as spectators, then click on the link and watch the message. If a particular type of video goes particularly viral, those who created it learn that this is what works best, this is what gets our attention, so if they want our attention they should do more of *this*. Even if *this* involves hijacking planes, driving trucks into crowds, or gruesome displays of power in conflict zones.

Are you evil for watching things online? Probably not. But you are probably helping terrorists to achieve what many of them want, which is to get their political message spread widely. I encourage you to be a conscious consumer of media reporting on terrorism, realising the larger impact that hiking up the number of views on a particular video might have in real life. Failing to prevent or discourage a harmful act might be almost as bad as directly committing the act itself.

Directly related to this is the 'bystander effect'. This line of research began as a response to the 1964 case of Kitty Genovese. Over the course of half an hour, Genovese was stabbed to death outside her apartment building in New York. The press widely reported on the murder, claiming that up to thirty-eight witnesses heard or saw the attack but none intervened to help her or called the police. This prompted the search for an explanation of what became known as 'Genovese syndrome', or the bystander effect.[20] The *New York Times*, the outlet that reported the story, was later accused of grossly exaggerating the number of witnesses and what they perceived.[21] Still, the case led to an interesting question: Why do 'good' people sometimes do nothing to stop vile acts?

In the first research paper on the topic, social psychologists John Darley and Bibb Latané wrote: 'Preachers, professors, and news commentators sought the reasons for such apparently conscienceless and inhumane lack of intervention. Their conclusions ranged from "moral decay," to "dehumanisation produced by the urban environment," to "alienation," "anomie," and "existential despair."'[22] But Darley and Latané did not agree with these interpretations and argued that 'factors other than apathy and indifference were involved'.

If you had taken part in this seminal experiment, it would have gone down as follows. Knowing nothing about the nature of the study, you arrive in a long corridor with doors opening to either side of it, into a number of small rooms. A research assistant meets you and takes you into one of the rooms, seating you at a table. You are given headphones and a microphone, and are told to listen for instructions.

Through the headphones you hear an experimenter explain that he is interested in learning about the personal problems faced by university students. It is explained to you that the headphones are there to preserve your anonymity, as you are going to be talking to other students. The researcher will listen to the tapes of your responses later, you are told, and because the researcher will not be present all those involved will need to take turns. Each participant gets the microphone on for two minutes, and during that time the others cannot talk.

You hear the other participants share their stories of adjusting to New York. You share yours. It's the first participant's turn again. He makes a few comments, but begins to grow louder and more incoherent. You hear:

> I-er-um-I think I-I need-er-if-if could-er-er somebody er-er-er-er-er-er- give me a little-er-give me a little help here because-er-I-er-I'm-er- h-h-having a-a-a real problem-er-right now and I-er-if somebody could help me out it would-it would er-er s-s-sure be good . . . because-er-there-er-ag cause I-er-I-uh-I've got one of the-er-sei er-er-things coming on and-and-and I could really use some help so if somebody would-er give me a little h-help-uh-er-er-er-er c-could somebody-er er-help-er-

uh-uh-uh [choking sounds] . . . I'm gonna die-er-er . . .
help-er-er-seizure [chokes, then quiet]

It's his turn to talk, so you cannot ask the others if they have
done anything. You are on your own. And, unbeknownst to
you, you're being timed. The question is, how long will it
take you to leave your research room to get help? Of those
led to believe that the experiment only involved themselves
and the person having the seizure, 85 per cent went to get
help before the end of the fit, and the average time it took
to get help was 52 seconds. Of those who thought that there
was 1 additional participant, 62 per cent helped before the
end of the fit, and it took them 93 seconds on average. For
those who believed there were 6 participants in total, 31 per
cent got help before it was too late, and it took them 166
seconds on average.

Now, this situation was incredibly realistic. (Can you
imagine the ethics they had to clear for this?) According to
the researchers, 'Subjects, whether or not they intervened,
believed the fit to be genuine and serious.' Yet a number of
participants still did not report it. And it wasn't apathy. 'If
anything, they seemed more emotionally aroused than did
the subjects who reported the emergency.' Instead, the
researchers argue their inaction had more to do with a sort
of decision paralysis, being stuck between two bad options
– potentially overreacting and ruining the experiment, or
feeling guilty for not reacting.

A couple of years later, in 1970, Latané and Darley
proposed a five-step psychological model to explain this
phenomenon better.[23] They argued that in order to intervene,
a bystander must i.) notice the critical situation, ii.) believe

that the situation is an emergency, iii.) have a sense of personal responsibility, iv.) believe they have the skills needed to deal with the situation, and v.) make the decision to help.

What stops us isn't a lack of caring. It's a combination of three psychological processes. The first is a diffusion of responsibility, where we think that anyone in the group can help, so why should it have to be us. The second is evaluation apprehension, which is the fear of being judged by others when we act in public – the fear of embarrassment (particularly in a place like Britain!). The third is pluralistic ignorance, the tendency to rely on the reactions of others when assessing the severity of a situation – if no one is helping, then there probably is no help needed. And the more bystanders there are, generally the less likely we are to help a person who is in need.

In 2011, Peter Fischer and colleagues reviewed 50 years' worth of studies in the area that included data from over 7,700 participants who took part in modified versions of the original experiment – some conducted in labs, and some in the wild.[24] Fifty years later, we are still affected by the number of bystanders. The more people there are around a crime scene, and also not helping, the more likely we are to disregard distressed victims.

But they also found that for physically dangerous emergencies where perpetrators were still present, people were highly likely to help, even if there were many bystanders. Accordingly, they said, 'Although the present meta-analysis shows that the presence of bystanders reduces helping responses, the picture is not as bleak as conventionally assumed. The finding that bystander inhibition is less pronounced especially in dangerous emergencies gives hope that we will receive help when help is really needed even if there is more than one witness of our plight.'

Like in the Kitty Genovese case, bystanders have many understandable motivations to not get involved. But doing nothing can be almost as bad as doing something harmful. If you ever find yourself in a situation where you are watching something unfold that is harmful or potentially an emergency, take action. Do something to intervene, or at least to report it. Don't assume that others will do it for you – as they might be thinking the same thing of you, with potentially fatal consequences. In some countries, not reporting crime can be a crime in its own right. I think the sentiment behind mandatory reporting laws goes in the right direction – if you know that a crime is being committed, you aren't off the hook just because you aren't the one committing it.

Now, let's turn it around. When would you become the perpetrator, not just the bystander? How about perpetrating one of the most highly publicised and violent types of attacks?

THE WRONG QUESTION

It's a question that comes up every time another terrorist attack is announced on TV: Why would anyone become a terrorist?

The word has a rather interesting history. It was first used in France in the late eighteenth century when 'terrorism' described the politically motivated violence carried out by the Jacobin government against its own people.[25] This flipped in nineteenth-century Europe when it turned from violent intimidation committed *by* governments to violent intimidation directed *towards* government. Terrorism was rebranded, and eventually gained the image we know today.

Terrorism involves the use of terror and violence to intimidate and subjugate as a political weapon or policy. And while many definitions, including that of the US State Department, limit terrorists to 'sub-national groups or clandestine agents',[26] many people take issue with this and highlight the need to be able to see states as agents of terrorism.

And we know at least one thing for sure: people do not become terrorists simply because they are homicidal psychopaths. Even more broadly there doesn't seem to be any particular kind of personality constellation that makes us more prone to becoming a terrorist. As summarised by psychologist Andrew Silke in 2003, in his book *Terrorists, Victims and Society*: 'Quite simply, the best of the empirical work does not suggest, and never has suggested, that terrorists possess a distinct personality or that their psychology is somehow deviant from that of "normal" people.'[27]

In 2017 this sentiment was further echoed by Armando Piccinni and colleagues, who found that: 'The popular opinion that terrorists must be insane or psychopathic is still widespread; however, no evidence exists that terrorist behavior may be caused either by prior or current psychiatric disorders or psychopathy . . . Moreover, most of these theories do not explain why, even if so many people are exposed to the same social factors or show the same psychological traits, only a tiny minority of them join a terrorist group.'[28] Terrorists may be portrayed as evil, but author and philosopher Alison Jaggar, who has tried to find a better definition of terrorism, claims that they are likely to see themselves as 'warriors fighting for a noble cause with the only means available to them'.[29]

But who is part of the 'tiny minority' of those who become terrorists? People like Amir. We don't know very much about Amir, but from what we do know he was a pretty regular teenager living in Turkey. After high school he went to college, but dropped out. His parents were pressuring him to find a wife and a job, to straighten out his life, when an easy solution seemed to appear. The terrorist group ISIS promised $50 per month along with a house and a wife. Amir crossed into Syria and signed up. When he spoke with NBC in 2015, an interviewer asked him 'How could you join an organisation like this?'[30] Amir broke down in tears, and explained: 'My life was hard and nobody liked me . . . I didn't have many friends. I was on the Internet a lot and playing games.' He claimed that ISIS offered him a reprieve from it all. He said that he was also shown 'videos that made it look amazing', further adding to the allure. But when things got real, and Amir was in the field tasked with killing opponents, he surrendered after just three days of fighting. It turned out he didn't feel able to kill, and ISIS couldn't actually give him whatever it was he was looking for – which probably included a sense of belonging, friends, a higher purpose, financial stability and love.

Most of us are not strangers to loneliness, or playing games online, or having nagging parents. Yet we don't become ISIS fighters. So, what's different about Amir?

It turns out we have no idea. Despite how much we talk about terrorism, we actually know very little about why individuals become terrorists. This explanation is deeply unsatisfying, which is probably why we almost never hear it. According to terrorism expert John Horgan, 'Faced with what appears to be an unending series of terrorist events, and equally invasive media coverage, a temptation for the seasoned pundit might be to offer a different, perhaps more honest answer: "Actually, we don't really know why people become terrorists," or "No, psychology cannot 'predict' who is vulnerable to becoming a terrorist."'[31] But this will not make us feel any more informed or comforted after a terrorist attack. After an attack we are looking for someone to give us clues regarding what to look for in individuals, so that we can gain control over the real sense of dread that comes with realising that such an attack can happen anywhere, to anyone.

Yet our governments are happy to provide us with the illusion of control, and useless advice. In 2018, US Homeland Security gave us the (trademarked) phrase: 'If you see something, say something,'[32] which they ambiguously explain is when 'you see something you know shouldn't be there – or someone's behavior that doesn't seem quite right'. It sounds a bit like a campaign for people who suddenly regain their sight. 'I see something! I see something!'

Taking a different approach, for the London Metropolitan Police in 2018 the signs of possible terrorist activity mostly have to do with making bombs and planning an attack.[33] They want to know: 'Have you noticed someone buying large or unusual quantities of chemicals for no obvious reason?' or 'Do you know someone who travels but is vague about where they're going?' or, my personal favourite, 'Have you seen someone who has several mobiles for no obvious reason?'

Presumably these instructions are so vague because

counter-terrorism units and police forces really have little idea what the public should be looking for. On top of that, particularly in big cities like London, with lots of weird people doing weird things all the time, even defining 'suspicious behaviour' becomes very difficult.

It's therefore unsurprising that many counter-terrorism procedures have little evidence to support their efficacy. Back in 2006, Cynthia Lum and colleagues critiqued the literature on counter-terrorism.[34] 'Not only did we discover an almost complete absence of evaluation research on counter-terrorism interventions, but from those evaluations that we could find, it appears that some interventions either did not achieve the outcomes sought or sometimes increased the likelihood of terrorism occurring.'

This concern was echoed in a 2014 review of counter-terrorism by Rebecca Freese, who argued that we were still largely 'flying blind' because counter-terrorism research 'has suffered from both a lack of sufficient rigour and lack of influence on policy-making'.[35] Going forward, we must be very careful that our response to threat does not increase our risk of attack.

Part of why the evidence base is lacking is because fortunately, compared to other types of crime, terrorism is such a rare event that it makes it very difficult to research and predict. In addition to that, terrorists can come from all walks of life. According to John Hogan, 'For every disenfranchised, angry young Muslim man who joins the so-called "Islamic State", we can find examples of well-off, well-integrated young men and women who leave their current lives, jobs, partners or spouses behind them. Sometimes, entire families join *en masse*. For every religious person that mobilises to join, we find others either completely ignorant of any religious practice or knowledge, and others again who are recent converts.'[36] This isn't just true for ISIS, it's true of many terrorist organisations, and even the so-called 'lone wolf' terrorists don't fit neatly into any psychological profile.

There is so much diversity and complexity, and a relative paucity of data, that asking 'Who becomes a terrorist?' is probably the wrong question.

Although we cannot say who will become a terrorist, scholars do know a few things about the process of radicalisation. One of the groups most associated with radicalisation and terrorism today are jihadi terrorists. According to the BBC, 'Jihadists see violent struggle as necessary to eradicate obstacles to restoring God's rule on Earth and defending the Muslim community, or *umma*, against infidels and apostates.'[37] Obstacles that must be eradicated can include western ideologies and lifestyles.

After reviewing the literature, and honing in on jihadi terrorism, in 2017 psychologists Clark McCauley and Sophia Moskalenko proposed the two-pyramids model of radicalisation.[38] They argue that there are two aspects of radicalisation that make it very difficult to understand. First, most people with extremist views never commit acts of terrorism. Second, some terrorists do not have radical or violent beliefs. Because of this insufficient link between beliefs and actions in their model, McCauley and Moskalenko split 'radicalisation of opinions' from 'radicalisation of actions'.

The first 'opinion' pyramid looks like this: 'At the base . . . are individuals who do not care about a political cause, higher in the pyramid are those who believe in the cause but do not justify violence (sympathisers), higher yet are those who justify violence in defense of the cause.' And we can put some numbers on the pyramid with the help of polling data. According to McCauley over half of Muslims in the US and UK believe the war on terror to be a war on Islam – these are individuals who can sympathise with the cause.[39] But only about 5 per cent of Muslims in the US and UK see suicide bombings in defence of Islam as 'often or some-times justified'. These 5 per cent are high on the belief pyramid.

Our former ISIS fighter, Amir, also spoke about this. While his motivations seemed to be more practical than ideological (finally, *a wife!*), the normalisation and justification of radical beliefs and behaviours was evidenced by his ISIS training. 'Nobody likes anyone to be killed without reason,' he said. According to Amir, ISIS leaders justified their beheadings by saying it was necessary to 'instil fear' and ensure that 'people run away from us'. The killing of homosexuals by throwing them off tall buildings was justified because they were 'half men, like women'. With regard to killing women more generally, this was justified by saying that all the women killed were 'adulterers'. So during training, ISIS was actively radicalising their recruits, and giving them justifications for extreme violence.

But being high on the belief pyramid is not itself enough to be a terrorist, which is probably one reason why Amir quit on day three. He just didn't really have it in him to kill. Referred to as a common 'push' factor that contributes to terrorists disengaging from their organisations, is the inability to cope with the psychological effects of violence,[40] and thus an inability to follow through with terrorist behaviour. To become, and stay, a terrorist one must also be high on the action pyramid.

McCauley and Moskalenko explain the action pyramid thus: 'At the base of this pyramid are individuals doing nothing for a political group or cause (inert); higher in the pyramid are those who are engaged in legal political action for the cause (activists); higher yet are those engaged in illegal action for the cause (radicals); and at the apex of the pyramid are those engaged in illegal action that targets civilians (terrorists).' Terrorists don't just need to adhere to an ideology, they must also adhere to a behavioural protocol.

So, what do we do with this information? For one, we stop assuming that individuals simply commit jihadist terrorist activities because they have made a rational choice to gain access to a rewarding afterlife. We must also dismiss the assumption that terrorists are evil psychopaths who will stop at nothing to do us harm. Instead, we should examine the often-incremental shift towards more radical beliefs and an acceptance of violence and crime, the same process that is associated with many other kinds of wrongdoing. The process that could, potentially, make any one of us into a terrorist.

Let's explore that idea further. What could make us cruel, and terrorists into the victims?

THE LUCIFER EFFECT

Many of us seem to find it quite easy to justify the torture of actual or potential terrorists. This is despite the legal, ethical and moral sanctions against it, and, according to psychologists Laurence Alison and Emily Alison, the lack of evidence for its efficacy.[41] After reviewing the evidence on torture, they conclude that it is mostly used as punishment, and usually doesn't give us reliable information. According to their work, 'Revenge-motivated interrogations regularly occur in high conflict, high uncertainty situations and where there is dehumanisation of the enemy.'

During the 'war on terror', the former Iraqi prison Abu Ghraib was made into a military prison by the western allies. In 2003 and 2004, stories and documentary evidence came to light showing that human-rights violations were happening at the prison – including torture, physical and sexual abuse, rape and murder. The crimes were perpetrated by the military staff, and many were documented. For some odd reason, the perpetrators had taken over 1,000 photos of their mess. Photos of naked, hooded, dirty prisoners forced to perform oral sex on one another, or stacked on one another in a human pyramid, or being punched or injected with substances. In a number of the photos the military staff were visible – sitting on the prisoners with their thumbs up, or smiling. When these photos leaked, the big question was 'What the hell happened?'

Social psychologist Philip Zimbardo became an expert witness for one of the Abu Ghraib guards, giving him access not just to one of the perpetrators, but to the photos taken during the crimes – what he referred to as one of the 'visual illustrations of evil'.[42] But he didn't think that these people were inherently evil, that they were just a bunch of 'bad apples'. No, he found that 'the system creates the situation that corrupts the individuals'. And he should know, because he conducted one of the most famous experiments of all time on the ability of a situation to corrupt 'normal' people.

Philip Zimbardo has spent most of his career researching the social and structural influences that explain how 'good people turn evil', or as he has called it, 'the Lucifer effect'.[43] His most famous experiment, indeed one of the most famous psychological experiments of all time, had an inconspicuous title: 'Interpersonal dynamics in a simulated prison'. More commonly, it is referred to as the Stanford prison experiment. Published in 1973 with Craig Haney and Curtis Banks, the study revolutionised how we think about the social influences on behaviour.[44] Although it has been criticized repeatedly, most recently in a long and very public bashing in 2018, the study will always be relevant.

In the original paper, the team write that a 'normal' group of male college students (yes, yet another study with an all-male participant pool – this was very popular until quite recently, partly because being female was seen as a confound. WTF, right?) were chosen, after extensive testing, for 'a psychological study of prison life in return for payment of $15 per day'. Twenty-one men were selected, of which ten were randomly assigned to play the role of prisoners, and eleven to be their guards. The 'prisoners' were told to be home on a specific Sunday, where they were to receive a call and the experiment would begin. Instead of a phone call, however, participants were unexpectedly arrested by a real police officer, who charged them with a crime, handcuffed them and drove them to the police station. After having their fingerprints and mugshots taken, they were blindfolded and taken to a mock prison, where they were stripped, sprayed and made to stand alone naked. They were then dressed in uniforms, assigned numbers, and taken to their cells, where they were supposed to spend the next two weeks.

In the paper, the prison is described as follows: '[It] was built in a 35-ft section of a basement corridor in the psychology building at Stanford University . . . three small cells were made from converted laboratory rooms by replacing the usual doors with steel barred, black painted ones, and removing all furniture. A cot (with mattress, sheet and pillow) for each prisoner was the only furniture in the cells. A small closet . . . served as a solitary confinement facility; its dimensions were extremely small (2 x 2 x 7 ft) and it was unlit.' Prisoners had to stay in their cells twenty-four hours a day.

The prison guards had a very different experience. They received their instructions the day before meeting the prisoners, where they were introduced to Zimbardo, the 'superintendent' of the prison, and a research assistant who assumed the role of prison warden. The guards were told that their job was to 'maintain a reasonable degree of order within the prison necessary for its effective functioning,' and that they would give the prisoners their meals, work and recreation.

They received little other instruction as to what to do, other than being told that physical punishment or aggression was explicitly and categorically prohibited, and that they should refer to the prisoners by their badge number. Unlike the prisoners, guards had eight-hour shifts, and got to go home in between. During their shifts, the guards had their own quarters, which had a recreation room.

Now, picture yourself in this position. How do you think you would perform as an impromptu guard? It seems like a simple situation, one in which it is easy to stay respectful and considerate of each other, particularly since you know researchers are watching your every move. But, as you probably already know or expect, that's not how it went down.

Mood plummeted rapidly, as did general outlook. Only a few hours after being assigned their roles, the guards began to harass the prisoners. At 2.30 in the morning, prisoners were awoken with whistles, and later prisoners were insulted and given ridiculous orders. Already on day two there was an uprising by the prisoners against their treatment by the guards, with the prisoners barricading themselves into their cells. The guards, in an effort to restore order, broke down the barricades. To punish the prisoners for their behaviour, they then stripped them of their clothing, put bags over their heads, and made them do push-ups and other humiliating exercises. The leader of the uprising was then locked into isolation for many hours. Prisoners started to have emotional meltdowns and one refused to eat.

The experiment had to end early, after just six days rather than the planned fourteen. According to the original write-up, 'We witnessed a sample of normal, healthy, American college students fractionate into a group of prison guards who seemed to derive pleasure from insulting, threatening, humiliating and dehumanising their peers – those who by chance selection had been assigned to the "prisoner" role . . . most dramatic and distressing to us was the observation of the ease with which sadistic behavior could be elicited in individuals who were not sadistic types.' Over the six days that the experiment took place, the guards engaged in escalating levels of harassment and verbal aggression. Statements taken from them after the end of the experiment showed how they quickly came to dehumanise the prisoners: 'Looking back, I am impressed by how little I felt for them'; 'I watched them tear at each other, on orders given by us'; 'We were always there to show them just who was boss.' The guards justified their aggression as 'just playing a role', although the reactions of the prisoners, including emotional breakdowns, were all too real. According to the prisoners:

> The way we were made to degrade ourselves really brought us down and that's why we all sat docile towards the end of the experiment.

> I began to feel I was losing my identity, that the person I call ——— , the person who volunteered to get me into this prison (because it was a prison to me, it still is a prison to me, I don't regard it as an experiment or simulation . . .) was distant from me, was remote until finally I wasn't that person, I was 416. I was really my number and 416 was really going to have to decide what to do.

> I learned that people can easily forget that others are human.

Why did this escalate and why didn't the participants just walk out of the study? Zimbardo argues that one of the main processes that led to the degrading environment was deindividuation, partly caused by uniforms, guards and prisoners who were made to feel like distinct groups, but not as distinct individuals within those groups. Deindividuation is the loss of self-awareness when we identify as part of a group. Once one of the guards – who was referred to as John Wayne, after the macho actor – started to misbehave, the whole group of guards was affected and began to see this as acceptable behaviour. Similarly, once a prisoner accepted the loss of control and behaved passively, the group began to act in ever more passive ways.

According to Zimbardo, 'the seven social processes that grease the slippery slope of evil' are:

1. mindlessly taking the first small step,
2. dehumanisation of others,
3. deindividuation of self,
4. diffusion of personal responsibility,
5. blind obedience to authority,
6. uncritical conformity to group norms, and
7. passive tolerance of evil through inaction, or indifference.

Now, similar to our terrorism pyramids, what is needed here is an incremental shift in opinions – i.e., justifying increasing levels of aggression as necessary to maintain control – and an incremental shift in action – actually perpetrating increasing levels of aggression.

Although the ethics of the study have been heavily criticised (including by Zimbardo himself), and the interpretations of the findings have been challenged in various ways (including by psychologists, journalists, and even the participants themselves), the conclusions have nonetheless had a tremendous impact on how we view aggressive behaviour within and between groups. As Zimbardo states while describing his own work and the work of Stanley Milgram's obedience study, 'Evil acts are not necessarily the deeds of evil men, but may be attributable to the operation of powerful social forces.' I think that understanding the social forces that influence us all helps us both in terms of understanding and empathising with those who become corrupted by and within organisations, and it can help us better protect ourselves from their influence. Knowledge is power, and knowing how easily we slip into bad behaviour, encouraged by the groups we function in, can help us spot and stop our own radicalisation.

The slope may be slippery, but we need to remember that we can probably get off it at any point.

PROBLEMS OF CONSCIENCE

This brings us right back to where this chapter started, the Nazis.

Adolf Eichmann was put on trial in 1961 for his leading role in the Holocaust, including coordinating mass deportations to ghettos and extermination camps. As the presiding judge stated during his sentencing, Eichmann's crimes 'are of unparalleled horror in their nature and their scope'.[45] The philosopher Hannah Arendt (who, perhaps ironically, was a racist herself)[46] reported on Eichmann's trial at the time. In a series of articles in the *New Yorker*, then in her popular 1963 book *Eichmann in Jerusalem*,[47] she summarises the unfolding of the trial and gives astute observations, trying throughout to make sense of the man behind the horror.

Although the prosecution tried to make out that Eichmann was a perverted sadist and a monster, what they found was an average man, who appeared to be more often concerned with *how* to get his job done rather than whether it *should* be done. Arendt depicts Eichmann as a man concerned more with timetables and travel costs than the realities of the suffering he was inflicting. 'The problem with Eichmann was precisely that so many were like him . . . terribly and terrifyingly normal.'

Nazis, including Eichmann, often internalised the propaganda that was sold to them, and many stopped thinking for themselves. According to Arendt, 'What stuck in the minds of these men who became murderers was simply the notion of being involved in something historic, grandiose, unique, which must therefore be difficult to bear. This was important, because the murderers were not sadists or killers by nature.' They believed they were working towards a noble, greater good, and that the death and devastation they were carrying out was a temporary burden they had to endure.

But this was easier said than done. Humans are naturally programmed to respond to human suffering with pity, with sadness, with guilt. All of these emotions serve to inhibit us from hurting each other. So high-ranking Nazis, who believed in their cause, helped individuals overcome their 'problems of conscience'. Arendt explains: 'The trick . . . consisted in turning these instincts around, as it were, in directing them towards the self. So that instead of saying: What horrible things I did to people!, the murderers would be able to say: What horrible things I had to watch in the pursuance of my duties, how heavy the task weighted upon my shoulders.'

Germans were taught to feel that they were the ones suffering, that they were sacrificing *themselves*. In this flipped reality, *not* killing people becomes deviant, the selfish thing to do. To ease one's own conscience was to sacrifice the greater good. Such circumstances make it difficult to know or to feel that one is doing wrong.

Yet can we excuse Eichmann for being a product of the

times? For believing that the Final Solution was the best course of action, and for playing a deciding role in making it a reality? I believe not.

The presiding judge at Eichmann's trial didn't buy the argument that he was just following orders: 'Even if we had found that the Accused acted out of blind obedience, as he argued, we would still have said that a man who took part in crimes of such magnitude as these over years must pay the maximum penalty known to the law, and he cannot rely on any order even in mitigation of his punishment.' The judge made it clear that blind obedience is not an excuse, not even a partial excuse, for causing such extreme suffering. This is in line with current laws that state that soldiers are not allowed to follow unlawful orders, and cannot simply claim that they were following orders as an excuse for wrong-doing. In the end, Eichmann was sentenced to death by hanging 'for the crimes against the Jewish People, the crimes against humanity and the war crime of which he has been found guilty'.

This issue is not about a particular human being, it's not just about Eichmann. As Arendt writes, 'Ultimately the entire human race sits invisibly behind the defendant in the dock'. The story of a normal person being at least partly responsible for the deaths of six million people is a tale of caution for all of us, a sign that the kinds of mechanisms I have explored in this chapter can compound, can escalate, and can lure us into causing an almost unthinkable magnitude of harm.

Throughout this chapter I have tried to explain how social situations can influence human behaviour, bringing out the worst in us. I have tried to explain why we all might find ourselves compelled to think in ways that other members of our group think, to act in line with how our group acts. But to explain is not the same as to excuse. Just because we can see how circumstances influence us in profound ways does not mean that we are justified in behaving badly. I would argue the exact opposite.

Arendt argues that evil is banal, and scholars like Zimbardo and Milgram argue that we are all capable of evil given the right circumstances. I go further and suggest that the fact that it is so commonplace detracts from the very integrity of the concept. If we are all evil, or are all capable of evil, does the word even still hold the meaning it is intended to have? If evil is not reserved for the worst possible opprobrium, what then is its purpose?

I challenge you to go through life without resorting to calling actions or people evil. Instead, to truly try to break down human atrocities, and the people who commit them, into their individual parts. Examine each part carefully, like a detective. You are looking for clues as to why it happened and, perhaps, what useful information you can glean that might help you prevent it from happening in the future.

Now that we understand some of the factors that influence wrongdoers, we carry even more responsibility to behave in line with our morality. By understanding concepts such as group pressure, bystander effects, authority and deindividuation, we carry the responsibility to fight these social pressures when they try to lure us into immoral behaviour. Be cautious. Be diligent. Be strong. Because any suffering you cause, directly or indirectly, is on you.

Whether we look at Hitler or the Nazis, at rapists or rape culture, at terrorists or radical belief systems, we can see how individuals are influenced by a combination of their brains, their dispositions, and the social systems they live in. Throughout this book we have alternated between exploring situations, thoughts and concepts that are extreme, and those that regularly touch our lives. We have wandered in and out of topics that many would normally not dare engage with, and you have probably felt yourself at times get uncomfortable, disconcerted and angry.

I know I have. Some sections of this book were very difficult to write, so I imagine they were difficult to read. I needed to step away from the material sometimes. Let it digest. Perhaps you did the same. I needed to remind myself that these thought experiments help us grow as human beings, that by understanding each other and ourselves we move forward as a society.

So, what do we do now? Now is the time for action. Now the discussion about evil can really begin.

CONCLUSION

'DISASTER TOURISM' IS a term used to describe people who travel to so-called 'traumascapes', areas that have been destroyed by natural disasters or been affected by horrific historical events. In many ways this is conceptually what we have done throughout this book. We have visited many instances throughout human behaviour where terrible things occured, and have looked at the science of how such things could happen.

Scholars like sociologist DeMond Miller believe that 'Disaster tourism serves as a vehicle for self-reflection.'[1] He believes that going to visit traumascapes allows a message to be conveyed to visitors in a way that allows them to interpret and better understand their own lives. It is also seen as an educational tool that can accelerate the time it takes for humans to heal after adversity. By seeing the full detail and complexity of a disaster, we can better understand what has happened and become less afraid of it. We can learn and move on.

This book is in no way an exhaustive exploration of evil. Instead, it is a tour through some key issues that society wrestles with today, with a focus on topics that are particularly close to my heart. The goal was to tear away the preconceived notions of evil, and the vast amount of misinformation that is routinely fed to us. The goal is to start informed conversations about evil. And the goal is to personalise evil, to make it about you and me, not just about abstract and unrelatable phenomena.

So, is there really such a thing as evil? Subjectively, yes. You can call sadistic torture, or genocide, or rape, evil. You may mean something very specific, and have well-reasoned arguments as to why you have called a particular person or act evil. But as soon as you have a discussion about it with others, you may find that what you think is an undeniable act of evil is not perceived that way by them. Certainly by the time you bring people who have committed the act into the discussion, you are likely to encounter a different perspective. To echo the philosopher Friedrich Nietzsche, evil is only created in the moment when we perceive something as such. And just as quickly as we can make evil, if our perception shifts, it can disappear.

We make evil when we label something so. Evil exists as a word, as a subjective concept. But I firmly believe there is no person, no group, no behaviour, no thing that is objectively evil. Perhaps evil only really exists in our fears.

You have probably heard the saying that one man's terrorist is another man's freedom fighter. Well the same thing rings true for many contexts – one person's soldier is another's insurgent, one person's sexual liberation is another's perversion, one person's dream job is another's source of all ills. When we learn that evil is in the eye of the beholder, we begin to question the beholder and the society they live in.

And when we turn our attention to ourselves we realise that we sometimes curiously even betray our own sense of morality.

Because of what I consider an insurmountable problem of subjectivity, I think that neither humans nor actions should be labelled evil. Instead, I cannot help but see a complex ecosystem of decisions, cascades of influences, multifaceted social factors. I refuse to summarise all of this into a single hateful word, 'evil'.

But not believing in evil as an objective phenomenon does not make me a moral relativist. I have strong views on what is objectively appropriate behaviour and what isn't. I believe in fundamental human rights. I believe that intentionally causing pain and suffering is inexcusable. I believe we need to take action when individuals violate the social contracts we make when we live as part of a society.

More importantly, though, knowing the various influences that can contribute to problematic behaviour makes us more likely to identify these influences and to stop them from having their full effect. Understanding that we are all capable of much harm should make us more cautious and more diligent. This is a powerful gift indeed.

THE BRIGHT SIDE OF YOUR DARK SIDE

Reading this book, you might get the impression that humans are awful creatures. But that's not the point I'm trying to make. I am actually far more interested in showing that things we often refer to as evil are part of the human experience. We may not like the consequences, but human tendencies are neither inherently good nor bad – they just *are*.

Confusingly, the foundation of much that makes us do harm also leads us to do things society benefits from. For example, there is research by behavioural scientists Francesca Gino and Scott Wiltermuth that shows that dishonesty can lead to an increase in creativity – because breaking rules and 'thinking outside the box' involve similar thought patterns. They both involve a feeling of not being constrained by rules.[2] Creativity has given us modern medicine, modern technology and modern civility, but it has also given us cyanide, nuclear weapons and bots that threaten democracy. Great benefit and great harm can readily come from the same human proclivity.

Similarly, deviance can be a good thing. Deviating from the norm can make us villains, but it can also make us heroes. Like the kid at school who stands up to bullies on behalf of another, or the soldier who disobeys orders to kill civilians, or the therapist who refuses to write off paedophiles.

Even the author of the Stanford prison experiment, Philip Zimbardo, who showed how easily we can be led to behave badly, has turned his attention over the past few years to studying extreme pro-social behaviour. In a nod to Hannah Arendt's work, he makes an argument for the banality of heroism. Like evil, heroism is often seen as only a possibility for outliers – people who are abnormal, special. But Zimbardo asks: 'What if the capability to act heroically is also fundamentally ordinary and available to all of us?' They say we should never meet our heroes, lest they disappoint us when we find out how normal they really are. But we should all be so lucky as to realise this.

As Zimbardo's prison experiment supported (and as Irish statesman Edmund Burke is often misattributed as saying),

'The only thing necessary for the triumph of evil is for good people to do nothing.' So how do we teach people to do something? Zimbardo argues that we should foster 'heroic imagination'.

To do this, we need to do three things. First, we need to share stories of normal people standing up for their values. We need to give people's imaginations a boost, make them think about normal heroes, realise that they can be one. Because not all heroes wear capes. Second, we need to put ourselves in a state of readiness to act heroically when the opportunity arises, through imagining acting heroically and having a plan as to what we would do in an emergency. And third, we need to teach people that heroes don't have to act alone. They can recruit others, therein changing the wider personal, political or social landscapes.

This book seeks to inform and empower. When we understand what leads to harm, we can begin to fight against it. This involves taking action to stop harm, fighting against our own urges to do harm, and helping people who have done harm to get better. And whatever we stand for, fight for, feel for, we must *never* dehumanise each other.

TEN THINGS EVERYONE NEEDS TO KNOW ABOUT EVIL

1. Calling people evil is lazy.
2. All brains are a bit sadistic.
3. We are all capable of murder.
4. Our creepiness radars suck.
5. Technology can amplify dangerousness.
6. Sexual deviance is pretty common.
7. All monsters are human.

8. Money distracts from harm.
9. Culture cannot excuse cruelty.
10. We must speak of the unspeakable.

Finally, I have but one wish: *please*, stop calling people or behaviours or events 'evil'. It ignores the important nuances of the underlying behaviours.

I encourage you instead to think the unthinkable, speak of the unspeakable, explain the unexplainable, because only then can we begin to prevent that which others have deemed unpreventable.

It's time to rethink Evil.

'Of all evil I deem you capable: therefore I want good from you.'

Friedrich Nietzsche,
Thus Spake Zarathustra

ACKNOWLEDGEMENTS

Ute Shaw, my mom. Thank you for creating me, caring for me, and loving me. I was going to dedicate this book to you, but it felt too weird to dedicate a book on evil 'To Mom'. Consider this an informal dedication instead. Your support throughout my studies in criminal psychology was absolutely crucial to providing me with the foundations for writing this book.

Paul Livingston, my love. Thank you for your ocean of love and support, and for reading all my first and second and third and fourth drafts.

Simon Thorogood, my UK editor. Thank you for tirelessly putting up with my writing, and somehow helping me fit all the pieces of this book together.

Christian Koth, my German editor. Thank you for your unshakable belief in me as a person and a writer.

Jamison Stoltz and Tim Rostron, my American and Canadian editors. Thank you for helping to craft this book into something I am proud of.

Annette Brüggemann, my publicist. Thank you for always

pushing me to do more, and supporting me to face the challenges of public outreach.

DGA, my publishing agency. Thank you for making this book possible and always encouraging me to grow as a writer.

Susanna Lea Associates, my foreign-rights agency. Thank you for allowing my writing to reach more parts of the world than I could ever have dreamed.

NOTES

INTRODUCTION

1. Nietzsche, F. *Morgenröte: Gedanken über die moralischen Vorurteile* [*The Dawn of Day*]. Munich: DTV, 1881.
2. Original text: '*Die Leidenschaften werden böse und tückisch, wenn sie böse und tückisch betrachtet werden.*'
3. Bushman, B. J., Jamieson, P. E., Weitz, I., & Romer, D. 'Gun violence trends in movies'. *Pediatrics*, 132 (6) (2013), pp. 1014–18.

1. YOUR INNER SADIST: THE NEUROSCIENCE OF EVIL

1. Langer, W. C. *The Mind of Adolf Hitler: The Secret Wartime Report*. New York: Basic Books, 1972.
2. Redlich, F. *Hitler: Diagnosis of a Destructive Prophet*. Oxford: Oxford University Press, 1998
3. Reimann, M., & Zimbardo, P. G. 'The dark side of social encounters: prospects for a neuroscience of human evil'. *Journal of Neuroscience, Psychology, and Economics*, 4 (3) (2011), p. 174.
4. Jones, S. 'UN human rights chief denounces *Sun*'. *Guardian*, 24 April 2015. <https://www.theguardian.com/global-development/2015/apr/24/katie-hopkins-cockroach-migrants-denounced-united-nations-human-rights-commissioner>

5. See, for example, Cillizza, C., 'That Trump read "The Snake"'. CNN, 1 May 2017. <http://edition.cnn.com/2017/05/01/politics/trump-the-snake/index.html>

6. Baumeister, R. F., & Campbell, W. K. 'The intrinsic appeal of evil: sadism, sensational thrills, and threatened egotism'. *Personality and Social Psychology Review*, 3 (3) (1999), pp. 210–21.

7. Buckels, E. E., Jones, D. N., & Paulhus, D. L. 'Behavioral confirmation of everyday sadism'. *Psychological Science*, 24 (11) (2013), pp. 2201–09.

8. Aragón, O. R., Clark, M. S., Dyer, R. L., & Bargh, J. A. 'Dimorphous expressions of positive emotion: displays of both care and aggression in response to cute stimuli'. *Psychological Science*, 26 (3) (2015), pp. 259–73.

9. Lorenz, K. '*Die angeborenen formen möglichen erfahrung* [The innate forms of potential experience]'. *Zeitschrift für Tierpsychologie*, 5 (1943), pp. 245–409.

10. Baron, R. A., & Richardson, D. R. *Human Aggression*. New York: Plenum Press, 1994.

11. Richardson, D. S., & Green, L. R. 'Direct and indirect aggression: relationships as social context'. *Journal of Applied Social Psychology*, 36 (10) (2006), pp. 2492–508.

12. Leisring, P. A. 'Physical and emotional abuse in romantic relationships: motivation for perpetration among college women'. *Journal of Interpersonal Violence*, 28 (7) (2013), pp. 1437–54.

13. Bushman, B. J., DeWall, C. N., Pond, R. S., & Hanus, M. D. 'Low glucose relates to greater aggression in married couples'. *Proceedings of the National Academy of Sciences*, 111 (17) (2014), pp. 6254–57.

14. Richardson, D. S., & Green, L. R. 'Direct and indirect aggression: relationships as social context'. *Journal of Applied Social Psychology*, 36 (10) (2006), pp. 2492–508.

15. Richardson, D. S. 'Everyday aggression takes many forms'. *Current Directions in Psychological Science*, 23 (3) (2014), pp. 220–24.

16. Warren, P., Richardson, D. S., & McQuillin, S. 'Distinguishing among nondirect forms of aggression'. *Aggressive Behavior*, 37 (2011), pp. 291–301.
17. Richardson, D. S., & Hammock, G. S. 'Is it aggression? Perceptions of and motivations for passive and psychological aggression'. *The Psychology of Social Conflict and Aggression*, 13 (2011), pp. 53–64.
18. Paulhus, D. L., Curtis, S. R., & Jones, D. N. 'Aggression as a trait: the dark tetrad alternative'. *Current Opinion in Psychology*, 19 (2017), pp. 88–92.
19. Paulhus, D. L. 'Toward a taxonomy of dark personalities'. *Current Directions in Psychological Science*, 23 (6) (2014), pp. 421–6.
20. Balsis, S., Busch, A. J., Wilfong, K. M., Newman, J. W., & Edens, J. F. 'A statistical consideration regarding the threshold of the psychopathy checklist – revised'. *Journal of Personality Assessment*, 99 (5) (2017), pp. 1–9.
21. Augstein, H. F. 'J. C. Prichard's concept of moral insanity – a medical theory of the corruption of human nature'. *Medical History*, 40 (3) (1996), p. 311.
22. Hare, R. D. *The Hare Psychopathy Checklist – Revised*, 2nd ed. Toronto, ON: Multi-Health Systems, Inc., 2003.
23. Poeppl, T., Donges, M., Rupprecht, R., Fox, P., . . . & Eickhoff, S. 'Meta-analysis of aberrant brain activity in psychopathy'. *European Psychiatry*, 41 (2017), S349.
24. Stromberg, J. 'The neuroscientist who discovered he was a psychopath'. *Smithsonian*, 22 November 2013. <http://www.smithsonianmag.com/science-nature/the-neuroscientist-who-discovered-he-was-a-psychopath-180947814/>
25. Fallon, J. *The Psychopath Inside: A Neuroscientist's Personal Journey into the Dark Side of the Brain*. London: Penguin, 2013.
26. Konrath, S., Meier, B. P., & Bushman, B. J. 'Development and validation of the single item narcissism scale (SINS)'. *PLOS ONE*, 9 (8) (2014). <https://doi.org/10.1371/journal.pone.0103469>

27. Goldbeck, J. 'The one question that can tell us who's a narcis-
     sist: a new study finds a surprising insight about personality'.
     Psychology Today, 16 September 2014. <https://www.psychol-
     ogytoday.com/blog/your-online-secrets/201409/
     the-one-question-can-tell-us-whos-narcissist/>

28. Krizan, Z., & Johar, O. 'Narcissistic rage revisited'. *Journal
     of Personality and Social Psychology*, 108 (5) (2015),
     pp. 784–801. <https://doi.org/10.1037/pspp0000013>

29. Jones, D. N., & Paulhus, D. L. 'Machiavellianism'. In: M. R.
     Leary & R. H. Hoyle (eds), *Handbook of Individual Differences
     in Social Behavior*. New York: Guilford Press, 2009, pp. 93–108.

30. Muris, P., Merckelbach, H., Otgaar, H., & Meijer, E. 'The
     malevolent side of human nature: a meta-analysis and critical
     review of the literature on the dark triad (narcissism,
     Machiavellianism, and psychopathy)'. *Perspectives on
     Psychological Science*, 12 (2) (2017), pp. 183–204.

31. Christie, R., & Geis, F. L. *Studies in Machiavellianism*. New
     York, NY: Academic Press, 1970.

32. Buckels, E. E., Jones, D. N., & Paulhus, D. L. 'Behavioral
     confirmation of everyday sadism'. *Psychological Science*, 24
     (11) (2013), pp. 2201–09.

33. Campbell, W. K. 'Is narcissism really so bad?' *Psychological
     Inquiry*, 12 (4) (2001), pp. 214–16.

2. MURDER BY DESIGN: THE PSYCHOLOGY OF BLOODLUST

1.   Darimont, C. T., Fox, C. H., Bryan, H. M., & Reimchen,
     T. E. 'The unique ecology of human predators'. *Science*, 349
     (6250) (2015), pp. 858–60.

2.   Kenrick, D. T., & Sheets, V. 'Homicidal fantasies'. *Ethology
     and Sociobiology*, 14 (4) (1993), pp. 231–46.

3.   Duntley, J. D., & Buss, D. M. 'Homicide adaptations'.
     Aggression and Violent Behavior, 16 (5) (2011), pp. 399–410.

4.   United Nations Office on Drugs and Crime. *Global Study on
     Homicide 2013: Trends, Contexts, Data*. New York: UNODC, 2013.

5. Roberts, A. R., Zgoba, K. M., & Shahidullah, S. M. 'Recidivism among four types of homicide offenders: an exploratory analysis of 336 homicide offenders in New Jersey'. *Aggression and Violent Behavior*, 12 (5) (2007), pp. 493–507.

6. Liem, M. 'Homicide offender recidivism: a review of the literature'. *Aggression and Violent Behavior*, 18 (1) (2013), pp. 19–25.

7. Archer, J. 'Sex differences in aggression in real-world settings: a meta-analytic review'. *Review of General Psychology*, 8 (4) (2004), p. 291.

8. Dabbs, J. M., Riad, J. K., & Chance, S. E. 'Testosterone and ruthless homicide'. *Personality and Individual Differences*, 31 (4) (2001), pp. 599–603.

9. Cooper, S. E., Goings, S. P., Kim, J. Y., & Wood, R. I. 'Testosterone enhances risk tolerance without altering motor impulsivity in male rats'. *Psychoneuroendocrinology*, 40 (2014), pp. 201–12.

10. Berthold, A. A. '*Transplantation der Hoden* [Transplantation of the testes]'. *Archiv für Anatomie, Physiologie und Wissenschaftliche Medicin*, 16 (1849), pp. 42–46.

11. Berthold, A. A., & Quiring, D. P. 'The transplantation of testes'. *Bulletin of the History of Medicine*, 16 (1944), p. 399.

12. Carré, J. M., Ruddick, E. L., Moreau, B. J., & Bird, B. M. 'Testosterone and human aggression'. In: *The Wiley Handbook of Violence and Aggression*, Peter Sturmey (ed.), Hoboken, NJ: Wiley-Blackwell, 2017.

13. Mazur, A., & Lamb, T. 'Testosterone, status, and mood in human males'. *Hormones and Behavior*, 14 (1980), pp. 236–46. <https://doi.org/10.1016/0018-506x(80)90032-x>

14. Crockett, M. 'The trolley problem: would you kill one person to save many others?' *Guardian*, 12 December 2016. <https://www.theguardian.com/science/head-quarters/2016/dec/12/the-trolley-problem-would-you-kill-one-person-to-save-many-others/>

15. Skulmowski, A., Bunge, A., Kaspar, K., & Pipa, G. 'Forced-choice decision-making in modified trolley dilemma situations: a virtual reality and eye tracking study'. *Frontiers in Behavioral Neuroscience*, 8 (2014).
16. Bleske-Rechek, A., Nelson, L. A., Baker, J. P., Remiker, M. W., & Brandt, S. J. 'Evolution and the trolley problem: people save five over one unless the one is young, genetically related, or a romantic partner'. *Journal of Social, Evolutionary, and Cultural Psychology*, 4 (3) (2010), pp. 115–27.
17. Greene, J. D., Morelli, S. A., Lowenberg, K., Nystrom, L. E., & Cohen, J. D. 'Cognitive load selectively interferes with utilitarian moral judgment'. *Cognition*, 107 (3) (2008), pp. 1144–54.
18. Garrigan, B., Adlam, A. L., & Langdon, P. E. 'The neural correlates of moral decision-making: a systematic review and meta-analysis of moral evaluations and response decision judgements'. *Brain and Cognition*, 108 (2016), pp. 88–97.
19. Jentzen, J., Palermo, G., Johnson, L. T., Ho, K. C., . . . & Teggatz, J. 'Destructive hostility: the Jeffrey Dahmer case: a psychiatric and forensic study of a serial killer'. *American Journal of Forensic Medicine and Pathology*. 15 (4) (1994), pp. 283–294.
20. Terry, D. 'Jeffrey Dahmer'. *New York Times*, 29 November 1994. <http://www.nytimes.com/1994/11/29/us/jeffrey-dahmer-multiple-killer-is-bludgeoned-to-death-in-prison.html?m-cubz=0>
21. Terry. 'Jeffrey Dahmer'.
22. Wiest, J. B. *Creating Cultural Monsters: Serial Murder in America*. Boca Raton, FL: CRC Press, 2016.
23. Hodgkinson, S., Prins, H., & Stuart-Bennett, J. 'Monsters, madmen . . . and myths: a critical review of the serial killing literature'. *Aggression and Violent Behavior*, 34 (2017), pp. 282–89.
24. *The Works of Plato*, F. Sydenham and Thomas Taylor (trans.), S. Cornish & Co., 1839 <http://bigthink.com/21st-century-spirituality/fear-of-death>

3. THE FREAK SHOW: DECONSTRUCTING CREEPINESS

1. McAndrew, F. T., & Koehnke, S. S. 'On the nature of creepiness'. *New Ideas in Psychology*, 43 (2016), pp. 10–15.

2. Bar, M., Neta, M., & Linz, H. 'Very first impressions'. *Emotion*, 6 (2006), pp. 269–78. <http://dx.doi.org/10.1037/1528-3542.6.2.269>

3. Porter, S., England, L., Juodis, M., Ten Brinke, L., & Wilson, K. 'Is the face a window to the soul? Investigation of the accuracy of intuitive judgments of the trustworthiness of human faces'. *Canadian Journal of Behavioural Science / Revue canadienne des sciences du comportement*, 40 (3) (2008), p. 171.

4. Petridis, A. 'One person's "edgy" model is another's gun-toting "street terrorist"'. *Guardian*, 3 July 2014. <https://www.theguardian.com/lifeandstyle/lostinshowbiz/2014/jul/03/edgy-model-gun-toting-street-terrorist-jeremy-meeks>

5. Nisbett, R. E., & Wilson, T. D. 'The halo effect: evidence for unconscious alteration of judgments'. *Journal of Personality and Social Psychology*, 35 (4) (1977), p. 250.

6. Thorndike, E. L. 'A constant error in psychological ratings'. *Journal of Applied Psychology*, 4 (1920), pp. 25–29.

7. Gibson, J. L., & Gore, J. S. 'You're OK until you misbehave: how norm violations magnify the attractiveness devil effect'. *Gender Issues*, 32 (4) (2015), pp. 266–78.

8. Hosoda, M., Stone-Romero, E. F., & Coats, G. 'The effects of physical attractiveness on job-related outcomes: a meta-analysis of experimental studies'. *Personnel Psychology*, 56 (2) (2003), pp. 431–62.

9. Phelan, S. M., Burgess, D. J., Yeazel, M. W., Hellerstedt, W. L., . . . & Ryn, V. M. 'Impact of weight bias and stigma on quality of care and outcomes for patients with obesity'. *Obesity Reviews*, 16 (4) (2015), pp. 319–26.

10. Adolphs, R., & Tusche, A. 'From faces to prosocial behavior: cues, tools, and mechanisms'. *Current Directions in Psychological Science*, 26 (3) (2017), pp. 282–87.

11. Korva, N., Porter, S., O'Connor, B. P., Shaw, J., & Brinke,

L. T. 'Dangerous decisions: influence of juror attitudes and defendant appearance on legal decision-making'. *Psychiatry, Psychology and Law*, 20 (3) (2013), pp. 384–98.

12. Wilson, J. P., & Rule, N. O. 'Facial trustworthiness predicts extreme criminal-sentencing outcomes'. *Psychological Science*, 26 (8) (2015), pp. 1325–31.

13. Santos, S., Almeida, I., Oliveiros, B., & Castelo-Branco, M. 'The role of the amygdala in facial trustworthiness processing: a systematic review and meta-analyses of fMRI studies'. *PLOS ONE*, 11 (11) (2016). <https://doi.org/10.1371/journal.pone.0167276>

14. Bonnefon, J. F., Hopfensitz, A., & De Neys, W. 'Can we detect cooperators by looking at their face?' *Current Directions in Psychological Science*, 26 (3) (2017), pp. 276–81.

15. McAndrew & Koehnke. 'On the nature of creepiness'.

16. Langlois, J. H., & Roggman, L. A. 'Attractive faces are only average'. *Psychological Science*, 1 (2) (1990), pp. 115–21.

17. Sofer, C., Dotsch, R., Wigboldus, D. H., & Todorov, A. 'What is typical is good: the influence of face typicality on perceived trustworthiness'. *Psychological Science*, 26 (1) (2015), pp. 39–47.

18. Wang, T. T., Wessels, L., Hussain, G., & Merten, S. 'Discriminative thresholds in facial asymmetry: a review of the literature'. *Aesthetic Surgery Journal*, 37 (4) (2017), pp. 375–85.

19. Halioua, R. L. 'Staring and perceptions towards persons with facial disfigurement'. Unpublished master's thesis, East Carolina University, 2010. <http://hdl.handle.net/10342/2930>

20. Stone, A., & Wright, T. 'When your face doesn't fit: employment discrimination against people with facial disfigurements'. *Journal of Applied Social Psychology*, 43 (3) (2013), pp. 515–26.

21. Tsankova, E., & Kappas, A. 'Facial skin smoothness as an indicator of perceived trustworthiness and related traits'. *Perception*, 45 (4) (2016), pp. 400–08.

22. Funk, F., & Todorov, A. 'Criminal stereotypes in the courtroom: facial tattoos affect guilt and punishment differently'. *Psychology, Public Policy, and Law*, 19 (4) (2013), p. 466.

23. Fincher, K. M., Tetlock, P. E., & Morris, M. W. 'Interfacing with faces: perceptual humanisation and dehumanisation'. *Current Directions in Psychological Science*, 26 (3) (2017), pp. 288–93.

24. Norman, R. M., Sorrentino, R. M., Gawronski, B., Szeto, A. C., ... & Windell, D. 'Attitudes and physical distance to an individual with schizophrenia: the moderating effect of self-transcendent values'. *Social Psychiatry and Psychiatric Epidemiology*, 45 (7) (2010), pp. 751–58.

25. Magin, P., Holliday, S., Dunlop, A., Ewald, B., ... & Baker, F. 'Discomfort sharing the general practice waiting room with mentally ill patients: a cross-sectional study'. *Family Practice*, 30 (2) (2012), pp. 190–96.

26. Sowislo, J. F., Gonet-Wirz, F., Borgwardt, S., Lang, U. E., & Huber, C. G. 'Perceived dangerousness as related to psychiatric symptoms and psychiatric service use – a vignette based representative population survey'. *Scientific Reports*, 8 (2017).

27. Pescosolido, B. A., Fettes, D. L., Martin, J. K., Monahan, J., & McLeod, J. D. 'Perceived dangerousness of children with mental health problems and support for coerced treatment'. *Psychiatric Services*, 58 (5) (2007), pp. 619–25.

28. Moore M., Petrie C., Braga A., & McLaughlin, B. L. *Deadly Lessons: Understanding Lethal School Violence*. Washington, DC: National Academies Press, 2003.

29. Sowislo et al. 'Perceived dangerousness'.

30. Peterson, J. K., Skeem, J., Kennealy, P., Bray, B., & Zvonkovic, A. 'How often and how consistently do symptoms directly precede criminal behavior among offenders with mental illness'. *Law and Human Behavior*, 38 (5) (2014), pp. 439–49.

31. Nesvåg, R., Knudsen, G. P., Bakken, I. J., Høye, A. . . . & Reichborn-Kjennerud, T. 'Substance use disorders in

schizophrenia, bipolar disorder, and depressive illness: a registry-based study'. *Social Psychiatry and Psychiatric Epidemiology*, 50 (8) (2015), pp. 1267–76.

32. Fazel, S., Gulati, G., Linsell, L., Geddes, J. R., & Grann, M. 'Schizophrenia and violence: systematic review and meta-analysis'. *PLOS Medicine*, 6 (8) (2009). <https://doi.org/10.1371/journal.pmed.1000120>

33. Milgram, S. 'Behavioral study of obedience'. *Journal of Abnormal and Social Psychology*, 67 (4) (1963), p. 371.

34. Baumeister, R. F., & Campbell, W. K. 'The intrinsic appeal of evil: sadism, sensational thrills, and threatened egotism'. *Person-ality and Social Psychology Review*, 3 (3) (1999), pp. 210–21.

35. Baumeister, R. F. *Evil: Inside Human Cruelty and Violence.* New York: W. H. Freeman, 1997.

36. McAndrew & Koehnke. 'On the nature of creepiness'.

37. Hurley, E. 'Overkill: an exaggerated response to the sale of murderabilia'. *Indiana Law Review*, 42 (2) (2009), p. 411.

38. Wagner, M. 'Beyond the Son of Sam: assessing government's first tentative steps towards regulation of the third party murderabilia marketplace'. *University of Cincinnati Law Review*, 80 (2011), p. 977.

39. Denham, J. 'The commodification of the criminal corpse: "selective memory" in posthumous representations of criminal'. *Mortality*, 21 (3) (2016), pp. 229–45.

4. TWO-FACED TECH: HOW TECHNOLOGY CHANGES US

1. Engle, J. 'US aviation security'. *Los Angeles Times*, 12 June 2011. <http://articles.latimes.com/2011/jun/12/travel/la-tr-airline-safety-timeline-20110612>

2. Fishel, J., Thomas, P., Levine, M., & Date, J. 'Undercover DHS tests'. ABC News, 1 June 2015. <http://abcnews.go.com/US/exclusive-undercover-dhs-tests-find-widespread-security-failures/story?id=31434881>

3. Neff, G., & Nagy, P. 'Automation, algorithms, and politics:

talking to bots: symbiotic agency and the case of Tay'. *International Journal of Communication*, 10 (2016), p. 17.

4. Weizenbaum, J. *Computer Power and Human Reason: From Judgment to Calculation*. San Francisco, CA: W. H. Freeman, 1976.

5. Neff & Nagy. 'Automation, algorithms, and politics'.

6. Garber, M. 'When PARRY met ELIZA: A ridiculous chatbot conversation from 1972'. *The Atlantic*, June 2014. <http://www.theatlantic.com/technology/archive/2014/06/when-parry-met-eliza- a-ridiculous-chatbot-conversation-from-1972/372428/>

7. de Lima Salge, C. A., & Berente, N. 'Is that social bot behaving unethically?' *Communications of the ACM*, 60 (9) (2017), pp. 29–31.

8. Floridi, L., & Sanders, J. W. 'Artificial evil and the foundation of computer ethics'. *Ethics and Information Technology*, 3 (1) (2001), pp. 55–66.

9. Medeiros, J. 'Stephen Hawking: I fear AI will replace humans'. *Wired*, December 2017. <http://www.wired.co.uk/article/stephen-hawking-interview-alien-life-climate-change-donald-trump>

10. Titcomb, J. 'AI is the biggest risk'. *Daily Telegraph*, 17 July 2017. <http://www.telegraph.co.uk/technology/2017/07/17/ai-biggest-risk-face-civilisation-elon-musk-says/>

11. Diamond, B., & Bachmann, M. 'Out of the beta phase: obstacles, challenges, and promising paths in the study of cyber criminology 1'. *International Journal of Cyber Criminology*, 9 (1) (2015), p. 24.

12. Grabosky, P. N. 'Virtual criminality: old wine in new bottles?' *Social & Legal Studies*, 10 (2) (2001), pp. 243–49.

13. Capeller, W. 'Not such a neat net: some comments on virtual criminality'. *Social & Legal Studies*, 10 (2) (2001), pp. 229–42.

14. Cohen, L. E., & Felson, M. 'Social change and crime rate trends: a routine activity approach'. *American Sociological Review*, 44 (4) (1979), pp. 588–608.

15. Pratt, T. C., Holtfreter, K., & Reisig, M. D. 'Routine online activity and internet fraud targeting: extending the generality of routine activity theory'. *Journal of Research in Crime and Delinquency*, 47 (3) (2010), pp. 267–96.

16. Wolfe, S. E., Marcum, C. D., Higgins, G. E., & Ricketts, M. L. 'Routine cell phone activity and exposure to sext messages: extending the generality of routine activity theory and exploring the etiology of a risky teenage behavior'. *Crime & Delinquency*, 62 (5) (2016), pp. 614–44.

17. Kigerl, A. 'Routine activity theory and the determinants of high cybercrime countries'. *Social Science Computer Review*, 30 (4) (2012), pp. 470–86.

18. Gupta, P. & Mata-Toledo, R. 'Cybercrime: in disguise crime'. *Journal of Information Systems & Operations Management*, 10 (1) (2016), pp. 1–10.

19. Eubanks, N. 'The true cost of cybercrime'. Forbes Community Voice, 13 July 2017. <https://www.forbes.com/sites/theyec/2017 /07/13/the-true-cost-of-cybercrime-for-businesses/#559396 c14947>

20. Morgan, S. 'Cybercrime damages $6 trillion'. *Cybercrime Magazine*, 16 October 2017. <https://cybersecurityventures. com/hackerpocalypse-cybercrime-report-2016/>

21. Ehrenfeld, J. M. 'WannaCry, cybersecurity and health information technology: a time to act'. *Journal of Medical Systems*, 41 (7) (2017), p. 104.

22. Bjerg, O. 'How is bitcoin money?' *Theory, Culture & Society*, 33 (1) (2016), pp. 53–72.

23. Barlett, C. P., Gentile, D. A., & Chew, C. 'Predicting cyberbullying from anonymity'. *Psychology of Popular Media Culture*, 5 (2) (2016), p. 171.

24. Rösner, L., & Krämer, N. C. 'Verbal venting in the social web: effects of anonymity and group norms on aggressive language use in online comments'. *Social Media + Society*, 2 (3) (2016). <https://doi.org/10.1177/2056305116664220>

25. Huang, G., & Li, K. 'The effect of anonymity on conformity

to group norms in online contexts: a meta-analysis'. *International Journal of Communication*, 10 (2016), p. 18.

26. Sticca, F., & Perren, S. 'Is cyberbullying worse than traditional bullying? Examining the differential roles of medium, publicity, and anonymity for the perceived severity of bullying'. *Journal of Youth and Adolescence*, 42 (5) (2013), pp. 739–50.

27. Cheng, J., Bernstein, M., Danescu-Niculescu-Mizil, C., & Leskovec, J. 'Anyone can become a troll: causes of trolling behavior in online discussions'. *Proceedings of the 2017 ACM Conference on Computer Supported Cooperative Work and Social Computing* (2017). arXiv:1702.01119 [cs.SI]. <http://doi.org/10.1145/2998181.2998213>

5: KINKY AS F*CK: THE SCIENCE OF SEXUAL DEVIANCE

1. Dawson, S. J., Bannerman, B. A., & Lalumière, M. L. 'Paraphilic interests: an examination of sex differences in a nonclinical sample'. *Sexual Abuse*, 28 (1) (2016), pp. 20–45.

2. American Psychiatric Association. *Diagnostic and Statistical Manual of Mental Disorders* (5th ed.). Arlington, VA: APA, 2013.

3. Joyal, C. C. 'How anomalous are paraphilic interests?' *Archives of Sexual Behavior*, 43 (7) (2014), pp. 1241–43.

4. Scorolli, C., Ghirlanda, S., Enquist, M., Zattoni, S., & Jannini, E. A. 'Relative prevalence of different fetishes'. *International Journal of Impotence Research*, 19 (2007), pp. 432–37.

5. Långström, N., & Seto, M. C. 'Exhibitionistic and voyeuristic behavior in a Swedish national population survey'. *Archives of Sexual Behavior*, 35 (2006), pp. 427–35. <http://doi.org/10.1007/s10508-006-9042-6>

6. Holvoeta, L., Huysb, W., Coppensa, V., Seeuwsd, J., . . . & Morrensa, M. 'Fifty shades of Belgian grey: the prevalence of BDSM-related fantasies and activities in the general population'. *Journal of Sexual Medicine*, 14 (9) (2017), pp. 1152–59.

7. Lammers, J., & Imhoff, R. 'Power and sadomasochism: under-
    standing the antecedents of a knotty relationship'. *Social
    Psychological and Personality Science*, 7 (2) (2016), pp. 142–48.

8. Leitenberg, H., & Henning, K. 'Sexual fantasy'. *Psychological
    Bulletin*, 117 (3) (1995), p. 469.

9. Engber, D. '"Cannibal Cop": an exclusive interview with
    Gilberto Valle'. *Slate*, 10 December 2015. <http://www.slate.
    com/articles/news_and_politics/crime/2015/12/cannibal_cop_
    an_exclusive_interview_with_gilberto_valle.html>

10. Weiser, B. 'Ex-officer's conviction in cannibal case shouldn't
    be reinstated, appeals court rules'. *New York Times*, 4 December
    2015. <https://www.nytimes.com/2015/12/04/nyregion/appeals-
    court-gilberto-valle-cannibal-case.html>

11. Volokh, E. 'Second Circuit rules for accused "cannibal cop"'.
    Washington Post, 3 December 2015. <https://www.washington
    post.com/news/volokh-conspiracy/wp/2015/12/03/second-
    circuit-rules-for-accused-cannibal-cop/?utm_term=.b96a52e
    809a9>

12. Bivona, J., & Critelli, J. 'The nature of women's rape fantasies:
    an analysis of prevalence, frequency, and contents'. *Journal
    of Sex Research*, 46 (1) (2009), pp. 33–45.

13. Joyal, C. C., Cossette, A., & Lapierre, V. 'What exactly is an
    unusual sexual fantasy?' *Journal of Sexual Medicine*, 12 (2)
    (2015), pp. 328–40.

14. Paul, P. *Pornified*. New York: Times Books, 2007.

15. Perry, S. L., & Schleifer, C. 'Till porn do us part? A longi-
    tudinal examination of pornography use and divorce'. *Journal
    of Sex Research* (2017), pp. 1–13.

16. Perry, S. L. 'Pornography consumption as a threat to religious
    socialisation'. *Sociology of Religion*, 76 (4) (2015), pp. 436–58.

17. Wright, P. J., Tokunaga, R. S., & Kraus, A. 'A meta-analysis
    of pornography consumption and actual acts of sexual aggres-
    sion in general population studies'. *Journal of Communication*,
    66 (1) (2016), pp. 183–205.

18. Kühn, S., & Gallinat, J. 'Brain structure and functional

connectivity associated with pornography consumption: the brain on porn'. *JAMA Psychiatry*, 71 (7) (2014), pp. 827–34.

19. Moran, C., & Lee, C. 'What's normal? Influencing women's perceptions of normal genitalia: an experiment involving exposure to modified and nonmodified images'. *BJOG: An International Journal of Obstetrics & Gynaecology*, 121 (6) (2014), pp. 761–66.

20. Hesse, C., & Pedersen, C. L. 'Porn sex versus real sex: how sexually explicit material shapes our understanding of sexual anatomy, physiology, and behaviour'. *Sexuality & Culture*, 21 (3) (2017), pp. 754–75.

21. Carroll, A. & Mendos, L. R., International Lesbian, Gay, Bisexual, Trans and Intersex Association. *State-Sponsored Homophobia 2017: A World Survey of Sexual Orientation Laws: Criminalisation, Protection and Recognition.* <http://ilga.org/what-we-do/state-sponsored-homophobia-report/>

22. Sweeney, J. 'Sochi 2014: No gay people in city'. Interview with Anatoly Pakhomov for BBC *Panorama*, 27 January 2014. <http://www.bbc.com/news/uk-25675957>

23. Gates, G. J. 'How many people are lesbian, gay, bisexual and transgender?' The Williams Institute, UCLA School of Law (2011). <https://escholarship.org/content/qt09h684x2/qt09h684x2.pdf>

24. Duncan, P. 'Gay relationships are still criminalised in 72 countries, report finds'. *Guardian*, 27 July 2017. <https://www.theguardian.com/world/2017/jul/27/gay-relationships-still-criminalised-countries-report>

25. Sanders, A. R., Martin, E. R., Beecham, G. W., Guo, S., . . . & Duan, J. 'Genome-wide scan demonstrates significant linkage for male sexual orientation'. *Psychological Medicine*, 45 (7) (2015), pp. 1379–88.

26. Coghlan, A. 'Largest study of gay brothers homes in on "gay genes"'. *New Scientist*, 17 November 2014. <https://www.newscientist.com/article/dn26572-largest-study-of-gay-brothers-homes-in-on-gay-genes/>

27. Adams, H. E., Wright, L. W., & Lohr, B. A. 'Is homophobia associated with homosexual arousal?' *Journal of Abnormal Psychology*, 105 (3) (1996), p. 440.
28. Wagner, G. J. 'Internalised homophobia scale'. In: *Handbook of Sexuality-Related Measures*, Clive Davis, William Yarber et al. Thousand Oaks, CA: SAGE Publications, 1998, pp. 371–72.
29. Tskhay, K. O., & Rule, N. O. 'Internalised homophobia influences perceptions of men's sexual orientation from photos of their faces'. *Archives of Sexual Behavior*, 46 (3) (2017), pp. 755–61.
30. Alarie, M., & Gaudet, S. '"I don't know if she is bisexual or if she just wants to get attention": analyzing the various mechanisms through which emerging adults invisibilise bisexuality'. *Journal of Bisexuality*, 13 (2) (2013), pp. 191–214.
31. Herek, G. M. 'Heterosexuals' attitudes toward bisexual men and women in the United States'. *Journal of Sex Research*, 39 (4) (2002), pp. 264–74.
32. de Zavala, A. G., Waldzus, S., & Cypryanska, M. 'Prejudice towards gay men and a need for physical cleansing'. *Journal of Experimental Social Psychology*, 54 (2014), pp. 1–10.
33. LaCour, M. J., & Green, D. P. 'When contact changes minds: an experiment on transmission of support for gay equality'. *Science*, 346 (6215) (2014), pp. 1366–69.
34. Williams, C. J., & Weinberg, M. S. 'Zoophilia in men: a study of sexual interest in animals'. *Archives of Sexual Behavior*, 32 (6) (2003), pp. 523–35.
35. Sangeeta, S. 'Health risks of zoophilia/bestiality'. *Journal of Biological and Medical Sciences*, 1 (1) (2017), e101.

6. TO CATCH A PREDATOR: UNDERSTANDING PAEDOPHILES

1. Kennedy, A. C., & Prock, K. A. '"I still feel like I am not normal": a review of the role of stigma and stigmatisation among female survivors of child sexual abuse, sexual assault, and intimate partner violence'. *Trauma, Violence, & Abuse* (November 2016). <https://doi.org/ 10.1177/1524838016673601>

2. Blakemore, T., Herbert, J. L., Arney, F., & Parkinson, S. 'The impacts of institutional child sexual abuse: a rapid review of the evidence'. *Child Abuse & Neglect*, 74 (2017), pp. 35–48.
3. McCartan, K. '"Here There Be Monsters"': the public's perception of paedophiles with particular reference to Belfast and Leicester'. *Medicine, Science and the Law*, 44 (4) (2004), pp. 327–42.
4. Jahnke, S., Imhoff, R., & Hoyer, J. 'Stigmatisation of people with pedophilia: two comparative surveys'. *Archives of Sexual Behavior*, 44 (1) (2015), pp. 21–34.
5. Wurtele, S. K., Simons, D. A., & Moreno, T. 'Sexual interest in children among an online sample of men and women: prevalence and correlates'. *Sexual Abuse*, 26 (6) (2014), pp. 546–68.
6. American Psychiatric Association. *Diagnostic and Statistical Manual of Mental Disorders* (4th ed.). Washington, DC: APA, 2000.
7. Sea, J., & Beauregard, E. 'The hebephiliac: pedophile or teleiophiliac?' *International Journal of Offender Therapy and Comparative Criminology* (2017). <https://doi.org/10.1177/0306624X17723627>
8. Bailey, J. M., Hsu, K. J., & Bernhard, P. A. 'An internet study of men sexually attracted to children: sexual attraction patterns'. *Journal of Abnormal Psychology*, 125 (7) (2016), p. 976.
9. McPhail, I. V., Hermann, C. A., Fernane, S., Fernandez, Y. M., . . . & Cantor, J. M. 'Validity of phallometric tests for sexual interests in children: a meta-analytic review'. Assessment (2017), pp. 1–17.
10. Birrell, I. 'Horror of senior detective', *Daily Mail*, 21 June 2015. <http://www.dailymail.co.uk/news/article-3132896/Horror-senior-detective-discovering-1-35-men-sexually-attracted-children.html>
11. Birrell, 'Horror of senior detective'.
12. Stephenson, W. 'How many men are paedophiles?', BBC

News, 30 July 2014. <http://www.bbc.co.uk/news/maga-zine-28526106>

13. Stoltenborgh, M., Van Ijzendoorn, M. H., Euser, E. M., & Bakermans-Kranenburg, M. J. 'A global perspective on child sexual abuse: meta-analysis of prevalence around the world'. *Child Maltreatment*, 16 (2) (2011), pp. 79–101.

14. McLeod, D. A. 'Female offenders in child sexual abuse cases: a national picture'. *Journal of Child Sexual Abuse*, 24 (1) (2015), pp. 97–114.

15. Bailey et al. 'An internet study'.

16. Evans, M., 'One in 35 men has paedophile tendencies', *Daily Telegraph*, 22 June 2015. <http://www.telegraph.co.uk/news/uknews/11690451/One-in-35-men-has-paedophile-tendencies-crime-agency-claims.html>

17. Cantor, J. M., & McPhail, I. V. 'Non-offending pedophiles'. *Current Sexual Health Reports*, 8 (3) (2016), pp. 121–28.

18. Richards, K. 'Misperceptions about child sex offenders'. *Trends and Issues in Crime and Criminal Justice*, 429 (2011), p. 1.

19. Långström, N., Enebrink, P., Laurén, E. M., Lindblom, J., . . . & Hanson, R. K. 'Preventing sexual abusers of children from reoffending: systematic review of medical and psychological interventions'. *British Medical Journal*, 347 (2013), f4630.

20. Stoltenborgh et al. 'A global perspective'.

21. Radford, L., Corral, S., Bradley, C., Fisher, H., . . . & Collishaw, S. 'Child abuse and neglect in the UK today: research into the prevalence of child maltreatment in the United Kingdom'. NSPCC (2011).

22. Glasser, M., Kolvin, I., Campbell, D., Glasser, A., . . . & Farrelly, S. 'Cycle of child sexual abuse: links between being a victim and becoming a perpetrator'. *British Journal of Psychiatry*, 179 (6) (2001), pp. 482–94.

23. Widom, C. S., & Massey, C. 'A prospective examination of whether childhood sexual abuse predicts subsequent sexual offending'. *JAMA Pediatrics*, 169 (1) (2015). <https:// doi.org/ 10.1001/jamapediatrics.2014.3357>; and Lee, J. K., Jackson,

H. J., Pattison, P., & Ward, T. 'Developmental risk factors for sexual offending'. *Child Abuse & Neglect*, 26 (1) (2002), pp. 73–92.

24. Babchishin, K. M., Hanson, R. K., & VanZuylen, H. 'Online child pornography offenders are different: a meta-analysis of the characteristics of online and offline sex offenders against children'. *Archives of Sexual Behavior*, 44 (1) (2015), pp. 45–66.

25. Seto, M. C., Cantor, J. M., & Blanchard, R. 'Child pornography offenses are a valid diagnostic indicator of pedophilia'. *Journal of Abnormal Psychology*, 115 (3) (2006), p. 610.

26. Cantor, J. M. 'Gold star pedophiles in general sex therapy practice'. *Principles and Practice of Sex Therapy* (2014), pp. 219–34.

27. 'Are paedophiles' brains wired differently?' BBC News, 24 November 2015. <http://www.bbc.co.uk/news/magazine-348 58350>

28. Cantor, J. M., Kuban, M. E., Blak, T., Klassen, P. E., . . . & Blanchard, R. 'Physical height in pedophilic and hebephilic sexual offenders'. *Sexual Abuse: A Journal of Research and Treatment*, 19 (4) (2007), pp. 395–407.

29. Cantor, J. M., Klassen, P. E., Dickey, R., Christensen, B. K., . . . & Blanchard, R. 'Handedness in pedophilia and hebephilia'. *Archives of Sexual Behavior*, 34 (4) (2005), pp. 447–59.

30. Blanchard, R., Kolla, N. J., Cantor, J. M., Klassen, P. E., . . . & Blak, T. 'IQ, handedness, and pedophilia in adult male patients stratified by referral source'. *Sexual Abuse: A Journal of Research and Treatment*, 19 (3) (2007), pp. 285–309.

31. Cantor, J. M., Lafaille, S. J., Hannah, J., Kucyi, A., . . . & Mikulis, D. J. 'Independent component analysis of resting-state functional magnetic resonance imaging in pedophiles'. *The Journal of Sexual Medicine*, 13 (10) (2016), pp. 1546–54.

32. Cantor et al. 'Independent component'.

33. Joyal, C. C., Beaulieu-Plante, J., & de Chantérac, A. 'The neuropsychology of sex offenders: a meta-analysis'. *Sexual Abuse*, 26 (2) (2014), pp. 149–77.

34. Seto, M. C. *Pedophilia and Sexual Offending Against Children: Theory, Assessment, and Intervention*. New York: American Psychological Association, 2007.

35. Cantor, J. M., Lafaille, S., Soh, D. W., Moayedi, M., . . . & Girard, T. A. 'Diffusion tensor imaging of pedophilia'. *Archives of Sexual Behavior*, 44 (8) (2015), pp. 2161–72.

36. Houtepen, J. A., Sijtsema, J. J., & Bogaerts, S. 'Being sexually attracted to minors: sexual development, coping with forbidden feelings, and relieving sexual arousal in self-identified pedophiles'. *Journal of Sex and Marital Therapy*, 42 (1) (2016), pp. 48–69.

37. McGuinness, D. 'Germany urges paedophiles out of the shadows'. BBC News, 13 July 2015. <http://www.bbc.co.uk/news/magazine-33464970>

38. Troup Buchanan, R., 'In Germany, they treat paedophiles as victims'. *Independent*, 14 July 2015. <http://www.independent.co.uk/news/world/in-germany-they-treat-paedophiles-as-victims-not-offenders-10387468.html>

39. McGuinness. 'Germany urges paedophiles'.

40. McMillan, J. 'The kindest cut? Surgical castration, sex offenders and coercive offers'. *Journal of Medical Ethics*, 40 (9) (2014), pp. 583–90.

41. Grubin, D., & Beech, A. 'Chemical castration for sex offenders'. *British Medical Journal*, 304 (2010). <https://doi.org/10.1136/bmj.c74>

42. McMillan. 'The kindest cut?'

43. Lee, J. Y., & Cho, K. S. 'Chemical castration for sexual offenders: physicians' views'. *Journal of Korean Medical Science*, 28 (2) (2013), pp. 171–72.

44. Lewis, A., Grubin, D., Ross, C. C., & Das, M. 'Gonadotrophin-releasing hormone agonist treatment for sexual offenders: a systematic review'. *Journal of Psychopharmacology* (2017). <https://doi.org/10.1177/0269881117714048>

45. Berlin, F. S. '"Chemical castration" for sex offenders'. *New England Journal of Medicine*, 336 (14) (1997), pp. 1030–31.

46. 'Brian Hopkins, smuggler of child sex doll'. BBC News, 1 September 2017. <http://www.bbc.co.uk/news/uk-england-devon-41130328>

7. SNAKES IN SUITS: THE PSYCHOLOGY OF GROUPTHINK

1. 'Strategic Plan: 2013–2017', Compassion in World Farming. <https://www.ciwf.org.uk/media/3640540/ciwf_strategic_plan_20132017.pdf>
2. Murphy, H. 'Fish depression is not a joke'. *New York Times*, 16 October 2017. <https://www.nytimes.com/2017/10/16/science/depressed-fish.html>
3. Bastian, B., & Loughnan, S. 'Resolving the meat-paradox: a motivational account of morally troublesome behavior and its maintenance'. *Personality and Social Psychology Review* 21 (3) (2017), pp. 1–22. <https://doi.org/10.1177/1088868316647562>
4. Festinger, L. *A Theory of Cognitive Dissonance*. Evanston, IL: Row, Peterson & Co., 1957.
5. Festinger, L., & Carlsmith, J. M. 'Cognitive consequences of forced compliance'. *Journal of Abnormal and Social Psychology*, 58 (2) (1959), p. 203.
6. Festinger, L. *A Theory of Cognitive Dissonance* (Vol. 2). Stanford: Stanford University Press, 1962.
7. Grauerholz, L. 'Cute enough to eat: the transformation of animals into meat for human consumption in commercialised images'. *Humanity & Society*, 31 (4) (2007), pp. 334–54.
8. Bastian & Loughnan. 'Resolving the meat-paradox', pp. 278–99.
9. Fiske, A. P., & Tetlock, P. E. 'Taboo trade-offs: reactions to transactions that transgress the spheres of justice'. *Political Psychology*, 18 (2) (1997), pp. 255–97.
10. Tetlock, P. E., Kristel, O. V., Elson, S. B., Green, M. C., & Lerner, J. S. 'The psychology of the unthinkable: taboo trade-offs, forbidden base rates, and heretical counterfactuals'. *Journal of Personality and Social Psychology*, 78 (5) (2000), p. 853.

11. Tetlock, P. E. 'Thinking the unthinkable: sacred values and taboo cognitions'. *Trends in Cognitive Sciences*, 7 (7) (2003), pp. 320–24.

12. Judicial College. *Guidelines for the Assessment of General Damages in Personal Injury Cases*. Oxford: OUP, 2017. These amounts exclude compensation for things like loss of earnings, care costs and other expenses.

13. Kahneman, D., Schkade, D., & Sunstein, C. 'Shared outrage and erratic awards: the psychology of punitive damages'. *Journal of Risk and Uncertainty*, 16 (1) (1998), pp. 49–86.

14. Bales, K. *Ending Slavery: How We Free Today's Slaves*. Berkeley: University of California Press, 2007.

15. Bales, K. 'How to combat modern slavery'. TED Talk, February 2010. <https://www.ted.com/talks/kevin_bales_how_to_combat_modern_slavery>

16. Kelly, A. 'Human life is more expendable'. *Guardian*, 31 July 2017. <https://www.theguardian.com/global-development/2017/jul/31/human-life-is-more-expendable-why-slavery-has-never-made-more-money>

17. Baumeister, R. F. *Evil: Inside Human Cruelty and Violence*. New York: W. H. Freeman, 1997.

18. Lucas, T., Zhdanova, L., & Alexander, S. 'Procedural and distributive justice beliefs for self and others'. *Journal of Individual Differences*, 32 (1), (2011).

19. Lucas, T., Zhdanova, L., Wendorf, C. A., & Alexander, S. 'Procedural and distributive justice beliefs for self and others: multilevel associations with life satisfaction and self-rated health'. *Journal of Happiness Studies*, 14 (4) (2013), pp. 1325–41.

20. Lerner, M. J., & Simmons, C. H. 'Observer's reaction to the "innocent victim": compassion or rejection?' *Journal of Personality and Social Psychology*, 4 (2) (1966), p. 203.

21. Hafer, C. L., & Sutton, R. 'Belief in a just world'. In: *Handbook of Social Justice Theory and Research*. Clara Sabbagh &

Manfred Schmitt (eds). New York: Springer, 2016, pp. 145–60.

22. Furnham, A., & Gunter, B. 'Just world beliefs and attitudes towards the poor'. *British Journal of Social Psychology*, 23 (3) (1984), pp. 265–69.

23. Strömwall, L. A., Alfredsson, H., & Landström, S. 'Rape victim and perpetrator blame and the Just World hypothesis: the influence of victim gender and age'. *Journal of Sexual Aggression*, 19 (2) (2013), pp. 207–17.

24. Walters, J. 'Martin Shkreli: entrepreneur defends decision'. *Guardian*, 22 September 2017. <https://www.theguardian.com/business/2015/sep/21/entrepreneur-defends-raise-price-daraprim-drug>

25. 'Public Enemy'. *Harper's*, September 2017. <https://harpers.org/archive/2017/09/public-enemy/>

26. Mangan, D. 'Martin Shkreli slaps down rapper'. CNBC, 28 January 2016. <https://www.cnbc.com/2016/01/28/martin-shkreli-slaps-down-rapper-ghostface-killah-in-vulgar-video.html>

27. Keshner, A. 'Pharma Bro's just a Lie-vy League alum'. *New York Daily News*, 19 July 2017. <http://www.nydailynews.com/news/crime/columbia-registrar-no-records-shkreli-enrollment-article-1.3339005>

28. Rushe, D., & Glenza, J. 'Martin Shkreli jailed'. *Guardian*, 9 March 2018. https://www.theguardian.com/us-news/2018/mar/09/martin-shkreli-jail-sentence-how-long-pharma-bro-court-trial

29. Umphress, E., & Bingham, J. 'When employees do bad things for good reasons: examining unethical pro-organizational behaviors'. *Organization Science*, 22 (3) (2011), pp. 621–40. <https://doi.org/abs/10.1287/orsc.1100.0559>

30. Palazzo, G., Krings, F., & Hoffrage, U. 'Ethical blindness'. *Journal of Business Ethics*, 109 (3) (2012), pp. 323–38.

31. Elphick, C., Minhas, R., & Shaw, J. 'Dark figures'. Unpublished, Open Science Framework (2017). <https://osf.io/7skxh>

8. AND I SAID NOTHING: THE SCIENCE OF COMPLIANCE

1. Garber, M. '"First They Came": the poem of the protests'. *The Atlantic*, 29 January 2017. <https://www.theatlantic.com/entertainment/archive/2017/01/first-they-came-poem-history/514895/>
2. Niemöller, M. 'First they came for the Socialists', version used at the United States Holocaust Memorial Museum. <https://www.ushmm.org/wlc/en/article.php?ModuleId=10007392>
3. Connolly, K. 'Joseph Goebbels' 105-year-old secretary'. *Guardian*, 15 August 2016. <https://www.theguardian.com/world/2016/aug/15/brunhilde-pomsel-nazi-joseph-goebbels-propaganda-machine>
4. Milgram, S. *Obedience to Authority: An Experimental View*. London: Pinter & Martin Ltd, 2010.
5. Milgram, S. 'The perils of obedience'. *Harper's*, 12 (6) (1973).
6. Milgram, S. 'Behavioral study of obedience'. *Journal of Abnormal and Social Psychology*, 67 (4) (1963), p. 371.
7. Burger, J. M. 'Replicating Milgram: would people still obey today?' *American Psychologist*, 64 (1) (2009), p. 1; and Doliński, D., Grzyb, T., Folwarczny, M., Grzybała, P., . . . & Trojanowski, J. 'Would you deliver an electric shock in 2015? Obedience in the experimental paradigm developed by Stanley Milgram in the 50 years following the original studies'. *Social Psychological and Personality Science*, 8 (8) (2017), pp. 927–33.
8. Caspar, E. A., Christensen, J. F., Cleeremans, A., & Haggard, P. 'Coercion changes the sense of agency in the human brain'. *Current Biology*, 26 (5) (2016), pp. 585–92.
9. 'Following orders makes us feel less responsible'. UCL News, 18 February 2016. <http://www.ucl.ac.uk/news/news-articles/0216/180216-following-orders-reduces-responsibility>
10. McMahon, S., & Farmer, G. L. 'An updated measure for assessing subtle rape myths'. *Social Work Research*, 35 (2) (2011), pp. 71–81.

11. Horvath, M. A., Hegarty, P., Tyler, S., & Mansfield, S. '"Lights on at the end of the party": are lads' mags mainstreaming dangerous sexism?' *British Journal of Psychology*, 103 (4) (2012), pp. 454–71.

12. Hegarty, P., Stewart, A. L., Blockmans, I. G., & Horvath, M. A. 'The influence of magazines on men: normalizing and challenging young men's prejudice with "lads" mags'. *Psychology of Men & Masculinity*, 19 (1) (2018) pp. 131–44.

13. Savin-Williams, R. C. 'True or false: 20% of young women are sexually assaulted?' *Psychology Today*, 16 July 2017. <https://www.psychologytoday.com/blog/sex-sexuality-and-romance/201707/true-or-false-20-young-women-are-sexually-assaulted>

14. Muehlenhard, C. L., Peterson, Z. D., Humphreys, T. P., & Jozkowski, K. N. 'Evaluating the one-in-five statistic: women's risk of sexual assault while in college'. *Journal of Sex Research*, 54 (4–5) (2017), pp. 549–76.

15. 'Victims of sexual violence: statistics'. RAINN. <https://www.rainn.org/statistics/victims-sexual-violence>

16. Yon, Y., Mikton, C., Gassoumis, Z. D., & Wilber, K. H. 'The prevalence of self-reported elder abuse among older women in community settings: a systematic review and meta-analysis'. *Trauma, Violence, & Abuse*, April 2017. <https://doi.org/10.1177/1524838017697308>

17. Rawlinson, K. 'Judge accused of victim-blaming in comments on rape case'. *Guardian*, 10 March 2017. <https://www.theguardian.com/society/2017/mar/10/judge-accused-of-victim-blaming-during-sentencing-comments-in-case>

18. Larson, F. 'Why public beheadings get millions of views'. TED Talk, June 2015.

19. LaMotte, S. 'The psychology and neuroscience of terrorism'. CNN, 25 March 2016. <http://edition.cnn.com/2016/03/25/health/brain-and-terrorist-attack/index.html>

20. Dowd, M. '20 years after the murder of Kitty Genovese, the question remains: why?' *New York Times*, 12 March 1984.

<https://www.nytimes.com/1984/03/12/nyregion/20-years-after-the-murder-of-kitty-genovese-the-question-remains-why.html>

21. McFadden, R. D. 'Winston Moseley, who killed Kitty Genovese'. *New York Times*, 4 April 2016. <https://www.nytimes.com/2016/04/05/nyregion/winston-moseley-81-killer-of-kitty-genovese-dies-in-prison.html>

22. Darley, J. M., & Latané, B. 'Bystander intervention in emergencies: diffusion of responsibility'. *Journal of Personality and Social Psychology*, 8 (1968), p. 377–83.

23. Latané, B., & Darley, J. M. *The Unresponsive Bystander: Why Doesn't He Help?* New York: Appleton-Century-Crofts, 1970.

24. Fischer, P., Krueger, J. I., Greitemeyer, T., Vogrincic, C., . . . & Kainbacher, M. 'The bystander-effect: a meta-analytic review on bystander intervention in dangerous and non-dangerous emergencies'. *Psychological Bulletin*, 137 (4) (2011), p. 517–37.

25. Jaggar, A. 'What is terrorism, why is it wrong, and could it ever be morally permissible?' *Journal of Social Philosophy*, 36 (2005), pp. 202–17.

26. US Department of State. *Patterns of Global Terrorism 1997*, Department of State Publications, 10321. Washington, DC: United States Department of State, 1998.

27. Silke, A. (ed.). *Terrorists, Victims and Society: Psychological Perspectives on Terrorism and Its Consequences.* Chichester: John Wiley & Sons, 2003.

28. Piccinni, A., Marazziti, D., & Veltri, A. 'Psychopathology of terrorists'. *CNS Spectrums* (2017), pp. 1–4.

29. Jaggar. 'What is terrorism?'

30. Simmons, K., & Gubash, C. 'Captured ISIS fighter'. NBC News, 27 July 2015. <https://www.nbcnews.com/storyline/isis-terror/captured-isis-fighter-joining-extremists-syria-ruined-my-life-n398976>

31. Horgan, J. 'A call to arms: the need for more psychological research on terrorism'. *Social Psychological Review*, 18 (1) (2016), pp. 25–28.

32. US Department of Homeland Security. 'If you see something, say something' campaign, launched July 2010. <https://www.dhs.gov/see-something-say-something>

33. Metropolitan Police, UK. 'Signs of possible terrorist activity'. <https://www.met.police.uk/advice-and-information/terror-ism-in-the-uk/signs-of-possible-terrorist-activity/>

34. Lum, C., Kennedy, L. W., & Sherley, A. 'Are counter-terrorism strategies effective? The results of the Campbell systematic review on counter-terrorism evaluation research'. *Journal of Experimental Criminology*, 2 (4) (2006), pp. 489–516.

35. Freese, R. 'Evidence-based counterterrorism or flying blind? How to understand and achieve what works'. *Perspectives on Terrorism*, 8 (1) (2014) pp. 37–35.

36. Horgan. 'A call to arms'.

37. 'What is jihadism?' BBC News, 11 December 2014. <http://www.bbc.co.uk/news/world-middle-east-30411519>

38. McCauley, C., & Moskalenko, S. 'Understanding political radicalisation: the two-pyramids model'. *American Psychologist*, 72 (3) (2017), p. 205.

39. McCauley, C. 'Ideas versus actions in relation to polls of US Muslims'. *Analyses of Social Issues and Public Policy*, 13 (2013), pp. 70–76. <http://dx.doi.org/10.1111/asap.12014>

40. Altier, M. B., Thoroughgood, C. N., & Horgan, J. G. 'Turning away from terrorism: lessons from psychology, sociology, and criminology'. *Journal of Peace Research*, 51 (5) (2014), pp. 647–61.

41. Alison, L., & Alison, E. 'Revenge versus rapport: interrogation, terrorism, and torture'. *American Psychologist*, 72 (3) (2017), p. 266–77. <https://doi.org/10.1037/amp0000064>

42. Zimbardo, P. 'The psychology of evil'. TED Talk, February 2008. <https://www.ted.com/talks/philip_zimbardo_on_the_psychology_of_evil/transcript>

43. Zimbardo, P. G. *The Lucifer Effect*. Oxford: Blackwell Publishing Ltd, 2007.

44. Haney, C., Banks, C., & Zimbardo, P. 'Interpersonal dynamics

in a simulated prison'. *International Journal of Criminology and Penology*, 1 (1973), pp. 69–97.

45. From the transcript of the documentary 'The Trial of Adolf Eichmann', Great Projects Film Co., ABC News Productions, April 1997. <http://remember.org/eichmann/sentencing>

46. Owens, P. 'Racism in the theory canon: Hannah Arendt and "the one great crime in which America was never involved"'. *Millennium*, 45 (3) (2017), pp. 403–24. <http://sro.sussex.ac.uk/66694/>

47. Arendt, H. *Eichmann in Jerusalem: A Report on the Banality of Evil.* New York, NY: Penguin, 1963.

CONCLUSION

1. Miller, D. S. 'Disaster tourism and disaster landscape attractions after Hurricane Katrina: an auto-ethnographic journey'. *International Journal of Culture, Tourism and Hospitality Research*, 2 (2) (2008), pp. 115–31.

2. Gino, F., & Wiltermuth, S. S. 'Evil genius? How dishonesty can lead to greater creativity'. *Psychological Science*, 25 (4) (2014), pp. 973–81.

INDEX